God's Eternal Story Threaded
Through the Lives of Ordinary People

Edited by Judith Ford

HENRY T. FORD

Foreword by Dr.Steve Masterson, Director of
Spiritual Formation, Promise Keepers Canada

EVERY LIFE TELLS A STORY

ISBN:978-1-77069-334-0

Word Alive Press
131 Cordite Road, Winnipeg, MB R3W 1S1
www.wordalivepress.ca

Library and Archives Canada Cataloguing in Publication

Ford, Henry T., 1927-
Every life is a story : God's eternal story being threaded through the lives of ordinary people / by Henry T. Ford.

ISBN 978-1-77069-334-0

1. Ford, Henry T., 1927-. 2. Clergy--Ontario--Biography. 3. Children
of single parents--Ontario--Biography. 4. People with disabilities--Ontario--Biography. I. Title.

BR1725.F67A3 2011 277.10092 C2011-906316-6

DEDICATED TO:

My wife Jean, who has faithfully loved me and has prayerfully stood by my side for sixty years. She has been a help meet to me in my pastoral ministry and has lovingly ministered to me, particularly during these last many years in my struggle with post-polio syndrome.

TABLE OF CONTENTS

TABLE OF CONTENTS

ACKNOWLEDGEMENTS

First I want to thank my daughter Judith, who edited my manuscript. She was most patient with me and did not hesitate to criticize when necessary, but always with gentle kindness towards her father. She has literally spent hours sorting, correcting, proofing, and all the other things a good editor would do. Thank you, dear. Without you this book could never have been published.

To my wife Jean, who assisted me with some of the details, reading when she was able, and allowing me to spend hours alone, screening calls and other interruptions that possibly would have disturbed my train of thought.

Special thanks to my cousin, Lois Dalzell McKee, who gave me so much information about her mother, Daisy; to Bud (now in heaven) and Marge Elford, who wrote out their story in great detail to assist me; David and Roger Gast, who filled me in with parts of their parents' lives during the years when I had been out of touch with them; my friend from Bulgaria; to those friends from Westside Baptist Church who clarified some of the intricacies of which I was unaware; to the Poynters and Eileen Tindall, for their willingness to proof the finished chapters.

Thank you to Steve Masterson, Barry Lee, Greg Constable, Bruxy Cavey, Richard Holliday, and John Ghent for their friendship and spiritual input into my life as well as this book.

A WORD FROM THE AUTHOR

"Whether you turn to the right or to the left, your ears will hear a voice behind you, saying, 'This is the way; walk in it.'"
(Isaiah 30:21)

"When things get tough, always remember, faith doesn't get you around trouble, it gets you through it."
—*Selected*

Why, at seventy-six years of age (I am now eighty-three—editor's note: it has taken me a long time!), am I attempting to write a book? As a matter of fact, my first attempt! I have asked myself this question over and over again, but persistently, I keep thinking of things I want to share and stories I want to tell as I remember them.

Has it been the Spirit of God who has prompted me? I would have to answer "Yes." I honestly believe the Holy Spirit is urging me to put into writing experiences that I have had as a Pastor.

I will also include quotes from authors of by-gone days as well as contemporary ones, with poetry and other items I have collected through the years. I will also be introducing several of the gospel songs that some of my readers may not know but I believe will be blessed by them. There are some new choruses I will also be using and are sure to be a blessing as you read them.

One of my favourite writers is Mrs. Charles E. Cowman. I have read several of her books outlining her ministry with her husband. They were missionaries in the Orient, primarily Japan, and had to return from the mission field because of his frail health. She nursed him until his premature death and then travelled around the world speaking and writing books that bless us to this day.

Many of us have enjoyed reading her daily devotional book, *Streams in the Desert*. Originally, I planned to follow her style, in which she gleaned precious and appropriate truths from others, compiling them into a daily devotional. I will do this, but will also include personal experiences of dear ones I have come to love in the churches where I served, along with other friends and family who left meaningful memories for me.

I am sure all of my readers will agree that the Lord's desire for each one of us is to be guided, directed, and energized by His Holy Spirit. I have heard it said by many preachers that people will quite likely forget your sermon but remember your illustrations and stories (though no doubt embellished considerably!). The real names of some people have been changed to be sensitive to their privacy.

My hope and prayer is that every part of this book will bless your heart and challenge you to intimacy with the Saviour. The Apostle Paul declared in his letter to the Philippians in Chapter 3, verse 10, *"That I may know Him."* It has been well said, "We receive His blessings and know His Word, but do we know *Him*?"

I want to reach people of my generation (now the "senior" ones!); but I also want to touch the hearts of the younger age groups and everyone in between. All of us need to be reminded that "God's way is the best way."

As I struggle with post-polio syndrome, now "living" in a power wheelchair, Isaiah 40:29–31 has been a great encouragement to me: *"He gives strength to the weary and increases the power of the weak. Even youths grow tired and weary, and young men stumble and fall; but those who hope in the Lord shall renew their strength."*

A short poem from *Our Daily Bread* (Ministry of the Radio Bible Class) says:

We're often weary in life's race,
Driven by its hurried pace;
But when we wait upon the Lord,
His strength becomes our sure reward.
—*Author Unknown*

As Leanne Payne says in many of her books, "We must practice the presence of Jesus." To better explain this statement let me briefly tell you the story of "Brother Lawrence." As a young man of eighteen, he found Christ as his Saviour. He later became a lay brother among the barefooted Carmelites in Paris in the mid-1600s.

From that moment on, he grew and waxed strong in the knowledge and favour of God, endeavouring constantly, as he put it, "to walk as in His presence." A wholly consecrated man, he lived his life as though he were a singing pilgrim on the march. He was as happy serving his fellow monks and brothers from the monastery kitchen as he was serving God in the vigil of prayer and penance. Perhaps, God willing, there will be those who read his book—*Practicing the Presence of God*—and be drawn into a closer walk with the Lord, *"who loved us and gave Himself for us"* (Galatians 2:20).

> Thank You, Lord, for the hope of heaven. Use it in my earthly life to inspire and sustain my passion and purpose.
>
> —*Selected*

ABOUT HENRY

Life experience—rich, varied, full of hope and disappointment, intensive involvement in the lives of others—all of this provides a perspective for mature and wise contemplation. Henry Ford has a great deal of life experience and his reflections in this book mirror his life.

His mother raised Henry in Ottawa in the late 1920's and 30's. He suffered the emotional and economic rejection of his father and learned at an early age the stigma attached to growing up in a single-parent family.

As a pre-teen, he contracted polio and has been walking with two crutches and now in a wheelchair over these latter years of his life. He learned to deal with physical pain and the extreme inconvenience caused by lack of mobility. He also learned how to deal with being visibly different from everyone else.

Henry is a husband, a father to four children, and a grandfather. He has learned the joy, pride, trials, and disappointments inherent to raising a family.

Henry pastored several churches in Southern Ontario, particularly the Toronto area. He has seen life—with all of its beauty and ugliness, success and failure, brokenness and healing.

The one characteristic that defines Henry more than any other and which infiltrates all his life experience is his love for people. When self-pity might reasonably have been an influential force—it is replaced with a genuine interest and concern for others. And it is because of this others-centred attitude that this book is written—to share what he has learned. There is much to glean from this mature and wise man.

—John Ghent

FOREWORD

Dr. Steve Masterson
Director of Spiritual Formation
Promise Keepers Canada

All of life is a story…

One of the greatest wagers of faith is to believe that God is writing His story through each of our stories. Our stories are not ours to claim or own. Why? Because God is the greatest Author, Editor, Publisher and Choreographer of the story about our lives. When we grasp this truth we will hear and see more clearly that this is God's invitation calling us up into His bigger story that has eternity written all through it.

Henry Ford is the craftsman as he forms the stories of men and women of God, of song writers, hymns, and of poems and poetry that all have the fingerprint of God's authorship and penmanship.

This book transcends the writing of Henry Ford to take you, as a reader, into the very heart of an amazing God. You will know that you are reading God's story as told through the lives of ordinary men and women, all redeemed by the finished work of Jesus Christ on the cross. You will also come to know that Henry Ford's life has been captured and captivated by this amazing God who has told His story through Henry's life. This is how God receives the glory, honour and praise…because it is His eternal story.

In Ecclesiastes 3:11 God says, *"He has made everything beautiful in its time. He has also set eternity in the hearts of men; yet they cannot fathom what God has done from beginning to end."* Reading these God stories, you will discover this verse to be true in every life, including Henry

Ford's. Don't ever forget that *all of life is a story…God's story being told through these lives and being told through your life as well. To God be the glory, great things He has done.*

I WILL *Meet* YOU IN THE MORNING

"...now as always Christ will be exalted in my body, whether by life or by death. For to me, to live is Christ and to die is gain."
(Philippians 1:20b–21)

"Heated gold becomes ornament. Beaten copper becomes wire. Depleted stone becomes a statue. So the more pain you get in life the more valuable you become."
—*Selected*

Heartbreak When a Child Dies

Some time ago when Dr. W. A. Criswell was pastor of the First Baptist Church of Dallas, Texas, he told how on an airplane flight he was sitting beside and visiting with a well-known theologian. The man told how he had lost a son, who one day had come home from school with a fever that he and his wife thought was just a childhood sickness. Sadly it turned out to be meningitis. The doctor gave no hope for the boy's survival.

Near the end when the professor was sitting at his son's bedside, the child said, "Daddy, it's getting dark isn't it?"

The professor answered, "Yes, son, it is getting dark, very dark."

"Daddy, I guess it's time for me to go to sleep isn't it?" the boy continued.

"Yes, son, it's time for you to go to sleep."

As the child fixed the pillow on his bed as best he could in his weakened condition and, putting his head on his hands, he said, "Good night Daddy. I will see you in the morning." Those were the last words the professor's son said as he closed his eyes in death and passed from this life to enter God's heaven.

For a long time, Dr. Criswell said, the professor just sat looking out the window of the airplane. Later he turned again and looking at Dr. Criswell, with tears in his eyes, said, "Dr. Criswell, I can hardly wait till the morning."

Dear reader, are you sure that you are ready for God's heaven so that if you go first, you will be able to say to your loved ones with certainty, "I'll see you in the morning?" If not, pray this prayer right where you are: "Dear God, thank you for the assurance of heaven that you have promised to all who accept your Son, Jesus, as their Saviour. Please help me to know that I am ready to meet you face to face so that I will see all of my loved ones who've gone before me. Thank you for hearing and answering my prayer. Gratefully, in Jesus' name, amen."
—*Author Unknown*

Before I tell you the story of a dear Christian couple who suffered the loss of their baby, let me quote from the book, *Goforth of China*. Dr. Goforth wrote the following letter to friends in the homeland:

> Gertrude Madeline (their first child) is dead. Ours is an awful loss…but on July 24, she died, only six days after she was taken ill with dysentery. There is no burying place here for foreigners, so I took her body in a cart to Pangchwang… fifty miles away…A Chinese service was conducted by the missionary. Then the crude coffin, covered with flowers, was borne by four Chinese outside the village wall. There, in the

> dusk of evening, with scores of curious Chinese looking on, we laid our darling to rest beside two other dear little foreigners who were laid to sleep there before her.
>
> None but those who have lost a precious treasure can understand our feelings, but the loss seems to be greater because we are far away in a strange land…'All things work together for good.' The Lord has a purpose in taking our loved one away. We pray that this loss will fit us more fully to tell these dying millions of Him who has gained the victory over death.

In the meantime, Mrs. Goforth, broken-hearted and stricken with dysentery, read from her *Daily Light* devotional and found so appropriately for that sad day these comforting words from the Lord: *"It is the Lord. Let Him do what seemeth Him good"* (1 Samuel 3:18); and in Job 1:21, *"The Lord gave and the Lord hath taken away. Blessed be the name of the Lord"* (KJV).

Now to my sad story. While I was a student at Bible College I was given the privilege of serving the Lord for a summer in the small town of Strathroy in Western Ontario. I made many friends throughout that long, hot summer, and one couple, Loren and Jean Gast, stand out in my memory because of their devotion and faithfulness to the Lord, and the tragic loss of their baby boy.

I'll start at the beginning. This couple had come from a Presbyterian Church in town and sat under the ministry of Dr. John Honeyman, an evangelical who preached the whole counsel of God. This included the message that Jesus taught in John 3:3: *"I tell you the truth; no one can see the Kingdom of God unless he is born again."* The Gasts, along with many others in the church, believed this message and whole-heartedly accepted the "Gospel in a nutshell"—John 3:16: *"For God so loved the world that he gave his one and only Son that whoever believes in him shall not perish but have eternal life."* The Gasts became new creatures in Christ Jesus. *"Therefore, if anyone is in Christ, the new creation has come: the old has gone, the new is here!"* (2 Corinthians 5:17)

Dr. Honeyman left the church in Strathroy to take up the position of Professor of Greek and Hebrew at the London Bible Institute in

London, Ontario. The Gasts were saddened to see him leave, since he was the one who had pointed the way to their eternal salvation. They were then devastated when the new minister who came was a liberal, preaching a social gospel but leaving out totally the need for the new birth. They came to the church where I happened to be ministering as Assistant Pastor and continued being outstanding servants of the Lord.

With Loren and Jean there was no sitting in the grandstands watching the action! They jumped in and with hearts filled with the love of God and with His blessed Holy Spirit, served the Lord unreservedly. They had many gifts but one that always blessed their hearers was when they sang together.

Pastor Pittaway, the Senior Pastor, began a radio ministry in Sarnia, Ontario, where the broadcasts were spread over the entire Western Ontario region. Mrs. Pittaway, the Gasts, and I would travel to Sarnia every Friday evening for a "live" broadcast; I was the pianist for these broadcasts. Quite often Jean would invite me to stay with them for the weekend (this was after I had returned to school) and always treated me royally and made me part of their family, which included two little boys, Roger and David.

Loren and Jean were farmers, and I should add, successful ones with a very good income. Loren was the only male in his family and when he married, the large home in which he lived with his parents was divided into two homes. His parents were not exactly happy that they had left the church where the family had worshipped for many, many years. Regardless, the young couple, along with their two little boys, stood their ground. The following hymn reminds me of the commitment they made:

I'm pressing on the upward way,
New heights I'm gaining every day;
Still praying as I'm onward bound,
"Lord plant my feet on higher ground."
Lord lift me up and let me stand
By faith on heaven's tableland

A higher plane than I have found—
Lord, plant my feet on higher ground.
My heart has no desire to stay
Where doubts arise and fears dismay;
Tho some may dwell where these abound,
My prayer, my aim is higher ground.
I want to live above the world,
Tho Satan's darts at me are hurled;
For faith has caught the joyful sound,
The song of saints on higher ground.
I want to scale the utmost height
And catch a gleam of glory bright;
But still I'll pray till heav'n I've found,
"Lord, lead me on to higher ground."
—Johnson Oatman, Jr.

That summer I conducted a Vacation Bible School for children. I did all of the teaching, assisted by many of the women in the church. Vacation Bible Schools were a novelty in those days and as we offered prizes for inviting friends, the children kept coming until we had to move into the arena to safely hold all the children and workers.

It was during this evangelistic outreach that Loren and Jean's oldest son, who was around eight years of age, accepted the Lord as his own personal Saviour. Just a few years ago I met Roger at his parents' fiftieth anniversary celebration and he reminded me of that day when he was saved. He has not only gone on with the Lord through all these years but he and his younger brother are both serving the Lord in full-time ministry.

Roger, in his retirement years, is the pastor to seniors at Bethel Baptist Church in Strathroy, Ontario. David and with his wife Sharon, both accomplished musicians, have served the Lord here in Canada as well as abroad. David had to take an early retirement in order to deal with cancer and all that is involved in treatment.

That fall when I returned to school, Loren felt God leading him to go to bible school to prepare for full-time ministry. Much to his father's chagrin he enrolled and started classes.

This meant, of course, that he had to get up before daybreak, do his usual farm chores, then drive to the city to attend classes. Before too long, even with his elderly father and Jean doing the chores, Loren realized this was an impossible situation. He returned to the farm and his work but still carried on with ministry in their home church.

Shortly after this scenario, I learned that Loren and Jean were expecting a baby. This was a pleasant and happy surprise considering the two boys were much older. In due time a baby boy was born and he brought untold joy and happiness to the whole family.

While he was still a little toddler, near as I can remember around two years of age, he was left with a young girl who was a reliable babysitter. She knew the family well and especially the baby.

The family set off to attend a Christmas concert in a nearby town for the presentation of that old, old story of the birth of the Lord Jesus Christ. They were in what is often called the "Christmas Spirit" and they very well could have been singing as they drove along, a favourite of most children:

Away in a manger, no crib for a bed,
The little Lord Jesus laid down His sweet head;
The stars in the sky looked down where he lay—
The little Lord Jesus, asleep on the hay.
The cattle are lowing, the Baby awakes,
But little Lord Jesus no crying He makes;
I love Thee, Lord Jesus, look down from the sky,
And stay by my cradle till morning is nigh.
Be near me, Lord Jesus, I ask Thee to stay
Close by me forever, and love me I pray;
Bless all the dear children in Thy tender care,
And fit us for heaven, to live with Thee there.
—Martin Luther

The Christmas program was being enjoyed by a "full house" when someone rushed in to whisper to Loren and Jean that their home was on fire. As soon as they heard the news of the fire, their first thought was for their precious child and there is no doubt the parents were praying for his safety.

They bundled up in their outer clothes and drove home as quickly as the winter roads would allow. Before they even reached the country line where their house was located, they could see the huge fire and smoke rising into the frosty night sky.

The old farmhouse was in smoldering ashes and to their horror they were told that when the babysitter realized the house was on fire, the smoke and fire were so intense she couldn't possibly get upstairs to rescue the baby.

We read this dreadful news in the paper the next day, and through our tears, our prayers and thoughts went to our dear friends who were now facing, without a doubt, their greatest trial ever.

As I took a break from writing this painful episode (for only those who have lost a child can empathize), I listened to a Gaither video and jotted down the words of a touching hymn, not knowing who wrote it.

There's no other name so sweet as Jesus,
No one ever cared so much for me,
As to shed His precious blood to save me,
No one ever cared so much for me.
When I see Him face to face in Glory
And I kneel at His nail-pierced feet;
Then I'll thank Him for the place He suffered,
All because He cared so much for me.

Being human, I don't believe Loren and Jean ever fully recovered from that loss. They grieved and sorrowed, knowing that one day as told by the Apostle Paul to the Thessalonians, *"...the Lord Himself will come down from heaven, with a loud command, with the voice of the archangel and with the trumpet call of God, and the dead in Christ will rise first. After that, we who are still alive and are left will be caught up together with them in the clouds to meet the Lord in the air. And so we will be with the Lord forever. Therefore encourage each other with these words"* (1 Thessalonians 4:16–18).

Let me digress at this point to relate another sad incident in the lives of the Goforths of China. Mrs. Goforth wrote,

In the summer of 1898 the Goforth's little daughter Gracie showed signs of a strange disease. Several months passed before the child was diagnosed to be in a hopeless condition from an enlarged spleen brought on by pernicious malaria. During those last months Gracie spent as much time in her father's arms as his work would permit. Sometimes she lay in her little carriage beside her father's desk. At such time all she seemed to crave was to gaze on her father's face or slip her little hand into his when free.

One evening, Gracie partly rose and said in a commanding tone, "I want my papa." Not wishing to disturb the tired-out father, the mother hesitated, when again Gracie said, "Call my papa. I want my papa!"

A few minutes later Jonathon took his beloved little one in his arms, laying her head gently on his shoulder as he started to pace the floor. Gracie, resting quietly in her father's arms, suddenly lifted her head and looking straight into her father's eyes, gave him a wonderful, loving smile, closed her eyes, and without a struggle, was gone.

The following is a poem that has been put to music and was first published in *Sacred Songs and Solos*, compiled by Ira D. Sankey, to be used in D. L. Moody's revival services, both in the United States and Great Britain.

Himself
Once it was the blessing, now it is the Lord;
Once it was the feeling, now it is His Word;
Once His gifts I wanted now the Giver own;
Once I sought for healing now Himself alone.
Once 'twas painful trying, now 'tis perfect trust;
Once a half salvation, now the uttermost;
Once 'twas ceaseless holding, now He holds me fast;
Once 'twas constant drifting, now my anchor's cast.
Once 'twas busy planning, now 'tis trustful prayer;
Once 'twas anxious caring, now He has the care;

Once 'twas what I wanted, now what Jesus says;
Once 'twas constant asking, now 'tis ceaseless praise.
Once it was my working, His it hence shall be;
Once I tried to use Him, now He uses me;
Once the power I wanted, now the Mighty One;
Once for self I labored, now for Him alone.
Once I hoped in Jesus, now I know He's mine;
Once my lamps were dying, now they brightly shine;
Once for death I waited, now His coming hail;
And my hopes are anchored, safe within the vail.
—*A. B. Simpson*

Before I conclude this story, I want to stop and interject a rather touching story about a little boy. The story was told by author and lecturer Leo Buscaglia. He was asked to judge a contest, the purpose being to find the most caring child. The following was the winner:

> A four-year-old child lived next-door to an elderly gentleman who had recently lost his wife. Upon seeing the man cry, the little boy went into the old gentleman's yard, climbed onto his lap, and just sat there. When upon his return his mother asked him what he had said to the neighbour, the little boy replied, "Nothing! I just helped him cry."

Postscript

Since commencing the story of the Gasts, dear Jean slipped away to heaven on July 25, 2008. My wife and I had the privilege of attending the celebration of her life and faith in Bethel Baptist Church, Strathroy, Ontario. I wept through most of the service as the favourite hymns and gospel songs were sung.

I also laughed at some of the remarks her sons made. Roger mentioned that on one occasion he had a disagreement with his mother! He left, slamming the door! But he added (I can't remember what the disciplinary action was), "I never slammed the door again on my mother."

These words were part of the Order of Service: "She spent 32,278 days on earth…She is enjoying eternity in heaven." Many people commented on how lovely she looked in her casket but added that it didn't look like Jean without her usual smile.

The following are excerpts from the bulletin of the service with further information provided by David:

> Loren and Jean were married for over seventy years. They met in Strathroy when Jean was only 15 years old. Her parents were greatly opposed to her dating Loren for he was 22 years old at the time. When Jean turned 18, (her parents still strongly opposed to the relationship) they eloped! That was March 20, 1938. Jean's parents had warned her that if she married a farmer, she would be dead in three years from overwork! They farmed for over 25 years before moving into Strathroy in 1965. Jean had a lifelong passion to go into nursing and when they were settled in town her dream became a reality as she trained and served at the Strathroy hospital for nine years as a Registered Nursing Assistant.

Then a new chapter of life unfolded for Jean and Loren when they moved to Toronto in 1973 to serve at Toronto Bible College. Loren was to manage maintenance and Jean would become the receptionist. They served the Lord faithfully for several years at the college and enjoyed immensely interacting with the young people and staff.

In their so-called retirement years, they lived in Brampton and then moved to Palmerston where Roger was pastoring. They lived in Roger's and his wife Ruth's home, and had their own apartment there.

They moved back to Strathroy in 2001 along with Roger and Ruth. I found out at the funeral that Jean and Loren had a third son whom I had never met. Karl was considerably younger than his two brothers.

The following gospel song was sung at the memorial service of their beloved son Paul, who died in the fire at their home in 1952. David began singing it and the entire congregation joined in with him to conclude the celebration of a life lived for God.

If we could see beyond today
As God can see,

If all the clouds should roll away,
The shadows flee;
O'er present griefs we would not fret
Each sorrow we would soon forget,
For many joys are waiting yet
For you and me.
If we could know beyond today
As God doth know,
Why dearest treasures pass away
And tears much flow;
And why the darkness leads to light,
Why dreary days will soon grow bright,
Some day life's wrong will be made right,
Faith tells us so.
If we could see, if we could know
We often say,
But God in love a veil doth throw
Across our way.
We cannot see what lies before,
And so we cling to Him the more,
He leads us till this life is o'er,
Trust and obey.
—Norman J. Clayton

Death of a Believer

I had just arrived at a new pastorate in the city of Hamilton. I was asked if I would visit a former member who was very ill, dying with cancer.

I made an appointment to go and see him. His dear wife had propped him up in bed with clean, soft pillows. When I entered his room, I saw this elderly man lying peacefully in his bed.

His wife had introduced us, and as I sat on the edge of his bed and held his hand I said, "I am so sorry to see you so very sick, and to be honest I really don't know what to say."

He responded as he squeezed my hand by quoting the first verse of a hymn I had never heard before:

I am not skilled to understand
What God hath willed, what God hath planned;
I only know at His right hand
Is one who is my Savior.

Brushing away my tears, I prayed with this dear brother and left, thanking him for blessing my soul. I went right back to the church and found the rest of that hymn:

I take Him at His Word indeed:
"Christ died for sinners", this I read;
For in my heart I find a need
Of Him to be my Savior!
That He should leave His place on high
And come for sinful man to die,
You count it strange? So once did I,
Before I knew my Savior!
Yes, living dying let me bring my strength
My solace from this spring:
That He who lives to be my King
Once died to be my Savior!
—Dorothy Greenwell

Some time ago, Richard De Haan of the Radio Bible Class wrote a short article about his cousin Kurt De Haan, who had suddenly hastened home to be with the Lord.

He was only in his early fifties, and every lunch hour he would jog several miles. Dr. De Haan described his sudden home-going: "He fell into the arms of Jesus."

David C. Egner, in *Our Daily Bread,* remembers hearing the news of the death of Kurt De Haan. Thinking to himself, "He's in heaven," brought him great comfort.

A few days later, he was talking to his former pastor, who was now in his eighties. As Mr. Egner enquired about different friends in the church this pastor, Roy Williamson, replied: "He's in heaven, she's in heaven," and then with eyes twinkling, he said, "I know more people in heaven than I do on earth." (Many of us can relate to that statement.)

David Egner goes on to say: "What joy to know that when believers in Christ die, they are instantly with Jesus." The Apostle Paul put it like this: *"We are confident, yes, well pleased rather to be absent from the body and to be present with the Lord"* (2 Corinthians 5:8). No more pain. No more sadness. No more sin. Only peace. Only joy. Only glory. *"There is a time for everything, and a season for every activity under heaven: a time to be born and a time to die, a time to plant and a time to uproot"* (Ecclesiastes 3:1–2).

Sudden Death

Before I relate a story that happened many years ago, I need to explain something that happened beforehand and a matter that I discussed in Jonathon's home with him.

I had attended a convention where I heard a speaker whose name was Dr. Lee Roberson. At the time, he was the pastor of a large Baptist Church in Chattanooga, Tennessee, with a Sunday school numbering in the thousands. The main sanctuary of the church held six thousand. Therefore, whatever this man said about the Lord's work, I wanted to hear.

One thing I remember with certainty was his formula for allowing people to be involved in the work of the Sunday school. For those of my readers who were never involved in a Sunday school or perhaps don't even know what it is, I will explain.

Sunday school used to be held in most churches on Sunday afternoon at three o'clock. I would no sooner get home from the morning Worship Service, have lunch, then have to hurry back to attend Sunday school. After Sunday school I would hustle home, have supper, and then return to the church for the evening gospel service.

It made for a very busy and somewhat hectic Sunday, not at all what God intended for the Lord's Day. Years later it was changed to Sunday morning before the morning worship service, the hope being that everyone in Sunday school would remain for the eleven o'clock service. Most men and women, along with many of the children, usually stayed.

Now back to Dr. Roberson's requirements for all Sunday school workers. They must commit and promise to not only be on time for Sunday school but also be there well before the pupils started arriving. They must remain for the morning worship service and attend the evening service; in addition, attend the mid-week prayer meeting and the once-a-month teachers and officers meeting. This, of course, sounded rather autocratic to me, but then, who was I to judge the high standards of a church and pastor who were reaching thousands for the Lord? Obviously they were doing something right!

I returned home to my church and made a similar proposal to the Deacon's Board. They unanimously agreed that we, too, should adopt these standards. At the next Sunday school staff meeting I presented this plan to all who were present, with the exception of one man, Jonathon, who never attended such a meeting. Thus it was my task to make an appointment with Jonathon on an evening when his wife was out. He would be home with his three young children, who by this time were in bed or doing homework.

I explained the proposal to Jonathon in considerable detail, as well as considerable trepidation on my part, as Jonathon only came to Sunday school. In all fairness to this man, I should explain that he was the bus driver and had to leave his home quite early to pick up the children. We had urged him to make arrangements with the parents that the bus would take them home after the morning worship service, but he refused to do this. Therefore, by the time he had delivered everyone to his or her home, it made little sense for him to return to the church. This I could fully understand.

When I challenged him to start coming to the other meetings he was missing, he stopped me abruptly and said, "Pastor, let me make myself clear." His reply left me somewhat speechless, at least for a few moments.

"My philosophy for life," he went on, "is: first—my family (and he was a faithful husband and a good father). Second—my work (he was an electrical engineer and worked for one of the finest elevator companies in Canada at the time). Third—is God." This definitely surprised me.

Before I left that evening I prayed earnestly for Jonathon, mentioning specifically that he should sort out his priorities and focus first on His Lord and Saviour Jesus Christ.

I drove home that evening with a heavy heart, for I loved this man and respected what he had accomplished in his life. He was the only son of European immigrants who came to Canada after World War II. With great effort on the part of his parents, whom he loved dearly, and his own hard work, he had earned his degrees and was well on his way to climbing to the top of the ladder in his chosen field.

Well, though his wife and children continued to come to church and Sunday school, Jonathon never returned. Oh, we found someone to take his Sunday school class and God wonderfully provided a capable and skilled bus driver, but we lost to the Lord's work a man who was compassionate and caring. The boys in his class knew he loved and cared for them.

That was many years ago and I still look back on that particular situation with regret and sorrow. You see, I am much older now and have learned a great deal since then. Would things have turned out differently if I had gathered our prayer warriors together and fervently prayed for Jonathon? Or if I had gone back and encouraged him? If I had made him realize that I valued his friendship? But no, these things I never did.

To be perfectly honest, I was arrogant, and yes, autocratic and abused the leadership skills God had gifted me with to build up my self-esteem and feed my ego. James 5:16 says, *"Therefore confess your sins to each other and pray for each other so that you may be healed. The prayer of a righteous man is powerful and effective."* We also read in Chapter 3:17, *"But the wisdom that comes from Heaven is first of all pure; then peace-loving, considerate, submissive, full of mercy and good fruit, impartial and sincere."* Our Saviour said of Himself in Matthew 11:28, *"…for I am gentle and humble in heart…"* I fear humility was not exactly one of my strong points, and I confess this with genuine sadness.

Someone has well said: "Humility means affirming others, empowering and enabling others." I recently read the following in *Our Daily Bread*: "Knowing God makes us humble; knowing ourselves keeps us humble." But I must move on and as the Apostle Paul urged the Philippians in Chapter 3, *"...forgetting what is behind and straining to what is ahead...I press on toward the goal."*

I read a book by Isabel Kuhn entitled *Green Leaf in Drought-Time* when I was physically, emotionally and spiritually down, and I do mean *down.* The book is about the Mathews—the last missionaries to escape from the merciless hand of Chinese communists.

Accused of murder, they faced extreme persecution and hardship. The following words of Mrs. Mathews really uplifted me and helped start me on my way to recovery:

> I have come to think that there is an 'if' in every life...It is something that God could have made different, if He had chosen, because He has all power; and yet He has allowed that 'if' to be there. I do not discount the 'if' in your life. No matter what it is.
>
> Come to the Lord with your 'if'...Do not be thinking of your 'if'. Make a power out of your 'if' for God...say, "Nothing has ever come to me, nothing has ever gone from me, that I shall not be better for God by it." Face the 'if' in your life and say, *"For this I have Jesus."*

Quoting Anne Graham Lotz from her book *My Jesus is Everything*, she wrote:

> Knowing Jesus is my joy
> And reason for living.
> He is—
> The Wind beneath my wings,
> the Treasure that I seek
> The Foundation on which I build
> the Song in my heart
> The Object of my desire,
> the Breath of my life—
> He is my All in All.

Now back to my story about Jonathon! Not too many months later, as usual, he got up, shaved, showered, and ate a hearty breakfast. Before the children came down for breakfast, his wife noticed the car was still in the driveway. On her way to the front door, she looked in the living room and there sat Jonathon, as pale and grey as death itself.

Before he slipped into unconsciousness he mumbled that he wasn't feeling well and even before the ambulance arrived Jonathon slipped away from this earth to join the Saviour in his eternal home.

From my previous remarks and my own pilgrimage with its own failures and disappointments, it was not an easy service to conduct.

But dear reader, perhaps you are one who has drifted away from the Lord who so miraculously saved you. Indeed, you may be one who needs to be restored and brought back into fellowship with the One who has loved you unconditionally and has longed for your return just as the father did for his prodigal son as told in Luke 15.

I quote now from *Our Daily Bread*, November 12, 2005:

> Hosea 11:4, *'I drew them with gentle cords, with bands of* love'. The people in Hosea's day followed a similar pattern. Although God had rescued them from Egypt and nourished them, they turned their backs on Him. They insulted Him by worshiping the gods of the Canaanites. But still God loved them and longed for their return.

Do you fear you may have strayed too far from God to be restored? He who saved you and cares for you longs for your return. His arms are open in forgiveness and acceptance. He will never drive you away. "How glad we can be for our Father's love!" quotes David Egner in *Our Daily Bread.*

I've found a Friend, O such a Friend!
He loved me ere I knew Him;
He drew me with the cords of love,
And thus He bound me to Him.
—James G. Small

My sin—O the bliss of this glorious thought—
My sin, not in part but the whole,
Is nailed to the cross and I bear it no more
Praise the Lord, praise the Lord, O my soul.
—H. G. Spafford

So dear readers, please keep in mind that God loves you unconditionally and though His Spirit grieves when you wander away from Him into the paths of sin, God always keeps His promises and will keep on loving you still.

To conclude this section I would like to summarize what Neil T. Anderson has said in his book, *Victory Over the Darkness*:

What Happens When I Stumble In My Faith?

Have you ever thought God is ready to give up on you because, instead of walking confidently in faith, you sometimes stumble and fall? Do you ever fear that there is a limit to God's tolerance for your failure and that you are walking dangerously near that outer barrier or have already crossed it? Many Christians are defeated by that kind of thinking. They believe that God is upset with them, that He is ready to dump them or that He has already given up on them because their daily performance is less than perfect.

It is true that the walk of faith can sometimes be interrupted by moments of personal unbelief, rebellion, or even Satanic deception. During those moments, we think God has surely lost His patience with us and is ready to give up on us. We will probably give up if we think God has. We stop walking by faith in God, slump dejectedly by the side of the road and wonder, *What's the use?* We feel defeated, our purpose for being here is suspended and Satan is elated.

God Loves You Just The Way You Are

The primary truth you need to know about God for your faith to remain strong is that His love and acceptance are unconditional. When your walk of faith is strong, God loves you. When your walk of faith is weak, God loves you. God's love for you is the great eternal constant in the midst of all the inconsistencies of your daily walk.

God Loves You No Matter What You Do

God wants us to do good, of course. The Apostle John wrote: 'I write this to you that you might not sin…But if anybody does sin, we have one who speaks to the Father in our defense—Jesus Christ, the Righteous One. He is the atoning sacrifice for our sins, and not only for ours but also for the sins of the whole world' (1 John 2:1–2).

One reason we doubt God's love is that we have an adversary who uses every little offence to accuse us of being good-for-nothings. Your advocate, Jesus Christ, however, is more powerful than your adversary. He has cancelled the debt of your past, present and future sins. No matter what you do or how you fail, God will still love you because the love of God is not dependent upon its object; it is dependent upon His character. Because He loves you, He will discipline you in order that you 'may share His holiness' (Hebrews 12:10).

God says to you, 'I want you to know something. No matter what you do in life, I'm always going to love you. You can be honest with me and tell me the truth, I may not approve of everything you do, but I'm always going to love you.'

At this point in the chapter I feel led to give a personal word of testimony. Back some time ago (and I am not proud to relate part of this story), I was at a very low point in my spiritual life. My dear daughter, Judith (the editor of this book), pointed me to Hosea 14:4: *"I will heal their backsliding, I will love them freely: for my anger is turned away from him"* (KJV). I then wrote these words in my Bible (the Bible that I have designated to be Judith's after my home-going): "Judith, dear, because of your wise and loving counsel, Hosea 14:4 has been my experience of God's healing. Love, Dad."

Jill and Stuart Briscoe in their daily devotional, *In a Quiet Place*, invite us to read Titus 3:3–7:

At one time we too were foolish, disobedient, deceived and enslaved by all kinds of passions and pleasures. We lived in malice and envy, being hated and hating one another. But when the kindness and love of God our Savior appeared, he saved us, not because of righteous things we had done, but because of his mercy. He saved us through the washing of rebirth and renewal by the Holy Spirit, whom he poured out on us generously through Jesus Christ our Savior, so that, having been justified by his grace, we might become heirs having the hope of eternal life.

The Restored Image

My mother acquired a lot of antiques for her beautiful manor house in England. To me they were rather ugly lumps of wood. I remember her bringing one piece in, and I said, "Oh, Mother, what on earth is that?" She replied, "It's the most beautiful piece!" and told me all about it. I said that it just looked like an old piece of wood. Her answer: "It's lost its image."

Well, my mother worked and worked on that piece. Eventually the image that had been lost came through. And it was indeed a beautiful piece of furniture. It's one of the precious things we brought with us from England. It stands in our home now, reminding me of a spiritual principle: that it cost my mom almost more to restore it than to buy it.

I cannot help thinking of my own life as an "ugly lump of wood"—loveless, carnal, selfish, irritable, impatient. And yet I know that somewhere in me is the image of God that needs to be restored. As you read your Bible during the next few days, look for clues about the divine image that God is restoring in you. What will you look and act like eventually, as that image becomes more defined?

Prayer

Lord, I need to remember what I used to be—it keeps me humble! But I must bear in mind what I will be—that keeps me going. Thank you, Lord. Amen.

"God…comforts us in all our trials so we can comfort others who are experiencing difficulties." In his book, *Beginning Again*, Terry Hershey writes,

> God not only says that failure is never the final word, but that your area of weakness will become your area of strength. Where you were weak and learned grace it will become a means whereby you can reach out and touch the lives of others who need the same good news…God is not only working to heal you, but to heal others through you, to make you what Henri Nouwen called a 'wounded healer.'
>
> Such healing doesn't happen through the man or woman who has all the answers. It happens through the man or woman who understands pain and grace. Nouwen explains, "…For a deep understanding of his own pain makes it possible for the [wounded healer] to convert his weaknesses into strength and to offer his experience as a source of healing to those who are often lost in the darkness of their own misunderstood suffering." I believe it was Ernest Hemingway who first used the phrase, "Growing strong in the broken places." The idea behind these words is that where a bone is broken and heals, it becomes the strongest part of the bone.
>
> The same is true of our broken places—where we have been hurt, have fallen or failed. When we bring these to Christ for his healing, his strength is then made perfect in and through our weaknesses. This is certainly true in ministering effectively to other people. They are helped, not through our brilliant logic or persuasive speech, but through the sharing of our struggles, and how, with God's help, we have overcome. It is a case of one beggar showing other beggars where to find bread.
>
> Suggested prayer: "Dear God, please heal me in my many broken places and use me to be a wounded healer to many others who have fallen, been wounded, hurt, or broken hearted. Thank you for hearing and answering my prayer. Gratefully in Jesus' name, amen."

I met this Christian brother at a seminar in Wheaton, Illinois, in the summer of 2004. Art came from California and, as it turned out, we were assigned a room to share. When I asked about his conversion, he told me a fascinating account of how God reached him while he was still a relatively young man.

He first told me that he had no history of being God-conscious whatsoever. In fact, he was a very worldly young man. Before he married, he had tasted and experienced all that the world had to offer. He lived and worked in Hollywood. He was a writer and soon became very successful, working with many actors who were famous and well-known.

By this time, he was married with children. None of them cared anything about God, let alone knowing that they could have a personal relationship with Him through His Son, the Lord Jesus Christ.

One day, without any warning whatsoever, he had a major heart attack. His heart stopped beating! Have you ever wondered, as I have, what is happening to someone when his or her heart stops beating?

This is what he related to me: "I felt someone or something pushing me down into a very dark hole." The paramedics arrived at this time and got his heart beating again. He was still unconscious, but not experiencing being pushed into this big, dark hole. His heart stopped at least two more times before they had him stabilized in the emergency room of the hospital. Each time he was being pushed into the abyss.

After regaining consciousness approximately three days later, he related the experience he had to his wife. When he returned home from the hospital, he began searching for someone who could tell him about God. He soon accepted Jesus Christ as his personal Saviour.

Art became a zealous Christian and soon his wife and children accepted the Lord. In those days, Hollywood was considered "sin city" and no place for a committed Christian to work or live. Art had the same mindset as Jonathon Goforth of China. Goforth said "…even before I gave myself to the Lord Jesus Christ, I had given up cards, dancing, the reading of questionable literature and other such things because I felt they were but a waste of precious time which might be spent in more worthwhile ways. After my conversion, I saw these and many other things were so many leakages of spiritual power."

Many years ago, an evangelist from the United States was not only an excellent speaker, but also a singer and guitar player. I have saved the sheet music all these years of a song he sang, written by Tim Spencer. If you are an unbeliever, not yet committed to the Lamb of God Who takes away the sin of the world, let this song touch and move your heart to accept Jesus Christ as your personal Saviour.

It's Your Life

It's your life, and you can kill it!
It's your heart and you can still it!
It's your grave and you can fill it!
But remember it's God's love you're throwing away!
It's your life for you to kill,
It's your life for you to still,
It's your grave for you to fill,
But remember it's God love you're throwing away!
It's your life, you can abuse it!
It's your soul, and you can lose it!
Heaven or hell, just as you choose it!
But remember it's God's love you're throwing away!
It's your life that you abuse
It's your soul for you to lose,
It's your hell for you to choose,
But remember it's God's love you're throwing away!

Art left his lucrative career with no regrets and faithfully served the Lord, often writing plays for church programs as well as making a comfortable living for his family. The words of the following hymn, by Frances R. Havergal, very fittingly describe Art's dedication to the Lord.

Take my life and let it be
Consecrated, Lord, to Thee;
Take my hands, and let them move
At the impulse of Thy love.

Take my feet, and let them be
Swift and beautiful for Thee;
Take my voice, and let me sing,
Always only for my King.
Take my lips, and let them be
Filled with messages from Thee;
Take my silver and my gold,
Not a mite would I withhold.
Take my moments and my days,
Let them flow in endless praise;
Take my intellect and use
Every pow'r as Thou shalt choose.
Take my will, and make it Thine,
It shall be no longer mine;
Take my heart, it is Thine own,
It shall be Thy royal throne.

At the time of this writing, Art is nearing his eightieth birthday and, along with his wife, children, and grandchildren, is still walking with the Lord.

The following appeared in an *Ann Landers* column some years ago. It was written by Robert Test and entitled *To Remember Me*.

> The day will come when my body will lie upon a white sheet neatly tucked under four corners of a mattress located in a hospital busily occupied with the living and the dying. At a certain moment, a doctor will determine that my brain has ceased to function and that, for all intents and purposes, my life has stopped.
>
> When that happens, do not attempt to instill artificial life into my body by the use of a machine. And don't call this my deathbed. Let it be called the Bed of Life, and let my body be taken from it to help others lead fuller lives.
>
> Give my sight to the man who has never seen a sunrise, a baby's face or love in the eyes of a woman.

Give my heart to a person whose own heart has caused nothing but endless days of pain.

Give my blood to the teenager who was pulled from the wreckage of his car, so that he might live to see his grandchildren play.

Give my kidneys to one who depends on a machine to exist from week to week.

Take my bones, every muscle, every fibre and nerve in my body, and find a way to make a crippled child walk.

Explore every corner of my brain. Take my cells if necessary, and let them grow so that, some day, a speechless boy will shout at the crack of a bat and a deaf girl will hear the sound of rain against her window.

Burn what is left of me and scatter the ashes to the winds to help the flowers grow.

If you must bury something, let it be my faults, my weaknesses and all prejudice against my fellow man.

Give my sins to the devil. Give my soul to God.

If, by chance, you wish to remember me, do it with a kind deed or word to someone who needs it. If you do all I have asked, I will live forever.

"Lord, remind me how brief my time on earth will be. Remind me that my days are numbered, and that my life is fleeing away" (Psalm 39:4, NLT). In his book, *The Purpose Driven Life*, Rick Warren states, "…earth is not our final home; we were created for something much better…at death you won't leave home—you'll go home."

If you rely upon God's strength
And live a life that's true,
Then what you do in Jesus' name
Will be His work through you.
—*Selected*

"My work for God in public is what I am in private."
—*Oswald Chambers*

JUST A *Little* COUNTRY GIRL

"Then he called the crowd to him along with his disciples and said: 'If anyone would come after me, he must deny himself and take up his cross and follow me. For whoever wants to save his life will lose it, but whoever loses his life for me and for the gospel will save it.'"

(Mark 8:34-35)

"Study the Bible to be wise; believe it to be safe; practice it to be holy."

—*Our Daily Bread*

I met this teenager and her sister in a roundabout way. I was visiting the mother of one of our junior Sunday school pupils. The child came in from the country via our Sunday school bus. Neither the mother nor the father attended our church.

When I arrived, the elder daughter of the family was also present. I spoke to both of these women and urged them to start attending church. The daughter said that she already attended a local church, but being farmers, it was not always possible to attend on a regular basis. But she asked if it might be possible for someone to pick up her two teenage daughters to attend Sunday school.

At first, to be frank, I was puzzled by the situation, for here was a twelve-year-old girl born to her parents after their daughter was married and had two girls. When I learned their ages, which were fifteen and sixteen, I asked the question as to whether or not they would want to come! She assured me they would be ready on Sunday morning waiting for transportation. In hindsight, I realized that, living in the country, they would be glad to get into town regardless of where they were going.

As it turned out, the bus did not travel on their side road so I went for them myself. I need to explain, especially for the younger reader, that in those days, women who professed to be Christians never wore makeup or earrings.

So here they were, standing in the laneway of the farm. As they climbed into the car, I wondered to myself how we would ever be able to reach these girls with the gospel. They had every kind of makeup on that was available and it was "plastered" on! They were provocatively dressed and, horrors, they were wearing earrings almost down to their shoulders! I was obviously forgetting that it is the power of the Holy Spirit to open up truth to someone's heart!

There wasn't a lot of conversation as we drove into town. However, when we arrived, they were assigned to my wife's class of young people. Well, as she and the other kids accepted them, my wife not only taught them the Word of God but also loved them right from the beginning. Both girls came to accept the Lord as their personal Saviour.

I'll call one Janet, who was the eldest, and the other Donna. They were quick to get involved in class activities, attending church morning and evening and always coming to the young people's meeting on Friday night. I cannot remember if Donna was ever baptized but Janet was and subsequently joined the church.

Sadly, after a year or so, Donna drifted away from the church and seemingly from the Lord. A few years later she married her long-time boyfriend and we rarely saw her throughout all those years.

Now to go into some detail about the subject of this chapter—our little country girl, Janet. When Janet first began coming to our little church, she had a boyfriend. He was "Mr. Wonderful." In order to be with Janet, he accompanied her to Sunday services and to the young people's group on Friday evening.

We had interesting and happy meetings, playing baseball in the summer, going out on Halloween, skating and tobogganing in the winter, with parties on various occasions. All activities were accompanied by messages, developed to help the young people grow and mature in the Lord.

During these years, "Mr. Wonderful" was in every respect a perfect gentleman: polite, courteous, reverent and always thoughtful of other people; but he did not, and would not accept Christ as his Saviour. Though he came from a godless home, he lived a very good life and no doubt thought his good life and works would save him.

Finally, Janet gave him an ultimatum—accept her Saviour as his own or they would have to break up. With no positive response from him, she gave him up. There is no doubt this was painful for both of them, but Janet was a committed and fully surrendered Christian and so, after making this decision, went on in her own path of dedication and service to the Lord.

The irony in this situation was that our "Mr. Wonderful" (we'll call him Brent), started dating another girl in our church. Like Janet, she was a Christian and eventually Brent made a profession of accepting Christ as Saviour and married and had a family with Dorothy.

Brent had an exceptionally good position in his career and he climbed to the top of his profession and became quite successful. He continued to always be the perfect gentleman. Not too many years ago we learned that Brent woke up one morning with severe chest pains and before Dorothy could get help, Brent slipped away in her arms and hastened home to heaven. We made it a point to visit Dorothy as soon as we were able and had a time of fellowship. We read comforting words from the Scripture, praying for God's strength to go on alone without Brent but with the presence of her Saviour by her side.

Now back again to our country girl who had now graduated from high school and was working in a small supermarket as a cashier. Most of the customers knew she was a born-again Christian.

One day, the owner of the only drycleaners in town came into the store. With all of the staff in listening distance, as well as a few customers, he said, oozing sarcasm in a loud voice, "Anyone here want to join me for a prayer meeting?" and laughing loudly left the store. Our little country girl, only five feet tall and weighing less than a hundred pounds, felt her face flush as this bulk of a man strolled out of the store. But she bravely continued with her work. I recall this episode and tell you about it to show you, dear readers, what an outstanding Christian she continued to be.

The following article entitled *Transformation*, aptly describes the tremendous change that took place in the life of this young woman.

> A woman was asked by a co-worker, "What is it like to be a Christian?" The co-worker replied, "It is like being a pumpkin. God picks you from the patch, brings you in, and washes all the dirt off of you. Then he cuts off the top and scoops out all the yucky stuff. He removes the seeds of doubt, hate, greed, and then He carves you a new smiling face and puts His light inside of you to shine for all the world to see."
> —*Author Unknown*

Now back to our story. Janet met up with a young man. He was unsaved and came from a religious family. Janet brought him out to all the services and gave him time to hear and accept the message of the gospel. You see, she knew well the verse in Scripture found in 2 Corinthians 6:14, *"Do not be yoked together with unbelievers. For what do righteousness and wickedness have in common? Or what fellowship can light have with darkness?"*

During Evangelistic meetings with Don Holliday and George Shuttleworth, Donald accepted the Lord. Both of these evangelists are still living today and though retired, still actively serve the Lord. Donald grew and matured in the faith and showed by his life that his experience was real.

They had a lovely and Christ-honouring wedding and commenced a life of "One in the Lord." This might be a good time to bring up the subject that, in spite of our so-called "enlightened age," is still taboo with many Christians…the subject of sex! Quoting from Promise Keepers Canada in a book compiled and written by Dr. Steve Masterson, the introduction plainly states God's perspective of this whole issue:

> Through the act of sexual love, the image of God, in its masculine and feminine aspects, is completed.
>
> Becoming one flesh, as Adam and Eve did before the fall, meant entering into a ONENESS, which is that mysterious Biblical description of sex, a blending of the two of them into the brilliant image of God.
>
> God designed sex to be the fusing of one male soul, through the body, to another female soul, through the body. The result is an entirely new reality…the full and complete display of God's image and likeness.
> (Genesis 2:24 and Ephesians 5:31)
>
> The Biblical concept of oneness is that, through the sex act, each participant irretrievably gives the other a part of his or her body, soul and spirit.
>
> In so doing, each person, the male and the female, is thereby changed and an entirely new entity created, one that in design is to never be separated. Why? Because the Oneness in the Godhead is never separated.
>
> Sexuality and sex worked wonderfully in Adam and Eve's marriage before the fall. They gave of the deepest parts of themselves in the context of sinless love, no shame, no self-consciousness and complete vulnerability and openness. They were changed and united forever. They knew in a way like no other, the deep union and intimacy of complete oneness.
>
> Adam and Eve fully completed one another and in becoming one flesh, brilliantly reflected God's image and likeness.
> (1 Corinthians 6:12–18)

I recommend that my readers look up for themselves the Scripture texts as indicated. And, dear readers, please do not take offence at this subject as stated above. Too long we have heard little or nothing about this from our pulpits from people who claim to preach the whole counsel of God.

Janet and Donald started a family and eventually had four boys. The children were carefully prayed for and nurtured in the things of the Lord. They were taken to Sunday school and church from babyhood on up to adulthood.

Another interesting part of their story is their eldest son. He met and married a Christian girl from their church and moved to the city. The amazing thing about this young woman is that she and her siblings were invited out to Sunday school. These children and their parents never attended a church of any denomination. In fact, we were horrified (maybe that's too strong a word for this day and age) to watch the father and his brother build their home on Sunday!

But through the children coming to Sunday school and church, the parents came and accepted Christ as personal Saviour. This became a truly Christian home. This was some time after we had moved on but it nonetheless thrilled us the way God used ordinary people to bring this other family to the Lord.

One of the realities in marriage is that every relationship has its ups and downs with hardships and trials. We usually don't need much teaching on the mountain tops of our lives but we certainly need to be reminded of what God can do with our painful moments.

Some of that hardship and unknown came about in a very difficult way. When Janet was still a comparatively young woman, she suffered a brain aneurysm and slipped home to heaven without ever regaining consciousness. Her sudden home-going was a shock to my wife and me, but we remembered with joy in our hearts a young teenage girl who came to dearly love the Lord and brought much pleasure and encouragement into our lives. I still look back to that day so many years ago when I went out to the country to bring two teenagers into Sunday school and church, one who would follow the Lord faithfully throughout her short but fruitful life.

It hurts to endure life's trials…Yet, without those deep hurts, we have very little capacity to receive godly counsel or make forward progress toward maturity.

Over the long haul, God is honing us through such tests. Stretching us. Breaking us. Crushing us. Reducing us to an absolute, open-armed trust, where we say, "Lord, I have come to the end of my own flesh."

The Lord also will be a stronghold for the oppressed,
a stronghold in times of trouble. (Psalm 9:9)
—Charles Swindoll

This I Know

I do not know what next may come
Across my pilgrim way;
I do not know tomorrow's road,
Nor see beyond today.
But this I know—my Saviour knows,
The path I cannot see;
And I can trust His wounded hand
To guide and care for me.
I do not know what may await
Or what the morrow brings;
But with the glad salute of faith,
I hail its opening wings;
For this I know—that in my Lord
Shall all my needs be met;
And I can trust the heart of Him
Who has not failed me yet.
—E. Margaret Clarkson

A praise chorus called *Jesus, All for Jesus* truly describes Janet's life.

Jesus, all for Jesus,
All I am and have and ever hope to be.
All of my ambitions hopes and plans,
I surrender these into Your hands.

For it's only in Your will that I am free,
For it's only in Your will that I am free,
Jesus, all for Jesus,
All I am and have and ever hope to be.
—Robin Mark

"Jesus is all we have, He is all we need, and all we want."
—Vance Havner, Evangelist

"Forget the former things; do not dwell on the past. See, I am doing a new thing! Now it springs up; do you not perceive it? I am making a way in the desert and streams in the wasteland."
(Isaiah 43:18-19)

"God often plants His flowers among rough rocks!"
—*Selected*

I will call him George. He was married with four daughters. His wife, after several years of marriage, left them to go and live with another man in a nearby city.

George faithfully looked after the children as best he could while working full-time. The children occasionally visited their mother on weekends and holidays. George brought them to Sunday school and church on a regular basis with the hope that they would accept Christ as Saviour and live a godly life that would bring glory and honour to the Saviour he loved. But sadly, when they were teenagers, they decided their father was too strict. They left him and went to live with their mother, whose lifestyle they preferred.

After all these years of raising his children, providing them with all their needs, and when possible, even their wants, George was left alone, really alone! Men who find themselves in this situation, abandoned and forsaken, often retreat from society and become reclusive. To some extent, this was the case with George. He continued to come to church faithfully but otherwise shunned social events and relationships with any of the people in the church.

How Can I Be Lonely?

One is walking with me over life's uneven way,
Constantly supporting me each moment of the day;
How can I be lonely when such fellowship is mine,
With my blessed Lord divine!
How can I be lonely
When I've Jesus only
To be my companion and unfailing guide?
Why should I be weary,
Or my path seem dreary,
When He's walking by my side!
Days may bring their burdens and their trials as I go,
But my Lord is near and helps to make them lighter grow.
Life may have its crosses, or its losses, or increases,
Jesus meets them all with peace.
In the hour of sad bereavement or of bitter loss,
I can find support and consolation at the cross;
Want or woe or suff'ring all seem glorified when He
Daily walks and talks with me.
In life's rosy morning when the skies above are clear,
In its noon-tide hours with many cares and problems near,
Or when evening shadows fall at closing of my day
Jesus will be there always.

—Haldor Lillenas

Now I want to tell you another somewhat sorrowful story (but keep reading, for as Corrie ten Boom often said: "The best is yet to come!"). I will call this dear lady Hilda. She married a fine Christian man several years older than she, and for a number of years they lived an idealistic life.

They had a beautiful old home in a fashionable area of the city, a late model car, a cottage in Muskoka, and Hilda could afford to buy her clothes from the upscale shops. Both were active in the church, he a deacon and trustee, she an accomplished and faithful organist who played every Sunday.

But calamity struck very, very suddenly. Hilda's husband, Tom, was stricken with a very debilitating stroke, loss of speech, and one whole side of his body completely paralyzed.

Thankfully this dear couple knew God and His Word. Hebrews 4:14 and 16 says, *"Therefore, since we have a great high priest who has gone through the heavens, Jesus, the Son of God, let us hold firmly to the faith we profess. Let us then approach the throne of grace with confidence, so that we may receive mercy and find grace to help us in our time of need."*

When life's afflictions batter you
Like waves upon the sand
Remember to look up to God
And take His outstretched hand.
—*Anonymous*

Tom was in the hospital for months, but physiotherapy did not seem to help very much. Since Hilda was working, she came to the conclusion that a nursing home would be the best place for Tom; she could and would visit him every day. All of these hospital and nursing home costs at that time were not covered by a government health plan.

When their savings were depleted, Hilda had some hard decisions to make on her own. She sold the car, then the cottage, and had to renovate the upstairs of their home and rent it to provide extra income.

Finally, Hilda had no choice but to bring Tom home. This greatly increased her workload, as she had to take care of all his needs. Tom sat in his wheelchair all day long with nothing or no one to stimulate him; remember, he never regained his speech.

Some of the men from the church visited him from time to time but it was always a difficult visit when Tom could not respond verbally. Eventually these visits were more and more sporadic.

Charles R. Swindoll, in his daily devotional *Bedside Blessings*, says the following:

> If I have learned anything during my journey on Planet Earth, it is that people need one another. The presence of other people is essential—caring people, helpful people, interesting people, friendly people, and thoughtful people. These folks take the grind out of life. By the time we are tempted to think we can handle things alone—boom! We run into some obstacle and need assistance. We discover all over again that we are not nearly as self-sufficient as we thought. *"A man's counsel is sweet to his friend." (Proverbs 27:9)*

I am sure Hilda knew well the gospel song written by Joseph Scriven, and I quote the third verse:

Are we weak and heavy-laden?
Cumbered with a load of care?
Precious Saviour still our Refuge –
Take it to the Lord in prayer.
Do thy friends despise, forsake thee?
Take it to the Lord in prayer,
In His arms He'll take and shield thee,
Thou wilt find a solace there.

A short time later, Tom slipped peacefully to his heavenly home, ending years of pain, emotional suffering, humiliation and loss of almost everything he enjoyed and cherished. But what about Hilda? She was totally alone.

She had been unable to attend church for years and after such a long period of time even her closest female friends, as well as couples, had pretty well forgotten her. She told me on my visit to her that she would often phone the operator to make sure her telephone was in working order. Now that's loneliness to the nth degree! How I wish Hilda could have heard one of our elderly deacons pray: "Lord, help us to trust You even though we can't trace You."

Being a pianist and organist I am sure she knew well this gospel song:

Sometime We'll Understand

Not now, but in the coming years—
It may be in the better land—
We'll read the meaning of our tears,
And there, sometime, we'll understand.
We'll know why clouds instead of sun
Were over many a cherished plan
Why song had ceased when scarce begun:
'Tis there, sometime, we'll understand.
Then trust in God thro' all thy days;
Fear not for He doth hold thy hand
Though dark thy way, still sing and praise;
Sometime, sometime we'll understand.
—*M. N. Cornelius*

Well, this story has a happy ending (aren't you glad?)! I certainly am! I am just about ready to cry the way I did when Hilda told me the heartache, pain, and desperate loneliness she experienced. Well now, you've guessed it! George and Hilda met, married and shared many happy years together.

Mrs. Cowman in her book, *Streams in the Desert,* quotes F. B. Meyer:

> The oriental shepherd was always ahead of his sheep. He was down in front. Any attack on them had to take him into account. Now God is down in front. He is in the tomorrows. It is tomorrow that fills men with dread. God is there already. All the tomorrows of our life have to pass Him before they can get to us.

God Is In Every Tomorrow

God is in every tomorrow,
Therefore I live for today,
Certain at finding at sunrise,
Guidance and strength for the way;
Power for each moment of weakness,
Hope for each moment of pain,
Comfort for every sorrow,
Sunshine and joy after rain.
—Anonymous

May I ask, dear reader, if sorrow, suffering, and the pain of loneliness have been experienced in your life? Have you been able to say as the Psalmist did in Psalm 23, *"The Lord is my Shepherd, I shall not want"*?

In Joel 2:32, we read: *"And everyone who calls on the name of the Lord will be saved."* Why not take God at His Word and call upon His name and know the joy of salvation? Have the assurance that your name is in the Lamb's Book of Life and you are on your way to that eternal home where *"...God will wipe away every tear from their eyes."*

Dear reader, may I also stop to ask you another pertinent question? Have you ever been lonely? I mean really, really, lonely! Lonely, perhaps so deep in the pit of discouragement, disappointment, loss of a close friend, or maybe abandoned by your spouse or one of your children. When despair and, yes, depression fall over you like a dark cloud, following you through the day and preventing sleep at night, most of us, if we would admit it, have been there! Sometimes in a group or even a crowd, you have felt so alone.

> Perhaps this has been a difficult year for you. The future stretching out before you may seem gloomy or threatening...In your rare moments of quiet, you may wonder, *Where is God?*
>
> He's right there at your side, my friend. He has never left. He has never removed His eye from you, nor has His attention wandered to other matters. Not even for a heartbeat. He has never ceased caring for you, thinking about you, considering

your situation, and loving you with a passion and intensity beyond comprehension.

My soul thirsts for God, for the living God. (Psalm 42:2)
—*Bedside Blessings* by Charles Swindoll

The Bible has told us, both in the Old Testament as well as the New, of many men and women who were left alone with what seemed like no hope. There was Joseph, Daniel, Elisha, David, Hosea, Paul, John, the apostles, and of course, Jesus, our precious Lord and Saviour. There are countless others, too numerous to name.

God has told us in Jeremiah 31:17, *"There is hope for your future, declares the Lord…"* so when we are lonely, truly feeling alone, we need to remember, there is *hope*. Jesus never fails.

We read in Hebrews 10:22, *"Let us draw near to God with a sincere heart in full assurance of faith…"* and verse 23, *"Let us hold unswervingly to the hope we profess, for He who promised is faithful."* However, to be honest, when we are in the pit of despair and extreme loneliness, we don't need a sermon. Read on, please.

I want to tell you about an interesting Christian author by the name of Barbara Johnson. I will be quoting from her book shortly. The publishers of her book, *Pain is inevitable but MISERY IS OPTIONAL so Stick a Geranium in Your Hat and Be Happy!*—write:

> Barbara's wit has helped her survive four devastating experiences, and to equip her with the credentials to help others work through their own pain. Her husband was in a near-fatal accident and slowly recovered from debilitating injuries. She lost one son in Vietnam, another son to a drunk driver, and a third to the homosexual lifestyle. And recently she was diagnosed as having adult-onset diabetes. Barbara has learned that though pain is inevitable to us all, we can choose to pick the flowers instead of the weeds.

Barbara writes, "Life is never perfect, but Jesus is. And He takes the imperfections—the broken pieces and the messes—and turns them into hope." After driving through Palm Springs, California, she and her husband saw a sign advertising 'DESERT SWEETENED GRAPEFRUIT' and she thought to herself, "That's the way it is with all of us when we go through a desert experience—when we're out there in the barren and dry wastes, not seeming to receive any encouragement from anybody. That's the time God uses to sweeten us as we learn to give our problems completely to Him."

I digress for a moment to quote verses written by Mosie Lister, who recently lost his struggle with cancer and went home to heaven. Elvis Presley recorded this gospel song and it became a number one hit on the charts.

Where No One Stands Alone

Once I stood in the night with my head bowed low,
In the darkness as black as could be;
And my heart felt alone and I cried,
"O Lord, don't hide Your face from me."
Hold my hand all the way,
Ev'ry hour, ev'ry day,
From here to the great unknown.
Take my hand; let me stand
Where no one stands alone.

Now back to Mrs. Johnson.

There are several steps we all go through when we try to give a problem completely to God…first…you CHURN. You feel as if your insides are full of knives, chopping you up in a grinder…your next step is to BURN…You literally feel as if you're burning inside.

In your third step you YEARN…you yearn for the happy past and this stage often lasts the longest of all.

But then you take your next step, which is to LEARN… You learn that you're in a long growth process. You become more understanding and compassionate. Spiritual values you learned in the past will suddenly become *real* to you. You will learn a great deal about unconditional love and reaching out to help others. The wonderful result is that that you relieve your own pain.

> And, finally, you take your last step—you TURN. You learn to turn the problem over to the Lord completely by saying, "Whatever, Lord! Whatever you bring into my life, You are big enough to get me through it...When you nail your problem to the foot of the Cross and say you have deposited that problem with the Lord and truly mean it, then you will be relieved of your crushing burden...you have a *door of hope ahead!*

She concludes this section of her book by saying, "Even in the midst of this messy old world, we can rejoice because we know our future—and our hope—is in Him!"

Let God Take You by the Hand

If you sometimes feel
just like a lonely traveler
Wandering through a dark,
unfriendly land
Far from your loved ones
and your Father's home...
Then it's time to let God take you by the hand.
For He alone can bring you
hope and comfort
When nothing goes the way
you might have planned,
When all your dreams
have turned to dust and ashes...
Then it's time to let God take you by the hand.
Remember that you have
no cares nor troubles
That He doesn't know about
and understand,
You have no problems
past His wise solution
If you only let God take you by the hand.
Prepare your heart
and you'll receive His guidance,

Open your mind
to hear His soft command
And you'll have peace
and strength in great abundance
BECAUSE YOU'VE LET GOD TAKE YOU BY THE HAND.
—Selected

NEVER ALONE

I'm never alone in the morning
As I rise at the break of day,
For Jesus who watched through the darkness
Says, "Lo I am with you always."
I'm never alone at my table
Though loved ones no longer I see;
Far dearer than all who have vanished
Is Jesus who breaks bread with me.
I'm never alone through the daylight,
Though nothing but trials I see.
Though the furnace be seven times heated
The 'form of the fourth' walks with me.
I'm never alone at the twilight
When darkness around me doth creep
And spectres press hard round my pillow.
He watches and cares while I sleep.
I'm walking and talking with Jesus
Each day as I travel along.
I'm never alone. Hallelujah!
The joy of the Lord is my song.
—Elizabeth Osborn

"Fallen threads I will not search for—I will weave."
—George MacDonald

NEVER TOO *Old* TO FALL IN LOVE

"Many waters cannot quench the flame of love, neither can the floods drown it. If a man tried to buy it with everything he owned, he couldn't do it."

(Song of Solomon 8:7, TLB)

"We must wait for God in the wind and the wet, in the thunder and lightning, in the cold and dark. Wait, and He'll come."

—Frederick Faber, English Writer

This is a story I know you will enjoy, whether you are young, middle-aged or a senior. It's a love story! Many years ago, when I was a young man of twenty-nine, I was invited to become the pastor of a small congregation in Hamilton, Ontario—Westside Baptist Church.

Dr. J. F. Holliday was a former pastor of the church when it had a large membership. He had advised me that the first thing he did when he commenced pastoring a new congregation was to visit the homes of every member and adherent of the church. This I did and one of my first encounters was with Jim MacKenzie. He was a Scotsman with a definite b-r-r-r-r-r in his speech. He was a gentle, kind, and generous man, a long-time member of the church attending one service a week.

Jim had retired from the hydro company where he had worked most of his life. He had a substantial pension from them, but to fill in his days, he worked part-time as, of all things, a bartender for a lawn bowling men's club. Jim was not comfortable doing such work. Few, if any, knew he was engaged in such a job. Those were the days when most evangelical Christians were total abstainers from alcoholic beverages.

His life, to some degree, had been a sad one. In his youth he had married an unsaved woman who had no use for religion and no time for church. They had one child, a daughter.

Jim faithfully took his daughter to Sunday school and church, but as she approached her teen years, she was not interested in attending church. Jim's wife then said she no longer had to attend church with her father.

Not too long after we arrived at this ministry, Jim asked me if I would visit his wife, explaining to me the fact that she was dying with terminal cancer. And so it was that I visited her and explained the message of the gospel.

When the Apostle Peter wrote to Christians scattered around the Roman Empire, he wrote to wives and husbands in Chapter 3 in his first letter. He said to the wives (although take note that Jack's situation was in the reverse), *"Wives, in the same manner be submissive to your husbands so that, if any of them do not believe the Word, they may be won over without words by the behaviour of their wives, when they see the purity and reverence of your lives. Your beauty should not come from outward adornment. Instead it should be that of your inner self, the unfading beauty of a gentle and quiet spirit, which is of great worth in God's sight" (1 Peter 3:1–4).*

I have quoted this passage because I believe it was this man's gentle and kind spirit that caused his wife to finally realize that her husband had a peace in his heart that she never had. I explained the gospel message to this dear lady; the gospel being that Christ Jesus, the Son of God, died on Calvary's cross to pay the price for all of her sin, past, present, and future. If she would accept Him as personal Saviour she could know the joy of sins forgiven. Her name would be written in the Lamb's Book of Life, securing for her a place in heaven. So it was my happy and joyful privilege to pray with her to accept God's forgiveness and love and become His child.

The truth I showed her comes from the Gospel of John 1:10–12. *"He was in the world, and though the world was made through Him, the world did not recognize Him. He came to that which was His own, but his own did not receive him. Yet to all who received Him, to those who believed in His name, He gave the right to become children of God…"*

Someone has well said, "Our action is to believe and receive; God's action is to give us power to become His children." Mrs. MacKenzie also believed the truth of Romans 5:6–8: *"You see, at just the right time, when we were still powerless, Christ died for the ungodly. Very rarely will anyone die for a righteous man, though for a good man someone might possibly dare to die. But God demonstrates His own love for us in this: While we were still sinners, Christ died for us."* She knew her name was recorded in heaven and that there would be rejoicing in heaven over her decision that day.

There is singing up in Heaven such as we have never known,
Where the angels sing the praises of the Lamb upon the throne,
Their sweet harps are ever tuneful, and their voices always clear,
Oh, that we might be more like them while we serve the Master here!
Holy, holy, is what the angels sing,
And I expect to help them make the courts of heaven ring;
But when I sing demption's story, they will fold their wings,
For angels never felt the joys that our salvation brings.
But I hear another anthem, blending voices clear and strong,
"Unto Him who hath redeemed us and hath bought us," is the song;
We have come through tribulation to this land so fair and bright,
In the fountain freely flowing He hath made our garments white.
Then the angels stand and listen, for they cannot join the song,
Like the sound of many waters, by that happy, blood-washed throng,
For they sing about great trials, battles fought and vict'ries won,
And they praise their great Redeemer,
who hath said to them, "Well done."

So, although I'm not an angel, yet I know that over there
I will join a blessed chorus that the angels cannot share;
I will sing about my Saviour, who upon dark Calvary
Freely pardoned my transgressions, died to set a sinner free.
—John Oatman, Jr.

It wasn't too long after that memorable visit and the saving of so precious a soul, that Jim's wife slipped away to heaven, ending a great deal of pain and suffering. But we all rejoiced with Jim that there was indeed, "a new name written down in glory."

Safe in the arms of Jesus,
Safe on His gentle breast;
There by His love o'ershaded,
Sweetly my soul shall rest.
Hark! 'tis the voice of angels
Borne in a song to me,
Over the fields of glory,
Over the jasper sea.
Safe in the arms of Jesus,
Safe on His gentle breast;
There by His love o'ershaded,
Sweetly my soul shall rest.
Safe in the arms of Jesus,
Safe from corroding care,
Safe from the world's temptations;
Sin cannot harm me there.
Free from the blight of sorrow,
Free from my doubts and fears;
Only a few more trials,
Only a few more tears!
Jesus, my heart's dear Refuge,
Jesus has died for me;
Firm on the Rock of Ages
Ever my trust shall be.

Here let me wait with patience,
Wait till the night is o'er;
Wait till I see the morning
Break on the golden shore.
—Frances J. Crosby

Anne Graham Lotz, in her small but powerful little book, *My Jesus is Everything* quotes:

Heaven has been opened! It is finished:
To receive salvation, forgiveness of sin,
acceptance by God, eternal life.
You don't have to do more good works than bad works.
You don't have to go to church every time the door opens.
You don't even have to go to church.
You don't have to count beads.
You don't have to climb the stairs to some statue.
You don't have to lie on a bed of nails.
You don't have to be religious.
You don't even have to be good!
It is finished! Salvation is free!
Sin is forgivable!
The price has been paid!
Jesus paid it all!
Hallelujah!
Hallelujah!
Hallelujah!
My Jesus is Everything
Jesus—the only One—makes God visible
And change possible
And happiness attainable
And resources ample
And suffering understandable
And sin forgivable
And heaven available!
My Jesus is Everything!

Right after the funeral Jim's life began to change. He quit his job at the bowling club and made a firm and lasting commitment to diligently and faithfully serve the Lord and be used by Him for the rest of his life here on earth. Jim was so happy that his wife's suffering was over and she was now at home in heaven.

Everyone who knew him could see the difference in his life. He made it known that his intent was to now do his utmost to honour, praise, and serve the Lord. His barber, the meat market owner, the clerks at the grocery store—all were given a verbal witness of his new-found joy and passionate love for the Saviour.

He attended every service faithfully, including mid-week prayer meeting and every pre-service prayer meeting. He loved the children and always had treats for them every Sunday. The young people grew to love him and treated him with the greatest of respect. He became my close friend, confidant, and mentor. It was always a joy to visit him.

Dr. Charles Stanley, in the December 2004 Issue of *In Touch* magazine, wrote, "Like Paul we must choose our response to pain and hardship. We can become resentful and bitter, consequently allowing a wonderful opportunity for spiritual growth to defeat us. Or we can turn to God, cry out for help, and be victorious."

This is exactly what occurred in Jim's life. He became a living example to all of us by living the Spirit-filled life, allowing God to transform him into the Christian man God wanted him to be.

A small book edited by D. L. Moody entitled *Thoughts for the Quiet Hour* quotes the following:

> "For the love of Christ constraineth us…" (KJV). The love of Christ is too large for any heart to hold it. It will overflow into others' hearts; it will give itself out, give itself away, for the enriching of other lives. The heart of Christ is a costly thing for anyone to have. It will lead those who have it where it led Him. If it cost Him the cross, it will cost them no less.
>
> *—J. M. Campbell*

Jim had been in the habit of returning to Scotland on a fairly regular basis to visit family. As well, he also enjoyed the beautiful countryside where he grew up. After his second consecutive visit there, he returned with the announcement that he had met a long-time friend, a school teacher, who was retired and still single. Her name was Catherine.

Jim soon realized after a few meetings and dates that he loved Catherine! She reciprocated that love. Let me tell you an interesting story concerning this woman that happened when she was younger.

Jim had an older brother to whom Catherine was engaged. She supported him through university with the intent that after graduation they would be married. But right after graduation, the Great War began and he was called into the service. After the war, he returned, unscathed, but broke the engagement with Catherine and married another woman!

Catherine told me this story one time when we were alone and admitted that, though hurt and humiliated, she made up her mind to forgive this scoundrel (my words, not hers) and get on with her life. And that is exactly what she did. She became the best teacher she could be. During her summer holidays she travelled, touring Europe, visiting Canada and the United States. She bought her own duplex apartment, served the Lord, and enjoyed life to the fullest.

The plan was that Jim, after settling his affairs in Canada and selling his home, would return to Glasgow, marry Catherine and settle down in her home. We were broken-hearted that he was leaving, for he had become an integral part of many of our lives. He sent us a lovely wedding photo, which we were glad to receive. Many of us wrote to him on a regular basis.

Catherine later told us that when a letter came from Canada she hardly knew what to do with it because, although Jim was glad to hear from us, it made him all the more homesick. Furthermore, we learned that though Catherine had a lovely duplex apartment, the only heat was the cook stove in the kitchen and the fireplace in the sitting room. The kitchen, bathroom, and bedroom were in between and they were as cold as any deep freeze. Jim, of course, was used to central, oil-fired, thermostatically controlled heat!

When spring arrived, Catherine asked Jim if he would like to go back to Canada, and if so, she would sell her duplex and go with him.

Well, that was all he needed to hear and by fall, everything was settled in Glasgow and the happy couple arrived back home in Hamilton.

What I failed to tell you was that Jim's daughter wisely advised him not to sell his home when he departed for Scotland to marry Catherine and settle there. As it so happened, his daughter's husband was transferred back to Ontario from British Columbia and they decided to stay in the house for at least a year. They wanted to be sure their father would stay in Glasgow. So Jim's home was ready for them.

Catherine was happy with the house and its furnishings. The only changes she made was to have all the dark woodwork painted pure white and all the walls papered with light, bright colours.

When winter and cold temperatures arrived, most of us were grumbling and complaining about the cold. But not Catherine! Jim bought her a fur coat and she came to love the winters with the cold but bright, sunshiny days.

At church, she entered into all the activities and we all came to love her as we did Jim. One of her comments after a blessed day in church, when asked how she enjoyed the day was, "I shall enjoy the after-glow for the rest of the week."

I had the privilege of baptizing her. They had several happy years together before Jim, now in his eighties, took sick and went home to Glory.

By this time we had left the church and moved on to another ministry. We were saddened by Jim's home-going but knew he would certainly hear the words of his blessed Saviour, the words He spoke to faithful stewards in Matthew 25:21: *"Well done, good and faithful servant!"*

A short poem comes to mind as I remember Jim:

When we say "yes" to Jesus as Lord,
We pledge to take Him at His Word.
If we're sincere He'll give us the grace
To follow 'til we see His face.
—*Author Unknown*

Lynn Anderson, in his book, *Finding the Heart to Go On*, says of King David, "David knew that God saw him as blameless..."

This quote could most certainly be said of Jim, this gracious and humble servant of the Lord. Personally, I will never forget him.

It appeared that Catherine was going to remain in Canada and Jim's daughter was more than happy for her to remain in the house as long as she wished. We were in Hamilton for a few days and brought her back to our home in Ottawa for a visit.

She loved our three children as they did her. Then when our precious chosen child joined our family at just ten days old, Catherine was smitten by the baby, Carrie, as were the rest of us.

We had an amusing experience when we were driving her back to Hamilton. We stopped on the highway at a rest station and when she came out of the ladies' room with Jean, both were laughing hilariously. The toilets were automatic flushers! In those days, this was something very new. They were both startled and amused!

When Catherine received word from Scotland that her older sister, who was unmarried, needed help to continue living on her own, Catherine felt it was time to go back and look after her sister. How she was missed by all of us!

Several years later, I was in Britain and made a special trip to Glasgow to visit Catherine in the senior's apartment she shared with her sister. What a wonderful time we spent together reminiscing over by-gone days.

One of the things I remember so clearly about our visit was Catherine saying, "The years I spent with Jim were the happiest and most fulfilling of my whole life." What a tribute to a man, who, like King David, *"was a man after God's own heart."* Oh, yes, I should tell you that we first visited in the sitting room with heat from the electric fireplace, after which the heat was turned off. We then moved to the kitchen, heated with a small heater, and enjoyed further fellowship; then a delicious lunch she had lovingly prepared. You see, it was Catherine who first introduced me to scones whenever I visited her and Jim in Hamilton. Her scones (similar to our tea biscuits) were so delicious with butter, jam and whipped cream! No wonder when I arrived back at my room that evening for supper I wasn't the least bit hungry!

I should also tell you that she remembered "our precious little lamb" Carrie, and gave me five British pounds to buy her a gift. When I arrived home I bought a lamp for Carrie's chest of drawers. I am now using the same lamp in our current home.

Dear reader, may I take the liberty here to tell you a personal incident I had with this man of God? When I visited them in their home I always read a Scripture portion and prayed for this dear couple. Jim would then continue, praying earnestly for me and the work of the Lord. He also prayed for the many missionaries serving the Lord at home (specifically for the Elfords who ministered in the far northwest of Canada) and those who served abroad.

He would always ask the Lord to keep him from sinning and enable him to live a godly life that would be well-pleasing to the Lord. As Jim would pray this prayer I would think to myself (and remember, I was not yet in my thirties), "Surely a man in his seventies would not have a problem of sin in his life!" Well, I am now an octogenarian and I know exactly how Jim felt. I quote for you now an important passage of Scripture necessary for each one of us to adhere to:

> *Finally, be strong in the Lord and in his mighty power. Put on the full armor of God so that you can take your stand against the devil's schemes. For our struggle is not against flesh and blood, but against the rulers, against the authorities, against the powers of this dark world and against the spiritual forces of evil in the heavenly realms. Therefore put on the full armor of God, so that when the day of evil comes, you may be able to stand your ground, and after you have done everything, to stand. Stand firm then, with the belt of truth buckled around your waist, with the breastplate of righteousness in place, and with your feet fitted with the readiness that comes from the gospel of peace. In addition to all this, take up the shield of faith, with which you can extinguish all the flaming arrows of the evil one. Take the helmet of salvation and the sword of the Spirit, which is the word of God. And pray in the Spirit on all occasions with all kinds of prayers and requests. With this in mind, be alert and always keep on praying for all the saints.* (Ephesians 6:10–18)

The flaming darts of the evil one are still being flung at me and I have learned how essential it is to *"put on the whole armor of God"* in order that I might stand firm and be steadfast in my Christian walk. Yes, it is absolutely a fact, no matter what our age, the enemy continues to track us down.

> *Be self-controlled and alert. Your enemy the devil prowls around like a roaring lion looking for someone to devour. Resist him, standing firm in the faith, because you know that your brothers throughout the world are undergoing the same kind of sufferings. And the God of all grace, who called you to his eternal glory in Christ, after you have suffered a little while, will himself restore you and make you strong, firm and steadfast.*(1 Peter 5:8–10)

I sadly admit that I have failed many times, but how glad I am for the grace and loving forgiveness of our Heavenly Father who freely forgives us. 1 John 1:9 says, *"If we confess our sins, he is faithful and just and will forgive us our sins and purify us from all unrighteousness,"* and He continues to cover us with His righteousness.

It has taken me years to learn that I must focus on Jesus and let the Holy Spirit who indwells me take over in my life. I need to let Him lead and control each day of my life. Many of us in evangelical circles have whole-heartedly and with earnest sincerity sung "All to Jesus I surrender, All to Him I freely give; I will ever love and trust Him, In His presence daily live," but do we truly understand what we sing and are we willing to surrender all? Simply put, it is a matter of focusing on Jesus and truly being serious and realistic as we sing.

For salvation full and free,
Purchased once on Calvary,
Christ alone shall be my plea—
Jesus! Jesus only!
Jesus only, let me see,
Jesus only, none save He,
Then my song shall ever be—
Jesus! Jesus only!

He my Guide from day to day,
As I journey on life's way;
Close beside Him let me stay—
Jesus! Jesus only!
May my Model ever be
Christ the Lord, and none save He,
That the world may see in me—
Jesus! Jesus only!
He shall reign from shore to shore;
His the glory evermore.
Heav'n and earth shall bow before—
Jesus! Jesus only!

I never intended to go into this subject of full surrender and its significance in the life of a Christian but I perceive there are many of God's children who want to go further, dig deeper, and climb higher. Jim MacKenzie's life is a true example of how full surrender can change one's life and their walk with Jesus.

May we come to understand the meaning of being filled and empowered by God's Holy Spirit to actually live a victorious life and have the power that the Apostle Paul speaks of in Philippians. *"I want to know Christ and the power of His resurrection."*

"As the years add up, God's faithfulness multiplies."
—*Selected*

A "COOL" *Missionary* COUPLE

"Then Jesus came to them and said, 'All authority in heaven and on earth has been given to me. Therefore go and make disciples of all nations, baptizing them in the name of the Father and of the Son and of the Holy Spirit.'"
(Matthew 28:18–19)

"In times like these we are not looking for something to happen, we are looking for Someone to come."
—*Vance Havner, Evangelist*

Dear reader, please don't get "turned off," because I am about to tell you the story of a unique couple, who, when they were very young, gave themselves to the Lord fully and completely. They committed to following the Lord's leading wherever He would call them to go! As I write their story, I am praying that God will burn into your heart and mind the passion and love they have for the Saviour to reach the lost for Jesus Christ. The following is a brief account of the ministry of Bud and Marge Elford.

I had been in a city church for about six months. It was a hot summer Sunday night. There was not a large attendance that evening. As we were singing, I noticed a new young woman in the congregation. In time, I then realized who it was! Marge Elford!

Our church supported the Elfords as missionaries. Since she was in her home city, I believe for a medical check-up, she, of course, wanted to attend our services. From the platform, I spontaneously asked Marge if she would come up to the pulpit and give us a brief testimony. I learned many years later that Marge did not particularly enjoy public speaking, even though she articulates extremely well and, in my opinion, excels at public speaking.

I don't remember all that Marge told us that evening but I am going to quote, in her own words, what she wrote about an experience they had in Churchill about two years later. From this you will learn, I am sure, why God used this couple so extensively throughout our country.

> Here in Churchill, Manitoba, the Lord dealt with both of us very deeply through the ministry of a Christian and Missionary Alliance missionary, Keith Bailey. The Lord showed us our evil hearts and we were smitten!
>
> I thought: I don't smoke, I don't drink, I don't dance, etc. but he showed me that in my heart was love of self, wrong motives, anger, jealousy, love of worldly things, etc. I was crushed. At that time we (I) surrendered fully to the Lord; not my will but Thine be done, turning everything over to the Lord—finances, houses, furniture, yes, even family. He would be first in my life. I guess many pastors would call this sanctification. It was death to the self-life indeed.

Now, I would like to tell you how, when, where, and under what circumstances I first met this amazing couple. I was just beginning my second year at the London Bible Institute in London, Ontario. A number of us were standing around in the autumn beauty of a warm September day in 1947.

To our amazement, a motorcycle roared into the driveway. In fact, everyone in the near vicinity simply "gawked" at this couple as they parked the vehicle and got off. Horror of horrors, a motorcycle! In those days we had a very legalistic view of Christianity, and a motorcycle represented a person who was probably gang-related or at the very least a troublemaker! We were shamefully very judgmental.

Bud introduced himself and Marge while we idiots (!) were standing there, for the most part, speechless! Bud was wearing black leather pants and a bomber jacket and Marge was wearing black satin pants!

Because they were a married couple and most of us were single guys, we didn't see that much of them, except in passing from time to time. Little did I realize then, in my pomposity and total lack of humility, that I was looking at a young couple who would put most of us to shame in their dedication, commitment and burning desire to serve the Lord faithfully wherever He would lead them. They actually took the words of one missionary we heard who laughingly said, "Where He leads me I will follow; what they feed me I will swallow," literally!

I believe it is significant to give you a bit of Marge's background, as she came from a non-Christian family. There were three girls, Marge being the middle one. There was no Bible teaching in the home and no thought of attending church. However, their parents were strict, instilling in them strong values and encouraging them to do their best as they were growing up.

Marge, when in high school, met a Christian girl who greatly impressed her and most certainly impacted her life. She showed kindness, friendliness and demonstrated a peaceful spirit, further showing by her life a sincere devotion to the Lord. Marge referred to her as her "religious girlfriend" and if she wanted to go to a movie, roller-skate, or attend a dance, she would ask her non-Christian girlfriend to go with her.

When Marge was eighteen years old, she went to church with her Christian girlfriend. It was there she first realized she needed to be saved. It was also at this same church that she met Bud, whom she has referred to as "the love of my life." It was Bud who urged her to give her life to the Lord. Marge did indeed accept the Lord as her personal Saviour and began the Christian walk with an earnest and sincere desire to mature and grow in the Lord.

Not too long after making her commitment to the Lord, Marge became quite ill and called on the Lord for healing. She promised the Lord if He would answer her prayer she would follow Him wherever he would lead her. God has reminded Marge over and over again of that promise she made to Him so many years ago, even to this day.

Little did this young Christian girl ever imagine where and to whom God would lead her and how many times throughout her life she would truly suffer the loss of all things for Jesus' sake. Like the Apostle Paul said in Philippians 3:7–8, *"But all these things that I once thought very worthwhile—now I've thrown them all away so that I can put my trust and hope in Christ alone. Yes, everything else is worthless when compared with the priceless gain of knowing Christ Jesus my Lord. I have put aside all else, counting it less than nothing in order that I can have Christ" (TLB).*

Bud's background was somewhat different from Marge's. His parents were pastoring a Methodist church in the Orillia, Ontario, area when he was born in 1924. In the early 1930's the family moved to beautiful Manitoulin Island where Bud's father pastored a Baptist Church. When Bud was fourteen years old his father was invited to become the pastor of a church in Mindemoya on the Island. This was the same church where Bud's grandfather had ministered in the early 1900s.

When Bud was fifteen years old, evangelist and radio preacher John Zoller came to the church and held what was called in those days "evangelistic meetings." It was during this campaign that Bud accepted the Lord Jesus Christ as his personal Lord and Saviour. Bud admitted that his life from that day on drastically changed.

I feel quite certain that back in those days the Hymn *Since Jesus Came Into My Heart* was sung on many an occasion!

What a wonderful change in my life has been wrought
Since Jesus came into my heart;
I have light in my soul for which long I have sought,
Since Jesus came into my heart.
Since Jesus came into my heart,
Since Jesus came into my heart;
Floods of joy o'er my soul like the sea billows roll,
Since Jesus came into my heart.
I have ceased from my wand'ring and going astray,
Since Jesus came into my heart;

And my sins which were many are all washed away,
Since Jesus came into my heart.
I'm possessed of a hope that is steadfast and sure,
Since Jesus came into my heart;
And no dark clouds of doubt now my pathway obscure,
Since Jesus came into my heart.
I shall go there to dwell in that City I know,
Since Jesus came into my heart;
And I'm happy, so happy as onward I go,
Since Jesus came into my heart.
—Rufus H. McDaniel

Bud quit school when he was sixteen and moved down to Southern Ontario to stay with an uncle. A year or so later Bud moved to Hamilton to get work and started attending the church where John F. Holliday was pastor.

Under Pastor Holliday's ministry in this fast-growing church, along with his Sunday school teacher, Charlie Hare, Bud received much of his discipling. As 2 Peter 3:18 exhorts, *"But grow in the grace and knowledge of our Lord and Saviour Jesus Christ. To Him be glory both now and forever! Amen."*

I have quoted this entire verse because the first part describes Bud's maturing in the faith. The last part of the verse describes how in fifty-two years of full-time service this couple has always given God the glory for anything that was accomplished in their faithful ministry. Someone has well said, "As you are growing, remember who Jesus is and what He has done."

This is probably a good place to tell you about Bud and the first time he saw Marge at the church. Like Marge, he too had said, "It was there that I met the 'love of my life.'" Quoting Bud's exact words,

> It was on Sunday morning in Sunday school class when Marjorie Jordanoff walked in with her good friend. I took one look at her and was smitten for life. I can tell you today what she was wearing and I said to my friend who was sitting beside

me, "There's the girl I'm going to marry." He said, "Forget it Bud, she's had a boyfriend for a year or two." [Bud's reply was so typical of him, as you'll see as you read on]. My response was "Jack, don't bother me with details!"

Dr. Charles Stanley, in his book *God's Perfect Timing,* wrote,

> We order our coffee to go, we use instant tellers, and the mere hint of living without a microwave is absolutely frightening. Even for Christians, the slightest delays seem to be some of life's most painful trials. Scripture, however, does not change, and our Father still calls His children to wait patiently.
>
> Waiting on the Lord's timing protects us from making bad decisions. How often do we run ahead of God by quickly making the wrong choice? Sadly, our desire not to miss out on the joys of life can cause us to act impulsively and disregard biblical truth. But for those who do practice self-control, the Savior will not withhold His very best. Whether you're buying a house, considering marriage, or contemplating a ministry opportunity, the Creator is always faithful to surpass your highest expectations when you wait on Him. Following His timetable sifts your motives, strengthens your faith, and prepares you to receive the Father's gift with humility and appreciation.

Bud and Marge married in September of 1947, and as newlyweds arrived for their bible school training. Bud spent five years studying and preparing for the ministry. Marge was only able to attend for one year as their first son Roan was born during that time.

Though Marge was unable to continue her studies at the Bible Institute, there is no doubt that God used her mightily in raising their three children. Later in this chapter I will tell you about these children; suffice it to say at this time that all three of them are in full-time ministry for the Lord. Praise God! 1 Timothy 1:5 says, *"I have been reminded of your sincere faith, which first lived in your grandmother Lois and in your mother Eunice and, I am persuaded, now lives in you also."*

Dr. Richard Dehaan said, "God has conferred on motherhood a true nobility, and she that fills that role can shape man's destiny." Abraham Lincoln quoted, "No man is poor who has had a godly mother."

Marge then became a full-time homemaker and mother. That is not to say that she settled down to a ho-hum lifestyle. During those years she was studying the Word of God, growing in her intimacy with the Lord, learning to pray earnestly and specifically, not only for themselves and their future place of service, but for family, friends and a myriad of other needs and burdens.

After graduation the time came to seriously seek the Lord's will in the place God would have them serve. There were possibilities of serving in Papua New Guinea. As they waited on God to open up doors, Bud spent two summers studying linguistics under Wycliffe Bible Translators at Caronport, Saskatchewan, where they now live in so-called retirement!

While there he met Stan Collie, founder and director of the Northern Canada Evangelical Mission. Bud and Marge were led to apply to this Mission.

While Bud was studying at the Summer Institute of Linguistics, Marge remained in Hamilton with Roan and worked to support Bud in his studies.

The most significant event of that summer was the way the Lord was leading this young couple to go north to minister to the Native Canadians. Marge had listened to a radio broadcast (no TV in those days!) and was challenged to consider a Northern ministry. At the same time, Bud was likewise challenged through his association with Stan Collie. Their letters crossed in the mail! Coincidence? I think not! They applied to the Northern Canada Evangelical Mission (NCEM).

The Next Step

Not year by year, or month by month,
Or even day by day;
I find my Father's will for me
Each moment as I pray.
I do not need to look ahead
To see tomorrow's task;
My Lord gives grace to help today

And strength each time I ask.
With every step He gives new light
To see one step ahead.
I cannot always see His hand
So gently I am led.
But as I look behind I see
Through every month and year,
That He has led me all the way,
And made the next step clear.
—Julie Dawn Smith

During the next year of 1951, they returned to London where Marge was able to take a year of Bible school with Bud working on and completing his Seminary degree.

From there they went to Caronport, Saskatchewan, where Marge took her first year of linguistics and Bud an advanced linguistics course. It was during this time that Papua New Guinea was opened up to North American missionaries, but both believed God had called them and was leading them to the North.

After approximately nine months' probation in Northern Saskatchewan with the director of the Mission, Bud and Marge returned to Caronport for more language training. Mr. Collie, with Holy Spirit discernment, arranged, at considerable expense for the Mission, to have a Chipewyan couple accompany them and assist them with the language in finer detail. Kit, their second son, was born during this period spent at Caronport.

Many years later, Bud, who wrote regularly in the Missions publication, said these words: "So, if you are no one in particular, just an ordinary believer in a lowly place, make yourself available to God's great purposes. Yield to His use, burn and be aglow with His Spirit. Who knows? You could attract some poor, discouraged wanderer back to God."

In the fall of 1953, Bud conducted a language training school for about six months, assisting new missionaries planning to serve in Northern Canada. He equipped them not only to speak the Chipewyan language but also to read it. There is no doubt that Bud himself was a "fast learner" and thus anxious to get going and reach the lost in the far North for Christ.

It was during this time that Bud spent weeks, eleven to be exact, reducing the Chipewyan language of the Dene people to writing, forming an alphabet, and preparing some pedagogical lessons. Bud admitted that the alphabet prepared at that time had the significant blessing of God upon it, for in over fifty years only one character needed to be changed. The government and other institutions working in that language now accept it.

That fall of 1953, the Mission called all of the missionaries working with the Denes to their headquarters in Meadow Lake, Saskatchewan, for a nine-month course. It was here that God gave Bud the strength to teach the lessons he had prepared, even though he himself was somewhat limited in his knowledge of the language.

This segment of Bud's life is quite significant for it was during this period that he made a commitment to the Lord that he followed through from that day until the present. Psalm 84:5 and 7 say, *"Blessed are those whose strength is in you, who have set their hearts on pilgrimage…they go from strength to strength."*

Now back to more of Bud's background. Bud joined the Canadian army in April of 1943 during World War II. After basic training in Canada and then Great Britain, July of 1944 found him in a slit trench involved in that horrific battle on the beaches of Normandy, France.

This was certainly not a particularly safe and comfortable place for a young man barely out of his teens. There, all alone, he made a covenant with the Lord that would change the direction of his life completely. In his own words Bud prayed, "Lord, if you get me out of this war alive, I will become a missionary." He further added, "I thought it was a good deal, and according to the outcome it looks like the Lord did, too."

So many of God's children, under duress and difficult circumstances, make promises to the Lord. When the difficulties and troubles have passed, they move on, forgetting, it seems, the promise they made to the Lord. Not so with Bud! He was able to return to Canada early near the end of the war, having volunteered for military service in the Pacific. However, the war ended a few months later (after atomic bombs were dropped on two cities in Japan) and Bud returned to civilian life and back to his church in Hamilton.

In his book, *The Best of A. W. Tozer*, Dr. Tozer has a chapter entitled *Marks of the Spiritual Man*. I refer to this chapter in part because it will help my readers to better understand this man who has such an insignificant nickname as "Bud."

I should also add that I have chosen to quote these words of Dr. Tozer because anyone who has known Bud and observed his life will totally agree that he is indeed like King David, "A man after God's own heart." Bud himself would refute this, but we who know him and have followed his ministry have found him to be a godly man.

> First is the desire to be holy rather than happy. John Wesley said of the members of one of the early Methodist societies that he doubted they had been made perfect in love because they came to church to enjoy religion instead of how they could learn to become holy.
>
> A man may be considered spiritual when he wants to see the honour of God advanced through his life even if it means he himself must suffer temporary dishonour or loss…The glory of God is necessary to him; he gasps for it as a suffocating man gasps for air.
>
> The spiritual man wants to carry his cross. Carrying a cross means to be attached to the Person of Christ, committed to the Lordship of Christ and obedient to the commandments of Christ.
>
> A Christian is spiritual when he sees everything from God's viewpoint. The ability to weigh all things in the divine scale and place the same value upon them as God does is the mark of a Spirit-filled life.
>
> Another desire of the spiritual man is to die right rather than to live wrong…He wants most of all to be right, and he is happy to let God decide how long he shall live…but he knows he cannot afford to do wrong, and this knowledge becomes a gyroscope to stabilize his thinking and his acting.

> The desire to see others advance at his expense is another mark of the spiritual man. There is no envy in his heart...If God is pleased, he is pleased...and if it pleases God to exalt another above him, he is content to have it so.
>
> The spiritual man habitually makes eternity-judgments instead of time-judgments...Such a man would rather be useful than famous and would rather serve than be served.
>
> All of this must be by the operation of the Holy Spirit within him. No man can become spiritual by himself. Only the free Spirit can make a man spiritual.

After these intense years of language study, the Elfords were sent to Churchill, Manitoba. This was 1953. If you were to get out your map you would easily find this significant northern town right on Hudson Bay—no place for southerners or those who want to remain in their comfort zone with all of the gadgets so many of us feel we couldn't live without. But Bud and Marge loved it there. Marge, in her own words, said, "A grand place—we loved the barrens, the rocks, the Hudson Bay, and especially the people."

Without minimizing the Elfords' gifts, talents and unique abilities, I quote from the book *Out of the Comfort Zone* by George Verwer, founder and International Director of Operation Mobilization, which has an international preaching ministry around the world:

> I am in full agreement with the practice of selecting mission candidates with care, but the long history of the Church shows that God sends out and uses all kinds of people with a huge range of gifts and talents. Stephen Gaukroger, in WHY BOTHER WITH MISSION? says, "The history of missions is a colourful history of 'unlikely heroes'—characterized by obedience rather than ability. Time after time God confirms His Word: 'Brothers, think of what you were when you were called. Not many of you were wise by human standards; not many were influential; not many were of noble birth. But God chose the foolish things of the world to shame the wise; God chose the weak things of the world to shame the strong.'" (1 Corinthians 1:26)

To me, there is no question that in the lives of Bud and Marge "heroes of the faith" obedience was just a "natural" for them. They had learned early on in their walk with the Lord that *"To obey is better than sacrifice"* (1 Samuel 15:22a).

Living in Churchill, they soon learned that they had an enemy, the devil. But thankfully they also learned how to resist him and maintain victory in the Lord Jesus Christ. *"God opposes the proud but gives grace to the humble. Submit yourselves then to God. Resist the devil and he will flee from you. Come near to God and He will come near to you"* (James 4:6–8).

While in Churchill, Bud led a young aboriginal man and his family to the Lord. This man helped Bud immensely with the language, translating hymns and Scriptures to be used in the services Bud held. A postscript to this experience is that this faithful Christian man suddenly had a heart attack and quickly entered the Pearly Gates of heaven. Bud was invited and gladly conducted the memorial service for this long-time servant of the Lord in February 2004. He had been a great help to the Elfords when they were in Churchill, getting the gospel out to his own people.

During their six years in Churchill, they had close association with the Cree people as well as missionaries to the Eskimos. In 1958, God gave them a beautiful baby girl who is now serving the Lord along with her husband at Briercrest Bible College.

In 1959, the Mission asked them to open a mission station in Brochet, Manitoba, a village not too far from the border of the Northwest Territories. Marge really loved Churchill and, having made many friends, was really not happy to have to leave. But she remembered the promise she had made to the Lord back in 1947: "I'll go where you want me to go."

Brochet, for a young mother and three children, was not an easy place to live to say the least! It was primitive and to those living in Southern Ontario or any of our Canadian cities, towns, or villages it was unimaginable—no electricity or running water, no doctor or nurse, no phone or law officers and no fresh food. There was a one-room school.

The only way to reach this village was by plane. Actually, one came in every two weeks (except for the weeks in the spring when the lake was thawing out) and brought with it the mail and other essentials for the village.

They were the first Protestant missionaries to live in the village and they were not warmly welcomed. In fact, the people made it abundantly clear they were not wanted.

If you will recall at the beginning of this chapter I recounted Marge's testimony of making that much-needed (for all of us) full and complete surrender to the Lord.

Now in Brochet, the people were terribly vulnerable to spirits. There were four different languages spoken in this native village. The main two were Chipweyan and Cree, with English as the trade language and French, the language of the Roman Catholic people.

When the chief and a counsellor asked why they had come to Brochet, Bud didn't hesitate a moment, or mince any words, but quickly replied: "Because Jesus Christ sent us." That was followed by a stony silence and then a quick departure.

Their home became "Open House" every evening. Bud would invite people in every night and because he could play the guitar and sing in Chip, they enjoyed it. But as soon as he would open up the Bible they would leave in haste.

Not to be turned off or discouraged, Bud developed a new tactic! He would take a hymn and explain the gospel from it. They were much more at ease with this and actually would come every night of the week. One of the reasons men, women and children would come to the Elford home is because they were the only white people who welcomed them into their home. Marge would have baked that day, in fact, every day, and after the meeting show true hospitality by feeding everyone who was there.

I mentioned to you previously that Bud and Marge were made aware, almost as soon as they arrived in Brochet, that many evil spirits were abiding in the small village. Bud would discover that for himself as soon as everyone left after an evening meeting. His mind would actually be paralyzed and he would find it almost impossible to pray. Furthermore, his hair would stand up and so would the hair on the dog's tail! They realized that the evil spirits were coming into the house with the people.

Most of us would be stymied at such a frightening situation. Not so with this godly couple. They decided that the next evening as the people started coming in they would silently pray and order the unclean spirits to stay outside! The response and the change in the atmosphere were immediate, particularly among the older people. Oswald Chambers says,

> We are ill-taught if we look for results only in the earthlies when we pray. A praying saint performs far more havoc among the unseen forces of darkness than we have the slightest notion of.

They came in, relaxed, and sat comfortably in chairs, and several remarked, "Boy, is your house ever nice on the inside!" These dedicated missionaries kept up that spiritual practice the entire time they lived in Brochet. Some twenty years later, Christians from that village told Bud and Marge that the reason they always wanted to go to their house was because it was the only house in the village where there were no demons.

It was in this village the Elfords learned spiritual warfare.

Fierce may be the conflict, strong may be the foe,
But the King's own army none can overthrow;
'Round His standard ranging, vict'ry is secure,
For His truth unchanging makes the triumph sure.
Joyfully enlisting, by Thy grace divine,
We are on the Lord's side—Savior, we are Thine!

This hymn was written by Frances R. Havergal, taken from the text found in Exodus 32:26: *"Who is on the Lord's side?"*

If any of my readers are sceptical about this matter of the reality of demons and evil spirits, we need only to read Romans 8:38–39 where the Apostle Paul states: *"For I am convinced that neither death nor angels nor demons…shall be able to separate us from the love of God that is in Christ Jesus our Lord."*

Then, who can doubt the truth of Mark 5 where Jesus, the Son of God, healed the demon-possessed man and sent the evil spirits into a huge number of pigs, two thousand, to be exact, who immediately raced into the lake and were drowned.

Paul also challenged the Ephesian Christians in Ephesians 5 to put on the full armour of God, as he states in verse 12, *"For our struggle is not against flesh and blood, but against the rulers, against the authorities, against the powers of this dark world and against the spiritual forces of evil in the heavenly realms."*

If there is still doubt in your mind about this satanic power when God's servants minister the truth, read what Author K.P. Yohannan has to say in his book, *Revolution in World Missions:*

> The only weapon that will ever effectively win the war against disease, hunger, injustice and poverty in Asia is the gospel of Jesus Christ. To look into the sad eyes of a hungry child or see the wasted life of a drug addict is to see only the evidence of Satan's hold on this world. All bad things are his handiwork. He is the ultimate enemy of mankind, and he will do everything within his considerable power to kill and destroy human beings. Fighting this powerful enemy with physical weapons is like fighting an armoured tank with stones.
>
> I can never forget one of the more dramatic encounters we had with these demonic powers. It was a hot and unusually humid day in 1970. We were preaching in the northwestern state of Rajasthan—the "desert of kings."
>
> As was our practice before a street meeting, my seven co-workers and I stood in a circle to sing and clap hands to the rhythm of Christian folk songs. A sizeable crowd gathered, and I began to speak in Hindi, the local language. Many heard the gospel for the first time and eagerly took our Gospels and tracts to read.
>
> One young man came up to me and asked for a book to read. As I talked to him, I sensed in my spirit that he was hungry to know God. When we got ready to climb aboard our gospel van, he asked to join us.
>
> As the van lurched forward, he cried and wailed. "I am a

terrible sinner," he shrieked. "How can I sit among you?" With that he started to jump from the moving van. We held on to him and forced him to the floor to prevent injury.

That night he stayed at our base and the next morning joined us for the prayer meeting. While we were praising and interceding, we heard a sudden scream. The young man was lying on the ground, tongue lolling out of his mouth, his eyes rolled back.

As Christians in a pagan land, we knew immediately he was demon-possessed. We gathered around him and began taking authority over the forces of hell as they spoke through his mouth.

"We are 74 of us...For the past seven years we have made him walk barefoot all over India...He is ours..." They spoke on, blaspheming and cursing, challenging us and our authority.

But as three of us prayed, the demons could not keep their hold on the young man. They came out when we commanded them to leave in the name of Jesus.

Sundar John was delivered, gave his life to Jesus, and was baptized. Later he went to Bible school for two years. Since then the Lord has enabled him to teach and preach to thousands of people about Christ. Several Indian churches have started as a result of his remarkable ministry—all from a man many people would have locked up in an insane asylum. And there are literally millions of people like him in India—demons and enslaved to their horrible passions and lusts.

In his own words, Bud said:

We learned to stand on the foundation of Colossians 2:15, "And having disarmed the powers and authorities, He made a public spectacle of them, triumphing over them by the cross." Also we stood on the truth of Revelation 12:11—"They overcame him by the blood of the Lamb and by the word of their testimony; they did not love their lives (self-lives) so much as to shrink from death."

2 Timothy 2:4 states, *"No one serving as a soldier gets involved in civilian affairs—he wants to please his commanding officer."*

These words could very well have been the text from which Isaac Watts, so many years ago, penned the words now found in many of our hymn books:

Am I a Soldier of the Cross

Am I a soldier of the cross,
a follower of the Lamb,
and shall I fear to own his cause,
or blush to speak his name?
Must I be carried to the skies
on flowery beds of ease,
while others fought to win the prize,
and sailed through bloody seas?
Are there no foes for me to face?
Must I not stem the flood?
Is this vile world a friend to grace,
to help me on to God?
Sure I must fight, if I would reign;
increase my courage, Lord.
I'll bear the toil, endure the pain,
supported by thy word.
Thy saints in all this glorious war
shall conquer though they die;
they see the triumph from afar,
by faith they bring it nigh.
When that illustrious day shall rise,
and all thy armies shine
in robes of victory through the skies,
the glory shall be thine.

Continuing with Bud's testimony:

We learned we had to give our testimony to Satan, face to face. I simply said "Look, I belong to Jesus Christ, my sins are all forgiven. I don't do them anymore and I have been renewed in the Holy Spirit, and Jesus told me I was to tell you about it." (Ephesians 3:10) This became a way of life for us, and has guided our lives ever since.

We found that the truth of James 4:7, "*Submit yourselves, then, to God. Resist the devil, and he will flee from you*" was not a one-time thing, but because it is in the present tense in Greek, it means to keep on submitting to God and keep on resisting the devil and he will keep on fleeing from you. Praise the Lord!

Marge, during this time in Brochet, had Sunday school every Sunday. She also ministered to the children when they came to their home to play with her own children. In her own words, I quote Marge at this point:

> We didn't know the influence we had on these children, but in later years different people have told us that kids got saved through our ministry. We just heard last year, 2003, that a young boy, five years old accepted the Lord and thirty-four years later has been having a Bible study in this village. He even led his father (who had no interest in spiritual things whatsoever) to the Lord before he died.

After settling down in Brochet with children, furniture, snowmobile (not a toy in that part of Canada in those days), boat and motor, and all the paraphernalia to survive in such a remote part of Canada, Marge confessed that it was a year of testing the promises they had made to the Lord—"All to Jesus I surrender." As I have already said, there was a total and complete dedication to the Lord with "no strings attached."

Bud commenced earnestly praying that God would send down the fire of the Holy Spirit on the village. Well, fire came, but not in a way they were expecting!

First, their outboard motor burned up. Then Bud was severely burned when a gasoline engine blew up in his face! That was followed by their storage shed burning to the ground! If that wasn't enough to dishearten the noblest of God's people, while they were attending their mission conference, lightning struck their home; and everything they possessed was destroyed.

Marge later told Bud that it would be more appropriate if, when he prayed, he would be more specific! Quoting Marge as she recalled this horrific year that probably would have sent most of us packing for home:

> We had fully surrendered these things to the Lord and it seemed like a testing to us but as we look back we can certainly say, "It was well with our souls." It was not ours; it was the Lord's and He could do with it whatever He wanted. It was a good lesson to let go of earthly things.
>
> They are going to burn up some day anyway. We have learned that everything belongs to God; we just use them.

This hymn is so descriptive of the testimony of their lives in the midst of such great difficulties:

God Leads Us Along

In shady, green pastures, so rich and so sweet
God leads His dear children along;
Where the water's cool flow bathes the weary one's feet,
God leads His dear children along.
Some through the water, some through the flood,
Some through the fire, but all through the blood;
Some through great sorrow, but God gives a song,
In the night season and all the day long.
Sometimes on the mount where the sun shines so bright,
God leads His dear children along;
Sometimes in the valley, in darkest of night,
God leads His dear children along.
Tho' sorrows befall us, and Satan oppose,
God leads His dear children along;
Through grace we can conquer, defeat all our foes,
God leads His dear children along.
Away from the mire, and away from the clay,

God leads His dear children along;
Away up in glory, eternity's day,
God leads His dear children along.
—G. A Young

May I tarry here for a moment and ask you, as I ask myself, is this our attitude to things, to stuff? Or, do we cling to our possessions as if they are going to live forever?

I am not sure if it was Dr. Sugden or Dr. Strauss who often said, "There are no U-hauls behind a hearse!" I am also reminded of the story about two old-timers discussing the death of a friend. One asked, "I wonder how much he left?" and the other replied, "He left it all!"

I once visited a young couple with small children who had immigrated to Canada from The Netherlands. They had rented an old house, but as I looked around it was a cozy and warm little home, tastefully furnished and decorated with articles from a thrift shop. When I commented on how lovely it was, this young man replied, "Ah Pastor, these things have just been loaned to us by God. And if He should see fit to bless and prosper us we will always remember everything we have is His and we are simply stewards to just use them."

Every Bible I have owned, I have always copied down the following poem, words I have often quoted in my preaching, but sadly, at times, I have forgotten. But God has been lovingly patient with me and has finally, through His blessed Holy Spirit, made me realize the truth of Matthew 6:33: *"But seek first His kingdom and His righteousness, and all these things will be given to you as well."*

Let me hold lightly things of this earth,
Transient treasures, what are they worth?
Moths can corrupt them, rust can decay
All their bright beauty fades in a day.
Let me hold lightly temporal things–
I who am deathless, I who wear wings.
Let me hold fast, Lord, things of the skies.
Quicken my vision, open my eyes.

Show me Thy riches, glory and grace
Boundless as time is, endless as space.
Let me hold lightly things that were mine–
Lord, Thou doest give me all that is Thine.
—*Author Unknown*

Surely, we as children of God should rejoice and be glad as we read the truth of God's Word in Romans 8:17: *"Now if we are children, then we are heirs—heirs of God and co-heirs with Christ, if indeed we share in His sufferings in order that we may also share in His glory."*

Recently I read an interesting statement: "The Canadian northlands experience only two seasons, Winter and July!" Well, this may not be entirely true, but for the Elfords, that was the least of their concerns. God in His love and mercy provided a new home for our missionary family. Bud had to build it but, though simply furnished, it was really quite lovely.

I can now tell you a little of life in Brochet as I had the privilege of visiting the Elfords. After an overnight trip from Winnipeg and a long day-trip in a very old passenger train attached to a freight train, I arrived in Lynn Lake, Manitoba.

After preaching and enjoying fellowship in a small but loving congregation, I left the next morning. Bud had arranged for a missionary to fly me into Brochet. When the small plane landed on the frozen ice, I was amazed the skis didn't break off. But the welcome from my missionary friends was well worth the getting there.

Bud commented that he had invited many pastors to come visit them and I was the first and only one who ever followed through on the invitation. Thankfully, since that time back in the sixties, it is more commonplace today, and pastors can visit the far-flung mission stations of the world. Short-term mission trips are also blessings to those on the field as well as to those who go. Many retirees are making themselves available to serve overseas. What a privilege!

Let us return to Brochet. I still remember Marge baking a pie for a needy family and asking Kit, who was just a young boy at the time, to deliver it. Marge cautioned him to be very careful where he walked. The village people, throughout the winter months, threw the contents of their slop pails out the door knowing the snow would soon cover it. But this was April and the snow was melting—no wonder you had to watch with great caution where you walked! Well, poor Kit—he dropped the pie! It was a bit of a balancing act to journey even a short distance, so he wasn't scolded. In fact, if I remember correctly, we laughed!

Throughout the day there was a constant flow of visitors who merely sat silently until Marge fed them and then they would leave. But in the evening we had a full house. I played the little pump organ and Bud led the singing, followed by a short devotional from the Word. Marge, ever given to hospitality *(1 Peter 4:9, "Offer hospitality to one another without grumbling."),* served so lovingly and graciously to everyone present.

For me, that was a week of blessing untold and I hated to leave. The ice was getting mushy and I reluctantly left on the last mail plane to come into Brochet until all the ice had melted. In the back of the plane was a small native baby being delivered to the hospital—but all alone—no parent, no nurse. Thank God since those years, there is more compassion shown to these dear people.

Evangelist Leighton Ford (son-in-law of Billy Graham) in his book *Good News Is for Sharing*, writes the following:

> In 1837 three young Methodist ministers—James Calvert, John Hunt, and Thomas Jagar—and their wives, set out from England for the Fiji Islands. Theirs was a difficult assignment. The venture was only three years old, and the people were still cannibals. They saw hardly any fruit during their first few years of service. Then in 1845 revival swept through the Islands… Within a few years the islands were completely transformed as the gospel took hold of the people there.
>
> Earlier, the captain of the ship that transported the three couples from England tried to dissuade them from going to the islands. He told James Calvert, "You'll lose your lives and the lives of those with you if you go among such savages."
>
> Calvert replied, "We died before we came here." In the

previous century, the founder of their movement, John Wesley, said, "Give me a hundred men who love God with all their hearts and fear nothing but sin, and I will move the world." Those three young missionaries were part of God's answer to Wesley's prayer—and a demonstration of living in resurrection power.

In 1965, the Elfords moved to Fort McPherson in the Northwest Territories, just one hundred miles or so from the Arctic Ocean. This Protestant village was a missionary's dream.

It was mid-January and everything in the house took days to thaw. But soon, very soon, the house was filled with children for Sunday school and the Sunday evening service crowded out the living room.

The school loaned our missionaries a portable classroom as the people came—many men, women, and children were saved during those two and a half years in Fort McPherson. That part of Canada has very dark, dark winter days and in the summer, sunshine all day and night! Marge claims they didn't need to sleep! I would wonder how they could sleep when the sun never set all summer long. Quoting Marge after she was transferred to another ministry:

> It was the hardest move I had to make. Even a year after we left my heart was still up there with those people. One day I received a newsletter from another mission. I read in it, "If you are discontent in the place where God has put you, it shows marks of immaturity." I matured very quickly!

The following hymn, written by Fanny J. Crosby, describes Bud and Marge's faith story throughout their missionary years in the North.

All The Way My Saviour Leads Me

All the way my Saviour leads me—
What have I to ask beside?
Can I doubt his tender mercy
Who through life has been my Guide?
Heav'nly peace, divinest comfort,
Here by faith in him to dwell—
For I know, whate'er befall me,

Jesus doeth all things well.
All the way my Saviour leads me,
Cheers each winding path I tread,
Gives me grace for ev'ry trial,
Feeds me with the living Bread.
Though my weary steps may falter,
And my soul athirst may be,
Gushing from the rock before me,
Lo, a spring of joy I see!
—Fanny J. Crosby

I digress from the Elfords for a moment to tell you another story. Many years ago I heard Reverend Tommie Titcombe, a passionate missionary who, along with his wife, spent years in what was then called "Dark Africa." The Titcombes went to a tribe in Africa where when twins were born they were immediately killed. The tribe believed that these babies were demon possessed. No matter what the missionaries said or did, they could not prevent the murder of these innocent babies.

Then, as the Lord would have it, the Titcombes themselves had twins, a boy, and a girl, named Emmerson and Edith. Because the Titcombes not only refused to kill their twins, but loved and cared for them, nurturing them as they grew, Tommie Titcombe was able to convince this tribe to cease this cruel treatment of newborn twins.

On a personal note, when we went to our first church in Ontario, long before there was Ontario Health Services, Emmerson was a family doctor in Thornbury, a short distance from where we lived in Meaford. He became our family doctor. For all those years he cared for us, delivered our last two babies, doing it all without charge! Praise God.

Reverend Titcombe also told the story of how he and his wife had to leave their young children with family in Hamilton, Ontario, when it was time for them to begin school. He wept as he recalled leaving the house for the last time. The children cried at the top of the stairs and screamed out the words, "Please, please don't leave us."

Years later, a home was established in Collingwood, Ontario for missionaries' children so they could at least be together as a family, where they were loved and nurtured by a godly couple. They could then attend local schools and be educated and prepared for higher education as the Lord led. This proved to be a good solution, although some of the children experienced severe trauma and suffered greatly being separated from their parents. Thankfully, most overseas missions today provide schooling in or near where their parents are serving so at least they can be with them on special holidays and vacation times.

I tell you the above story to relate to you Bud and Marge's testimony about their three children:

> All our children were raised on the mission field, some with more years than others. We made a covenant with the Lord that we would go anywhere He would lead and we would trust Him (and us) to undertake for their health, their education and to instil in them good, sound, Christian morals. Praise God, He was faithful, as were we, and although the education in many of the villages was less than satisfactory, they have all attended Bible College and earned degrees and better still, all three of the children are in full-time Christian ministry.

From this we can all learn a lesson: "God's way is the best way," and "It pays to serve Jesus." As it was said of Samuel, so it could be said of the Elford children: *"And the boy Samuel continued to grow in stature and in favour with the Lord and with men."*

In 1967, the Elfords moved to Cold Lake, Alberta. These were very busy years for both Bud and Marge.

Bud continued studying the language. He translated the Gospel of Mark, wrote tracts, put together a Dene Primer (used to this very day by the government), edited and published a dictionary, compiled a hymn book and made cassettes with a gospel message; all of this in the language the people could understand.

In addition, the government requested Bud teach the language to the Native people so they in turn could teach it in the schools. This material is still being used in the schools to this day.

Perhaps some of my readers are unfamiliar with how our government and various religious groups treated Canada's aboriginal peoples in the early days of our history. It was thought that the best thing to do for Canada's First Nations people was to teach them our culture, our language, our religion and integrate them into a productive society where they could support themselves and contribute to the growth of the nation. Big mistake!

Although our government at all levels has poured billions of dollars into helping these people, their needs today are astronomical. We are hearing constantly of alcohol and drug abuse, family abuse, sniffing glue, teenage suicides and the list goes on and on. These are just some of the consequences we are seeing today.

But, thanks be to God who has challenged many people of all ages to go with the gospel. We well know that the first thing any man or woman needs before they can ever hope to change and be free from the bondage of sin is the good news as recorded by the Apostle Paul in Romans 1:16: *"I am not ashamed of the gospel, because it is the power of God for the salvation of everyone who believes; first for the Jew, then for the Gentile."*

In 1979, Bud had been serving the Mission as Field Director for Western Canada as well as becoming Assistant General Director. He was asked to take on the General Director's position full-time.

Well, with such a decision to make and all that it involved—another move, up-rooting the family, more administrative work for both the Elfords, criss-crossing the country speaking in Bible colleges, seminaries, churches, youth groups—the first thing our dear missionaries did was *pray*. That is not surprising for these servants of the Lord, for their whole ministry as well as personal and family life was always bathed in prayer.

When I use the word "bathed" I am using the analogy of the difference between a quick shower in the morning and a bath, where one lingers, soaks, and totally relaxes. Waiting on God, as the Psalmist said in Psalm 37:7: *"Be still before the Lord and wait patiently for Him…"* We should also take heed of verse 14 in Psalm 27, *"Wait for the Lord; be strong and take heart and wait for the Lord."*

It has been well said: Waiting on God involves patience, quietness, trust, steadfastness, and courage. How many of us have missed God's will and blessings because we did not learn to wait! A preacher of by-gone days put it well when he said this concerning God's will and doing it, "I find doing the will of the Father leaves you no time disputing His plans."

Before I move on to finish this chapter, I feel led to briefly discuss with you, my readers, that knowing and discerning the will of God for our lives has almost always been a difficult task. Not that God so intended. He made it abundantly clear in Romans 12:1–2, *"Therefore, I urge you, brothers, in view of God's mercy, to offer your bodies as living sacrifices, holy and pleasing to God—this is your spiritual act of worship. Do not conform any longer to the pattern of this world, but be transformed by the renewing of your mind. Then you will be able to test and approve what God's will is—his good, pleasing and perfect will."* God also says in Jeremiah 29:11, *"For I know the plans I have for you, declares the Lord..."*

Because this is such a vital part of the Christian life, I want to share with you part of a message Dr. Charles Stanley preached, entitled *How Do We Discover The Will of God?* In this sermon he concludes by giving six practical keys to determining God's will for our lives, and they are as follows:

> 1—*Know the Word of God.* The Bible is God's instruction book for life, filled with guidance for every area of your life. If you are feeling led to do something that is in direct contradiction to God's Word, don't do it! It is not, and could never be, God's will.
>
> 2—*Pay attention to circumstances.* God is with you every moment of your life—not just during times of emergency. He is actively guiding the day-to-day circumstances of your life, and He will often use those seemingly random events—coincidences, new developments, open doors—to direct you. For a believer, there is no such thing as luck!
>
> 3—*Seek wise counsel.* Proverbs 11:14 declares that "Where there is no guidance the people fall, but in abundance of counselors there is victory." It's good to seek counsel, but be

careful! Not every counselor is wise or godly. That's why it's so important to examine the lives of our counselors carefully, to see if they, themselves, are living in God's will.

4—*Listen to your conscience.* God has given you a conscience to act as a filter for your decisions, and while it can't make you do the right thing, it can certainly make you feel the pain of violating it! Repeated sin can damage and dull your conscience—so make sure that it is reliable by carefully grounding yourself in God's Word.

5—*Use common sense.* There is nothing wrong with using human reasoning to weigh decisions and discern God's will—as long as it is balanced by Scripture, circumstance, wise counsel, and the guidance of the Holy Spirit.

Of course, sometimes God challenges us to do things that seem contrary to common sense; take the recently completed World Training Center at In Touch, for example. When God led us to begin that building, we didn't have the money to do it—but we knew it was God's will. And when God wills something, He provides for it.

Today, that building is funded and completed. More importantly, it is where the translation takes place for the broadcasts that beam the Gospel in 75 languages to hundreds of millions of people around the world!

So while common sense is important, be sure to leave room for God to act in spite of it—so that He can demonstrate His awesome power and generous provision for our lives.

6—*Finally, be sure you feel at peace.* When you are in God's will, your heart is at peace. I like to say that peace is God's umpire. If you don't have peace about a decision, don't do it! God may be sending you a signal, and either the action is wrong or the time is not right.

My friend, it doesn't matter if you are a car mechanic or a heart surgeon, a world traveler or a stay-at-home mom. The

> only contented people in the world, the only people who are at peace, the only ones who live life to its fullest, are those who know and walk in God's will.

It is my prayer that you will use these six keys to unlock that peace, and experience that fulfillment, all the days of your life.

The Elford family left Cold Lake and moved to Prince Albert in 1980 to fulfill the role of National Director for the Mission. These were blessed years with an increase in new candidates and the joy of seeing the attrition numbers dropping significantly.

Bud was missionary-evangelist extraordinaire, an excellent administrator and teacher, and an exceptional linguist. He also had a shepherd-heart filled with compassion and love, thus it was no wonder or surprise that few missionaries dropped away or moved on to other opportunities when Bud was the director.

During these busy years, Marge continued in her role as staff secretary, particularly typing all publications and material for the work. However, with all the added responsibilities of office administrator, Marge's greatest pleasure, and source of real joy, was the responsibility of taking on the new candidates from the very first contact and enquiry with the mission right through to the field destination.

Marge acknowledged that she felt very protective of these candidates, often young people, and watched over them like a mother hen. There is no question that Marge had the heart, as did the Apostle Paul when he wrote to the Thessalonians in 1 Thessalonians 2:7–8, *"Just as a nursing mother cares for her children, so we cared for you. Because we loved you so much, we were delighted to share with you not only the gospel of God but our lives as well."*

I cannot help but wonder how many young people who purposed to go to the mission field or full-time service were somehow derailed along the way because they did not have the love and encouragement they needed to press on!

From a publication by the Billy Graham Evangelistic Association of Canada, I quote:

> When William Carey left England in 1793 for a lifetime of missionary work (never to return), the former shoemaker preached to a small gathering of ministers and challenged them with these remarkable words: "Attempt great things for God! Expect great things from God!"
>
> Carey saw through the complacency and mediocrity that had gripped the church and challenged his fellow believers to answer God's call to evangelize the whole world. He laboured in a distant land for more than 40 years and is known today as the founder of the modern-day missionary movement.

Marge knew, as she nurtured these candidates for the hardness and harshness of the Northern mission field, that they would need strength, power, and grace that only Jesus could give them. This is why she would often assure them that Isaiah 41:10 was a promise they could always count on: *"So do not fear, for I am with you; do not be dismayed, for I am your God. I will strengthen you and help you; I will uphold you with my righteous right hand."* Nor would I be exaggerating if I did not tell you that Marge, many times, encouraged her new candidates with these words in 2 Corinthians 12:9: *"My grace is sufficient for you, for my power is made perfect in weakness."*

What I Need

I need a strength to keep me true
And straight in everything I do;
I need a power to keep me strong
When I am tempted to do wrong;
I need a grace to keep me pure
When passion tries its deadly lure;
I need a love to keep me sweet
When hardness and mistrust I meet;
I need an arm to be my stay
When dark with trouble grows my day;
And nought on earth can these afford,
But all is found in Christ my Lord.
—Selected

When Bud reached that magical retirement age of sixty-five, the Mission policy came into effect and Bud had to retire. Though Marge was somewhat younger than Bud (ahem!) she too, very reluctantly retired and together, they returned to Cherry Grove, Alberta—but not to retirement. No way!

This period of their lives was just a continuation of the work God had called them to do so many years before—lecturing at summer training camps for volunteers (a program which is widely used today but was quite significant in this mission back in the 1980s) and teaching in the Native Bible school, Kee-Way-Tin Bible Institute, as they had always done. Bud was invited across the country to speak in churches, Bible colleges and seminaries, as well as to participate as leader in seminars.

They then went to Arizona as volunteers with an Indian Mission (CHIEF) and served there for nine years. This teaching centre had bi-monthly seminars in which Bud participated. They were blessed with years of ministry meeting U.S. Natives, Eskimos from Alaska, and Peruvian and Mongolian Natives.

Though I know not what awaits me—
What the future has in store;
Yet I know that God is faithful,
For I've proved Him oft before.
—Author Unknown

We can trust our all-knowing God for the unknown future.
—Taken from Radio Bible Class Daily Bread

"I will never leave you nor forsake you." (Joshua 1:5c)
He has a purpose in our heartaches,
The Saviour always knows what's best;
We learn so many precious lessons
In each sorrow, trial and test.
—Author Unknown

Annie Johnson Flint was severely and painfully afflicted with crippling arthritis. Because of this she was confined to her bed for many years of her life. When writing a poem or gospel song, it became necessary for someone to pry her fingers loose so that she could write the words of the poem God had given her.

Many years ago a country and western award-winning songster Glen Campbell sang, *I Never Promised You A Rose Garden.* It became a number one hit on the charts but it didn't bring much comfort or encouragement to the ones who listened! But Annie Johnson Flint wrote one of her most famous poems that was put to music and has touched and blessed many a heart-broken and discouraged soul.

What God Hath Promised

God hath not promised skies always blue,
Flower-strewn pathways all our lives through;
God hath not promised sun without rain,
Joy without sorrow, peace without pain.
But God hath promised strength for the day,
Rest for the labour, light for the way,
Grace for the trials, help from above,
Unfailing sympathy, undying love.
God hath not promised we shall not know
Toil and temptation, trouble and woe;
He hath not told us we shall not bear
Many a burden, many a care.
God hath not promised smooth roads and wide,
Swift, easy travel, needing no guide;
Never a mountain, rocky and steep,
Never a river, turbid and deep.

Was life always a bed of roses for the Elford family? Certainly not! Was theirs such a perfect marriage that they never once had arguments or disagreements? Not very likely!

Many years ago Billy Graham and his wife Ruth were being interviewed on a popular television show. The interviewer asked Mrs. Graham (remember they had five children and her husband was often away from home for weeks at a time) if she and her husband ever argued or had disagreements. Mrs. Graham, for a second or two, was taken aback, but Billy quickly spoke up and said: "If two people always agreed, one wouldn't be necessary."

Marge jokingly told me that when Bud was off on a mission jaunt by plane, loaded with equipment necessary to camp out, including food, etc., sometimes a decision had to be made whether there was room for Marge or Bud's guitar; the guitar would win out! But Marge really didn't mind because she knew the guitar played an important part in Bud's ministry, as he could always draw a crowd playing and singing gospel songs. The following short poem written by Patricia Ann Boyes somewhat expresses the sentiment that Marge felt for Bud all through the years of marriage and service for the Lord.

My Husband

A shoulder to lean on
When life goes awry
A comforting soul mate
When a tear fills my eye
A person to laugh with
When fun fills the day.
A partner to share with
When thoughts go astray
A man for all seasons
Of life to the end
My partner, my soul mate,
My husband, my friend.

In 2001, our faithful couple moved back to Canada and settled in Cherry Grove, Alberta. Not too long afterwards, without going into great detail, Bud had three major surgeries. As he recovered from these traumas, still witnessing and serving the Lord, in 2004 he began to lose his sight and was soon unable to read or drive the car. Thankfully he was still able to get around on his own.

Since the two Elford sons were in ministry, some distance from Cherry Grove, Bud and Marge took their children's advice and moved to Caronport, Saskatchewan where their daughter and her husband are full-time on the staff of Briercrest Bible College and Seminary. Bud, who has always been so active in fixing, building, repairing etc., has had to sit back and let others renovate, repair and refurbish their new home.

Marge has had to pick up the slack and drive Bud wherever he needs to go, look up Scripture for him when he has opportunity to speak and just assist him in every way she can, always remembering this is important ministry and is being done out of love for her husband and love for her Saviour.

I quote now from a testimony Marge sent to me when I commenced this book:

> We thank the Lord for the direction in our lives today as well as the 52 years we spent on the mission field. Personally, if I had my life to live over I would want it to be just as it has been but with changes in many ways. For example, obedience, sins of the flesh, how I did things or how I thought about things and with more seriousness, devotion and love to the Saviour; to serve as He did, not thinking of Himself but others.
>
> Our hearts are filled with great joy for the Lord's goodness to us in every aspect of our lives—personally, physically, spiritually, and in ministry. (Marge then quoted the words of the chorus *How Great Thou Art.*)
>
> Then sings my soul,
> My Saviour God, to Thee;
> How great Thou art, how great Thou art!
> Then sings my soul, My Saviour God, to Thee;
> How great Thou art, How great Thou art!

Obviously this beautiful hymn meant a great deal to Marge. It was originally written in Swedish, translated to Russian and German and eventually to English. Space not permitting, I feel led to quote the last two verses, the third verse most certainly the Elford's testimony and the last verse, theirs and our blessed hope.

And when I think, that God, His Son not sparing;
Sent Him to die, I scarce can take it in;
That on the Cross, my burden gladly bearing,

He bled and died to take away my sin.
When Christ shall come, with shout of acclamation,
And take me home, what joy shall fill my heart.
Then I shall bow, in humble adoration,
And then proclaim: "My God, how great Thou art!"
—*Carl G. Boberg and R. J. Hughes*

Since I commenced this chapter on these servants of the Lord, Bud, who is now eighty years of age, has had cataract surgery on one eye, and at the same time had a cornea transplant. The cornea transplant takes several months to heal and receive its full benefit, but Bud, though he still can't read, can see the baseball games on television, ride his bike, and get around completely on his own. Again God has answered prayer and the praise and the glory all given to their Saviour and Lord.

The Elfords have always been students of the Word of God, and have also lived it in their daily lives. Dr. R. A. Tory, who many years ago was pastor of the great Moody Church in Chicago, and a close friend and associate of evangelist D. L. Moody, gives one of the reasons why D. L. Moody, with little formal education, was so blessed and used of God. "He was a deep and practical student of the Word of God…a profound and practical student of the one Book that is worth studying more than all other books put together; he was a student of the Bible."

I do not want to weary my readers by labouring this point of Bible study, but because it had a tremendous significance in the lives of these missionaries and their fruitfulness in the Lord's work, I want to quote from a book compiled by James S. Bell, Jr. entitled *The D. L. Moody Collection* and, again, the words of Dr. R. A. Tory:

> Oh, you may talk about power; but, if you neglect the one book God has given you as the one instrument through which He imparts and exercises His power, you will not have it. You may read many books and go to many conventions and you may have your all-night prayer meetings to pray for the power of the Holy Ghost, but unless you keep in constant and close association with the one Book, the Bible, you will not have power. And if you ever had power you will not maintain it

except by the daily, earnest, intense study of that Book. *Ninety-nine Christians in every hundred are merely playing at Bible study; and therefore ninety-nine Christians in every hundred are mere weaklings, when they might be giants, both in their Christian life and in their service.*

Bud has continued to write *Minute Message* for the Missions newsletter, a column he started many years ago when he was the President. The following is one of those articles:

> The law of gravity, discovered by Newton, assures us that objects are attracted to planet earth. It holds things so they do not go flying off into space.
>
> This law cannot be changed or broken, but can be overcome. When an aircraft flies, it does not cancel out the law of gravity. It interposes another law—that of aerodynamics. However, as soon as that law stops, gravity goes into effect and down goes the plane.
>
> Romans 8:2 talks about two laws—the law of sin and death, and the law of the Spirit of life in Christ Jesus. Paul says that this law sets us free from the law of sin and death. It does not destroy that law, but introduces another law. It is our duty to so live by faith and keep active the law of the Spirit of life in Christ Jesus, so we can walk in freedom. And no matter how old a person is in Christ, the moment he ceases to live by faith, he is victimized by the law of sin and death that is still very much in force, and down we come.
>
> An aircraft keeps flying as long as it overcomes the law of gravity. Likewise, we may walk free from the law of sin and death as long as we continue to walk in the Spirit by faith.
>
> Our pilots tell us there is nothing sweeter than—when flying on a beautiful summer's day with the motor purring, altitude perfect, and the aircraft trimmed correctly—to lean back and "enjoy" resting in the continual overcoming of the law of gravity by the plane.

Dear friend, it's so sweet to rest in Jesus' overcoming victory over the law of sin and death, resting in the law of the Spirit of life in Christ Jesus. Lean back and enjoy. That is living by faith.

Bud and Marge have had, as do many Christians, a verse that most describes their lives today as well as throughout over half a century of missionary service. Bud's is a verse found in 1 Thessalonians 1:9, *"We turn to God from idols and we serve the living and true God, and are waiting for His Son from Heaven"* (Paraphrase). Marge holds dear a verse her Sunday school teacher, Mrs. W. Harding, gave her when she first became a Christian, found in John 15:16. *"You did not choose me, but I chose you and appointed you to go and bear fruit—fruit that will last. Then the Father will give you whatever you ask in my name."*

After

After the trials the sun will shine,
But until then God's peace will be mine;
To cheer me, to guide me,
Give strength through the way,
To be my companion though stormy the day.
The Savior is watching and caring I know,
Though sunshine is hidden His beauties still glow.
Before me I see but the task we've begun,
And dreams of the Glory t'will be when He's done,
For my Lord will reveal beams from gold now refined,
When at ending of trials, radiant sunlight does shine.
—*Paul Durham*

Let us think often that our only business in this life is to please God, and that all besides is folly and vanity.
—*Brother Lawrence (17th century Monk)*

Postscript

It was with sadness that we learned our dear, long-time friend L. W. (Bud) Elford slipped away to heaven on September 20, 2008, into the loving arms of the Saviour He dearly loved and served so faithfully. Bud was in his eighty-fourth year and had been ill for some three years. But in between bouts of surgery, some very serious, he continued teaching his adult Bible class and occasionally preaching in the church at Briercrest Bible College in Saskatchewan.

When I learned of Bud's promotion to heaven, the words of King David came to mind when he spoke of Abner's death: *"A great leader and a great man has fallen today in Israel"* (2 Samuel 3:38, TLB). The word the Apostle Paul spoke in 2 Corinthians 5:8–9 well described Bud's life and testimony: *"And we are not afraid, but are quite content, for then we will be at home with the Lord. So our aim is to please him, always in everything we do whether we are here in this body or away from this body and with him in heaven" (TLB).*

We are not sure to whom we would credit the following poem but in my humble opinion it sounds like the Bud I knew.

From the Glory and the Gladness

From the glory and the gladness,
From His secret place,
From the rapture of His presence
From the radiance of His face,
Christ, the Son of God, hath sent me
Through the midnight lands;
Mine the mighty ordination
Of the pierced Hands,
Mine the message grand and glorious
Strange unsealed surprise
That the goal is God's Beloved,
Christ in paradise.

WOMEN WHO HAVE *Touched* AND INFLUENCED MY LIFE

"I am not ashamed of the gospel, because it is the power of God for the salvation of everyone who believes: first for the Jew, then for the Gentile."

(Romans 1:16)

"The one who takes your hand but touches your heart is a true friend."

—Selected

This was a difficult one for me to decide—who will I write about first? My mother, my grandmother, my wife's mother, my cousin Ann, or my great-aunt Daisy? Well, I have picked Aunt Daisy! Why? Perhaps because of all the women I have mentioned she is the most colourful, unique and fun!

Aunt Daisy was born into the Davidson family, January 5, 1903, in Ottawa, Ontario. Hers was a large family with six brothers and three sisters—ten altogether.

They were a good-living family, attending church regularly, but, sadly, never heard the simplicity of the gospel message. Daisy met and married my great-uncle George Dalzell in 1925.

Uncle George's parents were Wesleyan Methodist—very devoted, sincere and consecrated Christians. His father, my great-grandfather, was a lay preacher in his denomination and was well known and respected throughout the Christian community. Regrettably, none of his three children followed the Lord.

The newlyweds went to live with Uncle George's parents; as we well know, not always a good start for a new marriage. But for Daisy it was, as it was the godly influence and daily example of her husband's parents that introduced her to the gospel, a fact that the Bible makes clear. *"For it is by grace you have been saved, through faith—and this not from yourselves, it is the gift of God—not by works, so that no one can boast"* (Ephesians 2:8–9).

My first memory of Aunt Daisy was several years later. She and Uncle George had gone to Detroit, Michigan, as it was the depression years and unemployment was widespread. While there, two daughters, Lois and Georgia, were born. Shortly thereafter, the family returned to Ottawa. Aunt Daisy at this time was still not a Christian.

My mother and I had come to live with my grandparents and as George and my grandfather, Tom, were brothers, they were frequent visitors to our home. I don't remember how often they came but it was usually on a weekend. Another couple, Sue and Fred would join the two couples. I realize now that the reason they came to my grandparents' house was because of what they would be doing on these visits—the women playing euchre and the men smoking and drinking—a no-no in a strict Wesleyan Methodist home!

Now that you have the background of this family saga, I want to move on and tell you the best part of this account. My Aunt Jean, Aunt Daisy's niece, a young woman at the time, had been invited to a large church in Ottawa. In those days this church was called The Gospel Tabernacle. They were associated with the Christian and Missionary Alliance denomination.

They were having evangelistic meetings with two brothers who came from the United States. Aunt Jean accepted the Lord during those meetings and the first thing she did was invite her mother, Aunt Daisy, and Sue.

The first night Aunt Daisy went to one of the meetings, she was convicted by the Holy Spirit and stood up when the invitation to come forward for prayer and salvation was extended. She was prepared to take that all-important step that would seal her eternal destiny. *"Everyone who calls on the name of the Lord will be saved"* (Romans 10:13).

But her sister, who had also accompanied her, pulled her back down to her seat. She probably believed that "going forward" was not necessary for a girl brought up in the church, who really wasn't a sinner compared to so many they knew. This dear sister didn't realize at the time that the Bible explicitly states in Psalm 143:2b, *"...for no one living is righteous before You."* Or the verse in 1 Kings 8:46b, *"...for there is no one who does not sin."*

However, the next night she went back to the meeting and no one could hold her back! She practically ran to the altar and fell on her knees, and that night Aunt Daisy became a child of God. *"Yet to all who received him, to those who believed in his name, he gave the right to become children of God"* (John 1:12).

At the same meetings, my grandmother and Sue also accepted the Lord and became "new creatures" in Christ Jesus. 2 Corinthians 5:17 explains this: *"Therefore, if anyone is in Christ, he is a new creation; the old has gone, the new has come!"*

These three women were changed and transformed and they truly had an impact on their families. The New Living Translation says it this way in Colossians 1:13–14: *"For he has rescued us from the one who rules in the kingdom of darkness, and he has brought us into the Kingdom of his dear Son. God has purchased our freedom with his blood and has forgiven all our sins."*

Fanny Crosby put it so beautifully for us when she wrote *Blessed Assurance, Jesus is Mine*, and Aunt Daisy would soon learn (she became a woman of the Word) the assurance King David had when he wrote Psalm 32 and Paul wrote to the Christians in Romans 4:7–8, *"Blessed are they whose transgressions are forgiven, whose sins are covered, Blessed is the* [woman] *whose sin the Lord will never count against* [her]*."*

Aunt Daisy never looked back, never turned back. Though ridiculed by her brothers, she was, thankfully, always encouraged by Uncle George and led along by her husband's parents. She grew quickly in the faith and matured by attending Sunday school and all the church services with her two daughters. By this time the church was called The Metropolitan Tabernacle, where they were meeting in a theatre.

Farther along in this chapter I will show you how I know, without a doubt, that this dear lady matured and grew close to her Lord right from the beginning of her walk with God. The Apostle Peter put it so clearly to the saints scattered throughout the then-known world in his first letter, *"Like newborn babies, crave pure spiritual milk, so that you may grow up in your salvation, now that you have tasted that the Lord is good"* (1 Peter 2:2–3).

The following gospel song expresses the faith and determination Aunt Daisy had, not only when she was first born again but all through her long life.

I Have Decided To Follow Jesus

I have decided to follow Jesus;
I have decided to follow Jesus;
I have decided to follow Jesus;
No turning back, no turning back.
Though I may wonder, I still will follow;
Though I may wonder, I still will follow;
Though I may wonder, I still will follow;
No turning back, no turning back.
The world behind me, the cross before me;
The world behind me, the cross before me;
The world behind me, the cross before me;
No turning back, no turning back.
Though none go with me, still I will follow;
Though none go with me, still I will follow;
Though none go with me, still I will follow;
No turning back, no turning back.

—*Anonymous*

Before I move on and relate some of the ways God led this amazing woman, I would like to quote for you a poem written by Edgar A.

Guest (1881–1959). If this writer had remained in his original home in England, I am sure he would have become Great Britain's Poet Laureate. He lived and worked in Detroit, Michigan, and wrote and published more than eleven thousand poems. The following is one most quoted and loved by countless people around the world.

Sermons We See

I'd rather see a sermon than hear one any day;
I'd rather one should walk with me than merely tell the way.
The eye's a better pupil and more willing than the ear,
Fine counsel is confusing, but example's always clear;
And the best of all the preachers are the men who live their creeds,
For to see good put in action is what everybody needs.
I soon can learn to do it if you'll let me see it done;
I can watch your hands in action, but your tongue too fast may run.
And the lecture you deliver may be very wise and true,
But I'd rather get my lessons by observing what you do;
For I might misunderstand you and the high advice you give,
But there's no misunderstanding how you act and how you live.
When I see a deed of kindness, I am eager to be kind.
When a weaker brother stumbles and a strong man stays behind
Just to see if he can help him, then the wish grows strong in me
To become as big and thoughtful as I know that friend to be.
And all travelers can witness that the best of guides today
Is not the one who tells them, but the one who shows the way.
One good man teaches many, men believe what they behold;
One deed of kindness noticed is worth forty that are told.
Who stands with men of honor learns to hold his honor dear,
For right living speaks a language which to every one is clear.
Though an able speaker charms me with his eloquence, I say,
I'd rather see a sermon than to hear one, any day.

She also earnestly believed Christ showed His love by dying for us; we show our love by living for Him.

Another important Scriptural truth this new Christian learned very early in her Christian life was the plain, unadulterated instructions God gave to Christian wives whose husbands were unbelievers. I am referring to 1 Peter 3:1–6, especially the words in Verses 1b–2 "*...If any of them do not believe the Word, they may be won over without words by the behaviour of their wives, when they see the purity and reverence of your lives*" and Verse 4b "*...the unfaded beauty of a gentle and quiet spirit, which is of great worth in God's sight.*" Aunt Daisy "walked the talk." Her first love was the Saviour and after Him were her husband, children, church, extended family, friends, and neighbours.

The years I am referring to were called "the dirty thirties"; those were depression days with many, many thousands of men and women without work, unable to feed and clothe their families and keep a roof over their heads. Difficult years to say the least.

Aunt Jean and her husband Ira Corrigan had left Ottawa, gone up to Noranda, Quebec, and found work in the gold mines. Uncle George soon followed, and also found work in the gold and copper mines. That was the spring of 1937 and by October he had found them a place to live in Rouyn, an upper duplex overlooking the lake. Two more children, Wesley and Lloyd, had been added to their family by this time. Daisy took the train to the far north, not knowing what to expect, but knowing there would be a grand reunion with husband and father.

Rouyn-Noranda in those days was a far cry from Ottawa, Canada's capital city. It must have been a big adjustment for a city girl to move to that northern town, leaving home and family and settling into a completely different lifestyle—wooden sidewalks, muddy, unpaved side streets, no street cars or buses. But she never complained.

Their first Sunday there they joined Aunt Daisy's niece, Jean, at the little Baptist church in Noranda. They attended regularly every Sunday, through hot summer days and bitterly cold winters. In fact, Aunt Daisy attended the church for over forty years. In those days Sunday school was in the afternoon so it meant three trips to church on Sunday, and for Aunt Daisy, her weekly attendance at prayer meeting.

It was about this time that I truly came to know and love this dear one. It was the summer of 1938. I had just recovered from a long year of dealing with polio and its after-effects. My grandparents had by this time left Ottawa to find work in Noranda and I came up to visit them.

I was an only child, abandoned by my father. In a sense I also felt abandoned by my grandparents whom I loved and who adored me (being their first grandchild). My mother had to leave me on my own every day to work and support us, so I was a lonely and somewhat frail boy aged eleven.

The first thing I did was to make my way over to Rouyn to visit my cousins and Aunt Daisy. What a warm welcome I received! Aunt Daisy hugged and kissed me and for the first time I really felt part of a family.

I remember so clearly gathering around the kitchen table with my cousins and helping Aunt Daisy make peanut butter cookies. She would let us roll them into little balls, put them on the pan, press them with a fork, and then wait, not always patiently, while they baked. As soon as they were out of the oven and cooled, along with a cold drink, what a feast we would have!

Aunt Daisy absolutely adored her children. I doubt if they were ever spanked (a common disciplinary act in those days), probably yelled at once in a while but she was never too busy to be there for them. I can still remember sitting around the kitchen table playing *Snakes and Ladders* and other board games; but never card games or bingo, never! Her laugh was contagious and she laughed a lot. She was, as I mentioned at the beginning of this chapter, a lot of fun. How I loved her.

She also had a great sense of humour and was very good at one-liners! That same summer, I was at the Sunday school picnic and, being a curious boy, I decided to leave the picnic and go to visit a home where a family from the church lived.

When I got there they were not at home. They may have even been at the picnic. But the dog was home! Though he barked, growled, and showed his teeth, I, having no fear of dogs, kept right on blithely walking towards the door of the little house. Well, the inevitable happened. He lunged at me and gave me a nasty and painful bite on the leg.

Because I was bleeding profusely, it was suggested I should see the doctor. Aunt Daisy was assigned the task of taking me. After Dr. Linklater had cleansed the wound, sterilized and bandaged it, he asked if the dog was mad (meaning rabid), to which Aunt Daisy replied: "Well I don't know about the dog but Henry is!" The doctor really laughed at that one!

Was life always fun and games for Aunt Daisy? Certainly not! We could almost say that she had more heartache and sorrow than most would ever have to endure. But I will say it never changed her attitude. Isaiah 49:17 may well have been her comfort and stay for she was a woman of the Word—*"This is what the Lord says—your Redeemer, the holy One of Israel: 'I am the Lord your God, who teaches what is best for you, who directs you in the way you should go.'"* Her health failed on many occasions, but never her faith.

The LORD is gracious and righteous;
our God is full of compassion.
The LORD protects the simple hearted;
when I was in great need, he saved me.
Be at rest once more, O my soul,
for the LORD has been good to you.
For you, O LORD, have delivered my soul from death,
my eyes from tears, my feet from stumbling,
That I may walk before the LORD
in the land of the living.
(Psalm 116:5–9)

Her testimony was surely the following: "I'd rather walk with God in the dark than go alone in the light; I'd rather walk with Him by faith than walk alone by sight."

I can only mention a few of the set-backs, heartaches and sorrows this dear one endured but always with a firm belief in the truth of God's Word settled in her heart and mind. This brought her a sweet peace.

A few years ago while in India on a Missions trip, I ministered at a Christian school owned and operated by a fine Christian woman by the name of Evangeline Sita. I persuaded her to arrange an opportunity to minister at a leper colony. This was a unique and blessed experience. But, I am telling you this to tell you the following:

After we left the colony, we made another stop at a Christian brother's home. It was getting late by the time we arrived back at Evangeline's home. She insisted we come in. When we entered the house, her dear mother, whom I had met previously, did not hear us come in. As we came into the sitting room, we could see her in the bedroom reading her Bible.

Dear reader, are we missing the blessing and comfort that comes to us by failing to meditate daily on the Word of God? Author Eugene Peterson has said, "God's voice is speaking to us, inviting, promising, blessing, confronting, commanding, healing." There is a quote from *Our Daily Bread* that says, "Go to the Bible for your protection, correction and direction."

Anne Cetas wrote the following in the January 2006 issue of *Our Daily Bread:*

> Four pastors were discussing the merits of the various translations of the Bible. One liked a particular version best because of its simple, beautiful English. Another preferred a more scholarly edition because it was closer to the original Hebrew and Greek. Still another liked a contemporary version because of its up-to-date vocabulary.
>
> The fourth minister was silent for a moment, then said, "I like my mother's translation best." Surprised, the other three men said they didn't know his mother had translated the Bible. "Yes," he replied. "She translated it into life, and it was the most convincing translation I ever saw."
>
> Ezra 7:10 says, Ezra had prepared his heart to seek the Law of the Lord, and to do it, and to teach statutes and ordinances. As a scribe, he studied the Law, obeyed it, and taught it to the Israelites.
>
> Let's follow Ezra's example by seeking the Word of God and translating it into life.

The most important focus should be learning God's Word and doing it. James 1:21–22 says, *"Therefore, get rid of all moral filth and the evil that is so prevalent and humbly accept the word planted in you, which can save you. Do not merely listen to the word, and so deceive yourselves. Do what it says."*

This is what the LORD says to his anointed, "I will go before you and will level the mountains; I will break down gates of bronze and cut through bars of iron. I will give you the treasures of darkness, riches stored in secret places, so that you may know that I am the LORD, the God of Israel, who summons you by name."
(Isaiah 45:1–3)

Going back to those early days in Rouyn, Uncle George, who at best was not a strong, rugged man, came down with a serious case of pneumonia and was hospitalized for weeks. Most would think these circumstances, a husband desperately ill, and four children to support and care for, would have been enough to drag her down to the pit of despair but such was not the case!

Promised Strength

One day when my burden seemed greater
Than my body and spirit could bear,
Weighed down by the load, I faltered
Beneath my worry and care;
And I cried to the heedless silence
As I walked where I could not see:
'Where is the strength that is promised?
Where is the strength for me?'
And suddenly out of the stillness,
A voice came clear and true:
'My child, you are striving to carry
A burden not meant for you,

And the thought of the years outstretching
Before you has darkened the way,
While the only strength I have promised
Is the sure strength day by day.'
I took one step—and I found it
Quite easy, indeed to take,
And the burden slipped from my shoulders,
And my heart that was ready to break

Gave thanks that my eyes were opened
And my shoulders eased of their load,
As I saw, step by step I was strengthened
To walk on the roughest road!

Eventually Uncle George and Aunt Daisy bought their own home on Taschereau Street in Rouyn. By today's standards it was a small, three-bedroom bungalow, always neat, clean and tidy, and always "open-house" for one and all.

I remember having so much fun gathered around the kitchen table, playing games and eating chocolate marshmallow cookies and other assortments of what today we would call junk food. But what happy times they were! Aunt Daisy had an infectious laugh. Many times we would howl with laughter at the simplest of things.

Many of the neighbours on Taschereau Street were immigrants from Europe along with French-speaking Canadians. Aunt Daisy didn't have a biased/prejudiced bone in her entire body and I doubt if she even knew the word racist. She just loved them all and opened her heart and home for anyone who had a need. In fact, many of her neighbours became life-long friends.

Was she ever cross with her children? Did they ever annoy her? Did they ever make her angry? Did she ever yell at them? Well, I would probably have to say "yes." After all, they were normal kids, and there must have been times when she was totally exasperated with them. But the one thing we all knew, she absolutely and unconditionally loved and adored them.

There was one thing they could do that many children never could do and that was to share their hurts, feelings, dreams, or anything else that was bothering or troubling them. She was a good, kind and sympathetic listener and was always ready to give them good counsel and advice. I'm not sure if they always took her wise words seriously but I do know they turned out to be children who made her proud to be their mother and grateful to God for each one of them.

In 1940, when the girls were teenagers and the boys were not far behind in age, a lovely baby boy was born. I believe his name was William but we all called him Billy. He was a beautiful baby—great big brown eyes and dark curly hair. He was everyone's pet! He brought unspeakable joy to the whole family.

However, I need to stop here for a few lines and tell you about Billy's life. Somewhere along the way, Billy got off track and messed up his life and succumbed to the temptations of the world, the flesh, and the devil.

I have no knowledge of Billy's life over these years of rebellion, but I do know that he had a mother who brought him before the throne of grace on a daily basis. She followed the challenge that Augustine penned so many, many years ago: "Trust the past to God's mercy, the present to God's love, and the future to God's providence."

Let me tell you about a man named Frederick Arvid Blom. Aunt Daisy probably never knew his story, but I am sure she often sang one of the gospel songs he wrote—*He the Pearly Gates Will Open*. He was born in Sweden in 1867, came to the United States, went through seminary, worked with the Salvation Army, and pastored several churches.

Then something went terribly wrong in his life and he wound up in prison. While in prison, broken by his sin and failure, he repented and turned again to the Lord. He wrote this song while in prison. Please take note of the second verse, for it especially describes not only Billy, but many of us who are children of God.

He the Pearly Gates Will Open

Love divine, so great and wondrous,
Deep and mighty, pure, sublime;
Coming from the heart of Jesus—
Just the same thro' tests of time.
He the pearly gates will open,
So that I may enter in;
For He purchased my redemption
And forgave me all my sin.
Like a sparrow hunted, frightened,
Weak and helpless—such was I;
Wounded, fallen, yet He healed me—
He will heed the sinner's cry.

Love divine, so great and wondrous!
All my sins He then forgave;
I will sing His praise forever,
For His blood, His pow'r to save.
In life's eventide, at twilight,
At His door I'll knock and wait;
By the precious love of Jesus
I shall enter heaven's gate.

In the book *Hymns and Hymn Stories*, Cliff Barrows relates the following story:

> The hymn's message is very simple. Because of the love of God expressed in Christ our sins are forgiven, our lives are changed and we anticipate a joyful entrance into heaven. It is said that Fred Blom died in the custody of the law. While the gates of prison did not open for him, he knew that heaven's pearly gates would be swung wide by his Redeemer.

Spiritual failure doesn't have to be final. As God's children we are never beyond the touch of God's grace. Billy's mother certainly believed this with all of her heart and believed what God said in Jeremiah 32:27: *"I am the Lord, the God of all mankind. Is anything too hard for me?"*

> God of Second Chances
>
> As far as following God was concerned, Jonah failed hopelessly. He defiantly did the opposite of what he knew he was supposed to do. But did God reject him? No. God allowed him to experience failure. Getting thrown overboard and being swallowed by a whale (big fish) brought Jonah to his senses real quick. When he was ready to listen, "the Word of the Lord came to Jonah a second time."
>
> And so it is with us. No matter how many times we feel we've failed or blown it, God will continue to call us to himself. However, it is much wiser to "listen up" quickly so we don't

have to get hit over the head with a "4 by 4"—or be swallowed by a "whale of a problem" for God to get our attention.

So, if you feel you have failed, be encouraged. Now is the time to give God a chance. "He'll mend even a broken heart if you'll give him all the pieces." God calls us all to follow him, so why not respond to his call and, if you haven't already done so, ask him to come into your life as Lord and Savior? He can make a much better job of your life than you can if you will trust it to him.

"Then the word of the LORD came to Jonah a second time: 'Go to the great city of Nineveh and proclaim to it the message I give you.' Jonah obeyed the word of the LORD and went to Nineveh"

(Jonah 3:1–3, NIV).

A suggested prayer: "Dear God, thank you that you are a God of second (and third, and fourth, and fifth, and sixth, and seven times seventy) chances. Please help me to always live in harmony with your will so I will always be in tune to hear your word to me. Thank you for hearing and answering my prayer. Gratefully, in Jesus' name, amen." *—Author Unknown*

Like the prodigal son in Luke's Gospel, Chapter 15, one day Billy did return to his Heavenly Father. I am not sure of the details of his return to the Father's bosom but I am sure of the words of a hymn his mother often sang in her church:

Softly and tenderly Jesus is calling,
Calling for you and for me;
See, on the portals He's waiting and watching,
Watching for you and for me.
Come home, come home;
Ye who are weary, come home;
Earnestly, tenderly, Jesus is calling,
Calling, "O sinner, come home!"

Why should we tarry when Jesus is pleading,
Pleading for you and for me?
Why should we linger and heed not His mercies,
Mercies for you and for me?
Time is now fleeting, the moments are passing,
Passing from you and from me;
Shadows are gathering, death-beds are coming,
Coming for you and for me.
O for the wonderful love He has promised,
Promised for you and for me;
Though we have sinned He has mercy and pardon,
Pardon for you and for me.
—*William L. Thompson*

Was there a change in Billy's life? Absolutely. Written in one of my Bibles is a short poem that describes Billy.

I'd rather see a Christian
Than to hear one merely talk;
I'd rather see his actions
And behold His daily walk.
—*Author Unknown*

Billy lived in Niagara Falls. Having his mother's sense of humour, he would often say as we parted: "The next time you come over to the Falls, drop in!" When God laid hold of Billy, he became a living testimony to the grace and graciousness of our loving God.

Like his mother, he was a people-person and every life he touched was blessed by his cheery disposition and his servant-spirit. He could say as the Apostle Paul said in Romans 1:16–17, *"For I am not ashamed of the gospel. I see it as the very power of God working for the salvation of everyone who believes it, both Jew and Greek. I see it in God's plan for imparting righteousness to men, a process begun and continued by their faith, for as the Scripture says: 'The righteous shall live by faith'"* (J. B. Phillips Translation).

Sadly, Billy was plagued with serious heart trouble and underwent several open-heart surgeries and finally had to quit his work and go on a disability pension. Though his activities were somewhat curtailed, he kept on loving and serving his Saviour. He became all things to all men that he might bring them to a saving knowledge of the Lord Jesus Christ.

Just a few years ago, Billy hastened home to the Saviour he was so passionate about. His memorial service was one of triumph and victory. Many of his friends testified to how he was instrumental in leading them to the Saviour, helping them over and over again. It didn't matter how many times they failed and strayed away from the Lord.

All of us were sorely grieved at his home-going but happy for him that his days of suffering were at last over. We did not grieve as those who have no hope for we read the Apostle Paul's exhortation in 1 Thessalonians 4:13–18:

> *Brothers, we do not want you to be ignorant about those who fall asleep, or to grieve like the rest of men, who have no hope. We believe that Jesus died and rose again and so we believe that God will bring with Jesus those who have fallen asleep in him. According to the Lord's own word, we tell you that we who are still alive, who are left till the coming of the Lord, will certainly not precede those who have fallen asleep. For the Lord himself will come down from heaven, with a loud command, with the voice of the archangel and with the trumpet call of God, and the dead in Christ will rise first. After that, we who are still alive and are left will be caught up together with them in the clouds to meet the Lord in the air. And so we will be with the Lord forever. Therefore encourage each other with these words.*

When the Saints Go Marching In

I have a dear, sweet mother,
Singing 'round the white throne,
And I promised I would meet her,
'There we'll know as we are known.'
I have a living Saviour,
He redeemed me from sin;

Oh, how sweet 'twill be to meet Him,
When the saints go marching in.
—B. B. McKinney

Aunt Daisy gave birth to a stillborn baby in 1943. This was a disappointment and shock to the entire family, but she was the one who sustained the family and encouraged them to move on, knowing God never makes a mistake. Her daughter Lois commented how at times her health failed, but never her faith. There is an old Irish blessing that was so true in the life of this child of God:

God for the good day,
God for the bad day,
God for the pleasure,
God for the pain,
God for the rain,
God when our barns are empty,
God when they are full again.

In Deuteronomy 33:27 we read, *"The eternal God is your refuge and dwelling place, and underneath are the everlasting arms…"* (Amplified). This knowledge from the Word of God sustained Aunt Daisy over and over again throughout her long life.

Tis good to know that Jesus cares
When I'm too tired to say my prayers,
Tis grand to know He knows my need
When I'm too weak my wants to plead;
How restful is my sure belief
His arms eternal are beneath,
That round about me hour by hour
Are tender love, Almighty power,
That in His hands I safe may rest
And find that I am surely blest.
—Author Unknown

Around 1947, Uncle George sustained a serious accident at work. Both of his legs were broken. After his recovery, and as I mentioned previously he was not a robust man, going back to the mine was not an option. What were they to do?

Stephen Arterburn in his book *Healing is a Choice* has this to say when you may be at the end of your rope:

> ...You have one more choice to make and this is the choice to persevere.
>
> Holding on is never pleasant, but it protects you from a messy, premature end that flings turmoil all over everyone who felt they were close to you. There are some very important reasons to hold on when you don't feel that you can. The most important reason is that God loves you greatly and wants the very best possible for you. You are a valuable person to Him, and He wants you to persevere. To God, one day is worth a thousand years. Think about that. The Creator of infinite time, who has all the time in the world, values every minute of time you continue to live.
>
> Sometimes we think so small, we think in terms of what is before us on this earth. We can only understand the tangible, but there are some intangible dimensions of time that we are not aware of. Somehow the impact of one person remaining alive for one more day has an eternal value that equals one thousand years. I don't know how that works, but I believe it, because God's Word says it.

Well, Aunt Daisy knew how to persevere. And she knew how to pray. Over and over again in her long journey on this planet she had experienced and witnessed God answering prayer.

It's Me Again, Lord

Remember me, God? I come every day
Just to talk with You, Lord, and learn how to pray.
You make me feel welcome,
You reach out Your hand,

I need never explain for You understand,
I come to You frightened and burdened with care,
So lonely and lost and so filled with despair,
And suddenly, Lord, I'm no longer afraid,
My burden is lighter and the dark shadows fade.
Oh, God, what a comfort to know that You care
And to know when I seek You,
You will always be there!
—*Author Unknown*

God wonderfully answered prayer and Uncle George was offered a job as the custodian of a school in Noranda. This was ideal for both of them. The school provided an apartment, which was large and comfortable. This position also made it possible for Aunt Daisy to help her husband when there were jobs he found difficult to do.

Not only that, she became a friend and mentor to many of the children as well as several of the teachers. Many a time, during a break, a teacher would come in for a cup of tea, and one of her delicious squares, and receive counsel and comfort from Aunt Daisy.

This was somewhat of an irony, for these teachers were well educated, worldly-wise and quite sophisticated, but they sought out this dear woman for advice and encouragement. They knew that anything they shared with her would be held in the strictest confidence. Perhaps unknown to them, they would be added to her prayer list. She believed in the old adage "prayer changes things" and she also believed that prayer changes people.

O. Hallesby quotes this about prayer that well describes the heart of Aunt Daisy:

> The Spirit of prayer makes us so intimate with God that we scarcely pass through an experience before we speak to Him about it, either in supplication, in sighing, in pouring out our woes before Him, in fervent requests, or in thanksgiving and adoration.

I related at the beginning of this chapter that Aunt Daisy had accepted Christ Jesus as her personal Saviour. From that time on she never forgot that her eternal salvation and destiny was centred in Jesus Christ and His death on the cross at Calvary. In 1 Corinthians 1:18, we read *"The Message that points to Christ on the Cross seems like sheer silliness to those hell-bent on destruction, but for those on the way of salvation it makes perfect sense. This is the way God works, and most powerfully as it turns out"* (The Message).

Pastor C. J. Mahaney, in his book *The Cross Centered Life*, writes:

> You may forget this book and its author, but *never let the message of the cross slide into second or third place in your life. Never lay it aside. Never move on.*
>
> I can hear you asking, "But don't I need more than that?" In one sense the answer is no. Nothing else is of equal importance. The message of the cross is the Christian's hope, confidence, and assurance. Heaven will be spent marvelling at the work of Christ, the God-Man who suffered in the place of us sinners.
>
> And yet, in another sense the answer is yes, you do need more. You've been saved to grow, to serve in a local church, to do good works and to glorify God. But the 'more' that you need as a follower of Christ won't be found apart from the cross. The gospel isn't one class among many that you'll attend during your life as a Christian—the gospel is the whole building that all the classes take place in!
>
> Rightly approached, all the topics you'll study and focus on as a believer will be offered to you 'within the walls' of the glorious gospel.
>
> "The Spirit does not take his pupils beyond the cross", writes J. Knox Chamblin, "but ever more deeply into it."
>
> David Prior said it best in one of my favourite quotes: "We never move on from the cross, only into a more profound understanding of the cross." A lot has changed since I first trusted in Christ, but a lot has stayed the same. I'm grateful to say that what matters the most has remained the same. *The cross is still at the center.*
>
> I've come a long way since I heard the gospel in a drug-induced high. I've traveled many miles in this journey of faith.

But by His grace I've never moved on from the cross of Jesus Christ. And I never want to.

I have quoted the above because Aunt Daisy's life was indeed centred on the cross of her Saviour and the one she made Lord of her life. Today, in many of the churches, hymns that have to do with "the blood" have been eliminated from the new editions of their hymnals. And yes, in many of our evangelical churches, we sing "worship choruses" and few of them ever mention the blood. I often wonder if our young people today have ever heard this gospel song.

What can wash away my sin?
Nothing but the blood of Jesus!
What can make me whole again?
Nothing but the blood of Jesus!
—*Robert Lowry*

Hebrews 13:20 from the J. B. Phillips Translation says, *"Now the God of peace who brought back from the dead that great shepherd of the sheep, our Lord Jesus Christ, by the blood of the everlasting agreement, equip you thoroughly for the doing of His will."*

Without apology I quote an eighteenth century poet, Samuel Davies:

No Dye Too Dark

In wonder lost, with trembling joy
We take the pardon of our God;
Pardon for crimes of deepest dye,
A pardon bought with Jesus blood,
A pardon bought with Jesus blood.
O may this strange, this matchless grace,
This God-like miracle of love,
Fill the whole earth with grateful praise,
And all the Angelic Choirs above,
And all the Angelic Choirs above.

Florence Newby (Auntie Florence to our children and grandchildren) was a very close family friend who was connected to us through one of the churches where I was an interim pastor for two years. She was a teacher all of her life and was gifted in many ways. Florence is now in her eternal home with Jesus and we still miss her. She wrote the following two poems in response to a series of messages on Jesus' words from the cross. They were written in March and April, 1995.

Alone upon the cross He hung amid a jeering crowd
Hark to His oft-repeated cry through din of voices loud.
"Father, forgive; they do not know the things they seek to do."
They've never heard He came to die for them and all men too.
On a cross near Him there hung a thief condemned to death.
And from his lips there came a plea with almost his last breath.
"When in Your kingdom you will come, will you remember me?"
"Today with Me", the Lord replied, "In paradise you'll be."
Amid that jeering, howling mob a woman stands and weeps,
She sees her Son in agony, but she her vigil keeps.
And once again that suff'ring One speaks from the cruel tree,
"Woman, behold they son," He spoke. John said,
"Come home with me."
By these gracious words He cut all earthly, human ties.
No longer just the Nazarene—for all mankind He dies.
Now Mary fully understands that He's her Saviour too,
And with a new born sense of awe, she worships Him anew.
Darkness shuts from human view the travail of His soul,
As God withdraws His face from Him Who dies to make men whole.
"Why has Thou forsaken Me?"—a cry from deep within.
A holy God could only turn from Him Who was made sin.
"I thirst" escaped from parched lips, they quickly gave to Him
A sponge from out a vessel near, filled to the very brim
This was done so that the Word recorded in eons past
Might be fulfilled in God's own time to prove His word will last.
Ended now His work on earth, with every battle won,
Triumphantly He cries aloud, "It's finished! All is done!"

"Into Thy hands I now commit My spirit, God, to Thee."
With one last sigh His life He gave, on Calvary's blood-stained tree.
Sitting down they watched Him there, this crowd with feelings mixed.
Some taunting Him, some casting lots their eyes on Jesus fixed.
"That was the Son of God," said one, while Joseph bore away
The earthly form of God's own Son to rise on Easter Day!

Empty

An empty place in heaven's courts
While angels hush their praise
Think if you will of that great day
Bow your head in holy awe as God His love displays.
An empty spot in Pilate's hall as Peter slinks away.
Weep when you think of that great Jew who said,
"I know Him not, I am not His," and did His Lord betray.
An empty cell in Roman jail while Pilate, helpless, stands.
Look, if you can, on that dread scene—
Barabbas free instead of Him...he'd met the mob's demands.
One empty cross on Calvary's brow,
While Satan laughs in glee; weep as you must for blinded men
Who slew the King of Kings. He came to set men free.
An empty tomb in gardens fair while weeping women came;
Hark to the words the angel said—
"He is not here. He rose this morn. This news to men proclaim."
That empty place has now been filled as He returns to heaven.
Sing praise to Him who died for us,
And bow in thanks because He came that we might be forgiven.
An empty grave as we shall rise when Christ in power appears,
Shout, as you must, for Satan's grip o'er death is gone
Away with grief and fears.

In the 1950s the grandchildren began arriving. They were wonderful grandparents. I can just imagine Aunt Daisy saying, "If I knew grandchildren could bring me such joy, I would have had them first!"

Two of her granddaughters lived nearby and, of course, were with her more than the others. Barb said when she was young her grandma was her best friend; she could talk to her about anything. Doreen said that as far back as a small child she could remember her grandma sitting in her favourite chair reading her Bible. Both of these girls remember their grandma kneeling by her bed each night to pray. She often told them that things happened for the best, no matter what went wrong.

She obviously knew well the Scripture in Romans 8:28: *"And we know that in all things God works for the good of those who love him, who have been called according to his purpose."* This leads me to add from *Our Daily Bread*: "If our circumstances find us in God, we shall find God in all our circumstances."

The girls often remember Grandma singing them to sleep but the joke was that she would drift off to sleep before they did! Her home was always filled with her grandchildren. She always had time for them and never, it seemed, ever lost patience with any of them.

I would like to add a personal note here. When we would be visiting my wife's mother and sister in Rouyn, Kevin, our son, always wanted to spend the day with Aunt Daisy; in fact, as many days as he could. He would play in the gym in the school. She would come and get him for lunch and throughout the day provide him with delicious snacks. No wonder when I went to pick him up for supper, he wouldn't have much of an appetite! Kevin was a great-great nephew but that didn't matter to Aunt Daisy. She lavished her love upon him and he loved her, too.

In August of 1973 Uncle George suffered a massive stroke, and though only in his early 70s, passed away. He left a loving wife to go on alone, which she did for many years. His whole family missed him, including his extended family.

Then in the 1970s, great-grandchildren came on the scene. Sean and Tammy both remember her toast and tea routine; it was her comfort food. Sean remembers when he was around three years old how she would play with him and his "doctor's set" by the hour. He, too, remembers her praying by her bedside, always on her knees.

At this point in the story I was going to quote a beautiful gospel song by Bill and Gloria Gaither, *The Longer I Serve Him the Sweeter He*

Grows, but then I thought, no, I will quote one that she used to sing in Ottawa after she was saved and before she moved north. Here it is:

Sweeter As the Years Go By

Of Jesus' love that sought me, when I was lost in sin;
Of wondrous grace that brought me back to His fold again;
Of heights and depths of mercy, far deeper than the sea,
And higher than the heavens, my theme shall ever be.
Sweeter as the years go by, sweeter as the years go by,
Richer, fuller, deeper, Jesus' love is sweeter,
Sweeter as the years go by.
He trod in old Judea life's pathway long ago;
The people thronged about Him, His saving grace to know;
He healed the broken hearted, and caused the blind to see;
And still His great heart yearneth in love for even me.
'Twas wondrous love which led Him for us to suffer loss,
To bear without a murmur the anguish of the cross;
With saints redeemed in glory, let us our voices raise,
Till Heav'n and earth re-echo with our Redeemer's praise.
—*Leila N. Morris*

In the late 1980s, suffering from diabetes and high blood pressure, her family decided that since Noranda was almost totally francophone, and she had never learned to speak French, they would move her to Ontario. They found a lovely, luxurious senior's Lodge in Haliburton, Ontario. Upon arriving and settling in, she was simply overwhelmed and said she never thought she would ever live in such a beautiful home. Her cup was never half empty, but half full.

Jesus said in John 10:10b, *"I have come that they might have life and have it to the full."* The Weymouth Translation says, *"I have come that they might have life and have it in abundance."*

As she grew frailer and reached her ninetieth birthday, Aunt Daisy would remind her loved ones that God had left her here on earth that she might continue praying for all of them.

Aunt Daisy went to be with her Lord in August of 1993. The chapel was packed to its capacity for her memorial service with her extended family and friends, many who had come to a knowledge of Jesus Christ as personal Saviour through her spoken testimony and God-fearing life.

Author, editor, Gerald B. Smith compiled messages preached by A. W. Tozer on the subject of worship. Prior to Tozer's death in 1963, he expressed the opinion that "worship acceptable to God is the missing crown jewel in evangelical Christianity." With Aunt Daisy's home-going, the following excerpt from Smith's book, *Whatever Happened to Worship?* captures the essence of her life here with us and now around the throne in her eternal home.

> In Europe many generations ago, the dear old saint of God, Brother Lawrence, was on his deathbed. Rapidly losing his physical strength, he witnessed to those gathered around him: 'I am not dying. I am just doing what I have been doing for the past 40 years, and doing what I expect to be doing for all eternity!'
>
> 'What is that?' he was asked. He replied quickly, 'I am worshiping the God I love!
>
> Worshiping God—that was primary for Brother Lawrence. He was also dying, but that was secondary. He knew why he had been born into this world—and he knew why he had been born again.
>
> Yes, and Brother Lawrence is still worshiping God. He died and they buried his body somewhere, but his was a living soul, created in the image of God. So, he is still worshiping with all the saints around the throne of God.
>
> Sad, sad indeed, are the cries of so many today who have never discovered why they were born. It brings to mind the poet Milton's description of the pathetic lostness and loneliness of our first parents. Driven from the garden, he says 'they took hand in hand and through the valley made their solitary way.'

From the moment Aunt Daisy went down that aisle to accept Jesus Christ as her Saviour, she knew her destiny, who she was and who she belonged to. Her quiet life of trust displayed itself nobly till the end of her life here on earth and so the worshipping continues.

Aunt Daisy would probably blush to realize that a great nephew has written this chapter about her life; and as Hebrews 12:1 says: *"Surrounded then as we are by these serried* [in close formation] *ranks of witnesses, let us strip off everything that hinders us, as well as the sin which dogs our feet, and let us run the race that we have to run with patience, our eyes fixed on Jesus, the source and the goal of our faith"* (J. B. Phillips Translation).

O To Be Like Thee

O to be like Thee! blessed Redeemer,
This is my constant longing and prayer;
Gladly I'll forfeit all of earth's treasures,
Jesus, Thy perfect likeness to wear.
O to be like Thee! O to be like Thee,
Blessed Redeemer, pure as Thou art;
Come in Thy sweetness, come in Thy fullness;
Stamp Thine own image deep on my heart.
O to be like Thee! full of compassion,
Loving, forgiving, tender and kind,
Helping the helpless, cheering the fainting,
Seeking the wandering sinner to find.
O to be like Thee! lowly in spirit,
Holy and harmless, patient and brave;
Meekly enduring cruel reproaches,
Willing to suffer others to save.
O to be like Thee! Lord, I am coming
Now to receive anointing divine;
All that I am and have I am bringing,
Lord, from this moment all shall be Thine.
O to be like Thee! while I am pleading,
Pour out Thy Spirit, fill with Thy love;
Make me a temple meet for Thy dwelling,
Fit me for life and Heaven above.
—Thomas O. Chisholm

Little faith says, "I think God will."
Great faith says, "I know God will."
Perfect faith says, "It is finished."

I close this chapter with the words that are inscribed on the walls of an old church in England:

> I will not wish thee riches, nor the glow of greatness that wherever thou goest some weary heart shall gladden at thy smile, or shadowed life know sunshine for a while. And so thy path shall be a track of life, like angels' footsteps passing through the night.

Postscript

On February 7, 2011, Aunt Daisy's daughter, Lois, passed on to her eternal home. Lois was not only my cousin but one of my wife's best friends. As her health began failing we had the privilege of talking to her on the phone often over the months before she died. A number of years ago, Lois filled in many details of Aunt Daisy's life to help me write this chapter.

The following is taken from her Obituary:

> Lois' faith in the Lord Jesus Christ was the bedrock of her life and remained vibrant and unwavering to her last breath. Lois enjoyed no greater pleasure than being surrounded by her family as she poured herself into all of our endeavours. She loved us sacrificially and unconditionally. While we are deeply saddened we also draw great comfort from the assurance that to leave this earthly tent is to enter our heavenly dwelling in the presence of God.

This description of Lois' life seems to very readily mimic what I have written about her mother on these pages. It aptly describes the legacy that Aunt Daisy passed on to her children and grandchildren as she remained faithful throughout her life loving her Lord and Saviour.

MY MOTHER-IN-LAW

Jessie GRAHAM MATHESON CORRIGAN

"The LORD himself goes before you and will be with you; he will never leave you nor forsake you. Do not be afraid; do not be discouraged."

(Deuteronomy 31:8)

"God is glorified when we believe with all our hearts that those who trust in Christ can never be condemned."

—C. J. Mahaney

No doubt most of my readers have heard the definition of "Mixed Emotions"? It is when your mother-in-law drives your Mercedes Benz over Niagara Falls! Well, I am happy to say that was not the emotion I felt for Jessie (I always called her Mrs. Corrigan).

I loved her and greatly respected her as a woman who loved and feared the Lord. She taught me so many truths which she had gleaned from her long life, as well as many spiritual exhortations. Had I heeded them, I believe my own life would have turned out differently.

I recently read a funny story about an elderly man who was to undergo major surgery, a very delicate and difficult procedure, with a life or death outcome. The patient's son was the surgeon. Just before the anesthetist administered the medication that would put him to sleep, he whispered to his son: "Now do your very best, son, for if I die your mother is coming to live with you." Another rather corny joke, but I would have to say that this was not my attitude towards Jessie.

She would visit us, sometimes for up to three months, and I always hated to see her leave. And, by the way, she always came to visit us by plane! This would be back in the fifties when flying was a novelty and Toronto's Pearson International Airport was a small wooden building not much bigger than an average-sized residential bungalow.

Now to get on with the story of a remarkable woman. She only had a grade 4 education yet her wisdom and knowledge of the Word of God, King James Version of course, was indeed astounding. Charles Spurgeon once said: "Wisdom is the right use of knowledge. To know is not to be wise. Many men know a great deal, and are all the greater fools for it…but to know how to use knowledge is to have wisdom." Dr. Charles Stanley wrote a devotional on the Benefits of Wisdom (Proverbs 3:13–18) and concluded with this word: "Intimacy with God, clear guidance, Divine protection, human wisdom cannot provide any of these. They come from God through Christ's Spirit."

I first met Jessie when I was about twelve years old. I would often be at her home in Rouyn, Quebec, and there I would play Monopoly with her daughter Jean (who later, much later, would become my wife) and her older daughter Elsie. If you have ever played Monopoly you know that it can go on for hours. I was terribly thin at the time, having just recovered from Polio, and dear Jessie would keep bringing me cushions so I could keep playing. Her chocolate cake was out of this world! From this information you can now understand that I knew her for a very long time and so I am quite adequate, with the help of Jean, to tell her story and bless your heart as I know it will.

Jessie was born in Glasgow, Scotland, December 4, 1883. Sadly, her mother died while she was just a little toddler. She was the youngest of four children, the others being boys. Their father died six weeks after their mother. Her father had left specific instructions that the children were to be sent to Canada upon his death. Before this could be arranged with families in Canada, the children were placed in the Quarrier Homes in Glasgow. This was an excellent facility and most probably much ahead of the systems for orphans in North America. The homes consisted of individual bungalows on streets with Bible names. Several children would be in one home with surrogate parents to care for them. Since it was a Christian organization, church was a very important part of their lives and the children regularly attended Sunday school and church every Sunday.

Then the time came when the little family was to be sent to Canada. Jessie was just five years old. Her grandmother and aunt begged the authorities to let them keep Jessie and raise her, but to no avail. Their father's Will had to be carried out. Jessie learned this when she returned to Scotland as a married woman with her daughter Elsie, to visit her grandmother and aunt. At that time she also learned that while they were in the Quarrier Homes, her brother John was bitten by a rabid dog and died.

What happened next would be unthinkable in today's society. The three children were separated—the boys to farms out in western Canada and Jessie to a farm near Shawville, Quebec, a small Anglophone community, often referred to as the Bible belt of the Ottawa Valley. Fortunately Jessie was placed with a loving couple that had no children of their own. She had a truly happy childhood. Again, being in a Christian home, Jessie regularly attended Sunday school and church. Her adoptive parents attended the Methodist Church. Jessie happily enjoyed every opportunity to be in God's house and she learned at a very young age the importance of reverence for the Lord's house, true worship of the Saviour, and great loyalty to servants of the Lord. During her entire life she would often quote the Scripture *"Touch not mine anointed"* found in 1 Chronicles 16:22 (KJV) and was therefore always compassionate, kind, and generous to God's servants.

The Wesleyan Methodists regularly had evangelistic meetings, usually held in tents in a field with "the sawdust trail" (sawdust was put down in the aisles as they could be quite bumpy or even muddy) where men, women, boys and girls would go forward at the invitation for sinners to repent, backsliders to be restored and for many to re-consecrate their lives to the Lord. It very well could have been at one of these "Revival Meetings" that young Jessie gave her heart and life to the Lord.

Jessie loved the springtime when the little lambs would be born. She was always allowed to pick one to be her pet. How she adored these little lambs.

Remembering Jessie telling me about her pet lambs, I have decided to include a poem about God's little lambs.

Little Lambs

Said a precious little laddie to
His father one bright day:
"May I come and trust in Jesus
Let Him wash my sins away?"
"Oh, my son, you are too little,
Wait until you older grow;
Bigger folk, 'tis true, do need Him,
Little folk are safe, you know."
Said the father to his laddie,
As a storm was coming on,
"Are the sheep all safely sheltered,
Safe within the fold, my son?"
"All the big ones are, my father,
But the lambs I let them go;
For I didn't think it mattered;
Little ones are safe you know."
Oh, my brother! Oh my sister!
Have you, too, made this mistake?
Little hearts that now are yielding,
May be hardened then—too late.
E'er the evil days come nigh them,
"Let the children come to Me;
And forbid them not," said Jesus,
"For of such My fold shall be."
—*Author Unknown*

When Jessie reached her early teens, her adoptive mother died. This was a blow to this young girl, having lost her own mother when a very young child. It was a sorrowful loss. In Song of Solomon 8:5 we read, *"Who is this coming up from the desert leaning on her lover?"* Well, there is no question that by this time in her life, Jessie knew without a doubt who her lover was.

Lean Hard

Child of my love, lean hard,
And let me feel the pressure of thy care;
I know thy burden, child, I shaped it;
Poised it in My own hand, made no proportion
in its weight to thy unaided strength;
For even as I laid it on, I said,
I shall be near, and while he leans on Me,
This burden shall be Mine, not his;
So shall I keep My child within the circling
arms of My own love.
Here lay it down, nor fear to impose it on a
shoulder which upholds the government of
worlds.
Yet closer come; Thou are not near enough;
I would embrace thy care so I might feel My
child reposing on My breast.
Thou lovest Me? I knew it. Doubt not then;
But, loving Me, lean hard!
—May Prentiss Smith

Happily for Jessie, her adoptive father married a short time after his wife's death. His new wife was, Janie, who was also in her teens! Jessie and Janie, being so close in years, and Janie, being married to a much older man, became very close. Jessie loved her dearly and looked back on those years with great fondness. Life was quite normal for Jessie but unlike many rebellious teens, this teenager continued to love the Lord and walk in His ways. Like Enoch (Genesis 5:24), Jessie *"walked with God."*

Trust and Obey

When we walk with the Lord in the light of His Word,
What a glory He sheds on our way!
While we do His good will, He abides with us still,
And with all who will trust and obey.
Trust and obey, for there's no other way
To be happy in Jesus, but to trust and obey.
Then in fellowship sweet we will sit at His feet.
Or we'll walk by His side in the way.
What He says we will do, where He sends we will go;
Never fear, only trust and obey.

When Jessie was in her late teens, probably nineteen years old, she met and married Alexander Corrigan. Mr. Corrigan was not a farmer, to say the least, and when the lumber business opened up in Massey, Ontario, he, along with Jessie and their first-born son, Mervyn, left Shawville and settled in Massey. They bought a lovely home in the town and spent many happy years there, making many friends and, of course, finding a good church and attending regularly.

O Tender Shepherd, who does hold
Each little lamb within Thy fold,
With rod and staff who followest still
The wandering sheep o'er vale and hill;
While here we bide, or far we roam,
Hear this our prayer—
GOD BLESS OUR HOME!

The family lived in Massey some twenty years. Three more children were born to them during this time. Added to Mervyn were Arthur, Clem, and Elsie. By this time the Methodist Church was becoming extremely liberal, or modernistic. The Presbyterians, likewise, were also heading in the same direction spiritually. These two denominations joined together and formed a large denomination called The United Church of Canada. Thankfully, many of the Christians in the Massey

Presbyterian Church refused to move over to the United Church, so Jessie and the family became Presbyterians.

The Imperfect, Empowered Church

The New Testament tells about a church that had some real problems. But in spite of all these, it reached thousands of people for Christ.

This church was located in the wrong place. Most of the people in the community looked on the members of this church with scorn and ridicule. It didn't have a building in which to meet. Most of the members were on the verge of poverty.

The members of this church weren't trained for their jobs. Their membership was small—only about 120. The treasurer ran off with the church's money. What's more, the chief leader of this church had a way of putting his foot in his mouth. He was constantly making people angry.

To top it all off, there were divisions in this church. Several members were forced to flee to other cities because of persecution.

The one thing this church had going for it was the power of the Holy Spirit. It was the church in Jerusalem described in the Book of Acts. With all its problems, this church baptized 3,000 people after its first revival service.

What we need today are more imperfect churches empowered by the Holy Spirit.

—Leonard Ravenhill (English Evangelist)

When the lumber mills began to close in the Massey area, Mr. Corrigan moved the family farther north to Schumaker. Jessie never complained, but this was a difficult time in her life. This town, quite close to Timmins, Ontario, was fairly new and there were no established churches for the family to attend. To be honest, at that time, it was a rough town, mostly inhabited by miners and their families. It was not a town that Jessie would have chosen to raise her family. There was no gospel church or testimony in the town and as a result Jessie had nowhere to worship or have the family in church and Sunday school. This was a hardship and disappointment to her. But she had learned so many years before the words of the Psalmist: *"Your word is a lamp to my feet and a light for my path. I have taken an oath and confirmed it, that I will follow your righteous laws"* (Psalm 119:105–106).

I would like to tarry a moment here in my story and remind my readers how important it is to read and study the Bible. All of us need to *read* the Word, *reflect* (meditate) and *apply* the Word. Frances R. Havergal wrote a short poem:

Upon Thy Word I rest, so strong, so pure,
So full of comfort blest, so sweet, so sure
The Word that changest not, that faileth never!
My King, I rest upon Thy Word forever.

Pastor Bruxy Cavey, the teaching pastor of The Meeting House in Oakville, Ontario, preached a message on Sunday, March 12, 2006, entitled, *Eating Scripture*. The text he referred to is found in Ezekiel 3:1–3: *"And he said to me, 'Son of man, eat what is before you, eat this scroll; then go and speak to the house of Israel.' So I opened my mouth, and he gave me the scroll to eat. Then he said to me, 'Son of man, eat this scroll I am giving you and fill your stomach with it.' So I ate it, and it tasted as sweet as honey in my mouth."*

Another Scripture he referred to is Revelation 1:8. *"'I am the Alpha and the Omega,' says the Lord God, 'who is, and who was, and who is to come, the Almighty.'"* Pastor Bruxy commented, "The Bible is a portal, a window through which we can clearly see Jesus, the Word of God, enlaced. Jesus is the 'Alphabet' God uses to write His message of love to us."

"How can I use the Bible to change me?" he asked, and answered by saying: "It must be internalized!" In concluding this message we are exhorted to "Balance Eating with Exercise. Beware: reading without application is like a diet without exercising. The very food that nourishes your body will eventually make you fat and unhealthy. Just eating more is not necessarily better! When you close your Bible, take God with you." Matthew 7:24: *"Therefore everyone who hears these words of mine and puts them into practice is like a wise man who built his house on the rock."*

Reading the Bible for Spiritual Formation—Some ideas…

Learn the context (from the Bible, other books, and other Christ-followers). This is an ongoing task done best in spiritual community.

Ask God to guide you through each experience of Bible reading.

Enter the text, using your imagination to walk through the story, experiencing the emotion, allowing the questions raised to become as real as any answers you're searching for. Allow your imagination to help you 'rehydrate' the text, approximating the original form of the story, complete with smells, sights, and sounds.

Pray through the text, reading a bit, talking to God about it, reading some more, etc.

Meditate on the text's main point of contact with your spirit.

Envision yourself living out the key lessons of the text in your life.

Invite God to remind you of this vision throughout your day.

—*Bruxy Cavey*

The Bible is like a telescope. If a man looks *through* his telescope, then he sees worlds beyond; but if he looks *at* his telescope, then he does not see anything but that. The Bible is a thing to be looked through, to see that which is beyond.

—*Phillips Brooks (1835–1893)*

Now back to the life of Jessie Corrigan. As I said earlier, life was difficult in the town of Schumaker and had a long-term effect on the children. Merv and Clem remained there, marrying and establishing their families. But it did not affect Jessie's faith and trust in the Lord. The Word of God and prayer were still paramount in her life.

My Prayer Time

I love to come to the quiet hour,
My bible in my hand,
To give my need unto the Lord,

To find His presence grand.
Upon my knees to Him I go
And cast down all my care.
I praise Him and I thank Him
As we fellowship in prayers.
'Tis joy for me to meet Him,
From earth's joys to come apart,
And the wonder is, His presence
Keeps abiding in my heart.
For when the time is ended,
I have gained a peace sublime,
And it keeps me all the day long,
That sweet glow of my prayer time.
—Paul Durham

Fortunately for Jessie, she and her husband had decided to keep the house in Massey. It became their summer home. This was always a blessing to Jessie as she could then attend church, fellowship with friends, and enjoy the beauty of that small town.

When she and Alex were in their early forties, Graham was born and two years later, Jean came along. The older boys and Elsie were now adults so this was like a second family. But it was a happy family and Alex and Jessie derived a great deal of joy in having these two children in middle life.

Love in the Home

If I live in a house of spotless beauty
With everything in its place, but have not love,
I am a housekeeper—not a homemaker.
If I have time for waxing, polishing and decorative achievements, but have not love,
My children learn cleanliness—not godliness.
Love leaves the dust in search of a child's laugh. Love smiles at the tiny fingerprints on a newly cleaned window.
Love wipes away the tears before it wipes up the spilled milk.
Love picks up the child before it picks up the toys.

Love is present through the trials.
Love reprimands, reproves, and is responsive.
Love crawls with the baby, walks with the toddler, runs with the child, then stands aside to let the youth walk into adulthood.
Love is the key that opens salvation's message to a child's heart.
Before I became a mother I took glory in my house of perfection.
Now I glory in God's perfection of my child.
As a mother, there is much I must teach my child, but the greatest of all is LOVE.
—*Author Unknown*

I mentioned earlier in this chapter that Mr. Corrigan was not a farmer; neither was he a miner. He used his skills to put the power lines into many of these small northern towns. Jessie's greatest sadness of their stay in Schumaker was that the children, by this time young adults, did not follow their mother's Saviour. If only they had realized the truth that John Greenleaf Whittier writes of:

We search the world for truth. We cull
The good, the pure, the beautiful,
From graven stone and written scroll,
From all old flower-fields of the soul;
And, weary seekers of the best,
We come back laden from the quest,
To find that all the sages said…
…Is in the Book our mothers read.

In 1927, the family moved to Rouyn, Quebec. Elsie, Jean and Graham accompanied their parents; Elsie, now a young woman, Graham, four years old and Jean two years old.

Rouyn, back in those days, was not particularly a great improvement as far as the infrastructure of the town was concerned. There were gravel roads, some wooden sidewalks but no buses and many of the other things that would have made life bearable in the far north. The temperature during the long winters often reached minus-fifty degrees Fahrenheit.

But for Jessie, there was the beginning of a small Baptist church, organized and funded by a lady from a well-to-do family by the name of Miss Olive Copp. She dearly loved the Lord and gave up the comfort of her city home to come north to establish an Evangelical Baptist Church. Miss Copp and Jessie became close friends and the fellowship and friendship continued on for many years.

To give you an example of the uncomplaining and humble spirit of Miss Copp, she and Jessie were traveling together in an old railway coach that had wooden seats. Jessie mentioned to her friend that the seats were rather hard but Miss Copp replied: "Yes, but they are clean." Henry Ward Beecher, unknown to these dear Christian women once said, and this describes their humble spirit: "In this world it is not what we *take up*, but what we *give up*."

Miss Copp had actually started a church, previous to Rouyn-Noranda, in Timmins, Ontario. The Rouyn-Noranda work grew large enough to call a pastor. The first church was a very small building in Rouyn, a veritable shack, covered with tarpaper to help keep out the bitter cold. Eventually the small group of believers was able to build a functional and attractive clapboard church right on the main street bordering the two towns. This is the Baptist church I mentioned in the chapter about Aunt Daisy.

It was a very long walk to church for Jessie and the two children, but walk it they did, every Sunday. Jessie was absolutely thrilled to be able to attend church on a regular basis. Psalm 105:3 was her experience during these days: *"Glory in His holy name; Let the hearts of those who seek the Lord rejoice."* Mr. Corrigan, sadly, never went to church with his family but he always made sure there was fuel for the furnace and that Jessie was able to give generously to the Lord's work.

I believe that during these years in Jessie's life, while there were good times, there were also circumstances and happenings that caused her a great deal of inward pain and heartache. It was during these times that she learned:

My Secret

Shall I tell you what it is that keeps me singing,
Never minding whether it be shade or shine?
'Tis because His own glad song is singing in me,
'Tis because the Savior's joy is always mine.
Shall I tell you what it is that keeps me springing,
With a strength that smiles at sickness and decay?
'Tis because the life of Jesus fills my being,
And the Living Bread sustains me day by day.
Shall I tell you why my life is now so easy?
'Tis because this wretched self has ceased to be;
Once it caused me all my troubles, but it's buried,
And it is no longer I, but Christ in me.
Shall I tell you why I love to work for Jesus?
'Tis because His blessed Spirit works in me;
I have but to let Him use me, His the power,
Mine the recompense to share, the fruit to see.
Shall I tell you why I love to tell of Jesus?
'Tis because there's nothing else so good and true;
There's no other name or story worth the telling,
Without Jesus what could helpless sinners do?
Shall I tell you why I'm watching for His coming?
'Tis because of all my future, He's the sum;
This will be my joy forever—Jesus only—
And I long, and look, and pray for Him to come.

—A. B. Simpson

Yes, life for Jessie in Rouyn became better as the years flew by. She had a comfortable home, her husband had a thriving trucking business, hauling ore in from the smaller mines to the smelters at the large Noranda mine. Her daughter Elsie was still at home and of course, Graham and Jean.

In Whatsoever State—CONTENT

Sometimes with triumph I abound,
Sometimes I know defeat;

The secret I have learned, to take
The bitter with the sweet:
For, whatsoe'er my state may be,
All things through Christ who
strengthens me!
In sickness and in health alike
I have the selfsame creed;
It serves me when well satisfied
And when I suffer need;
For, whatsoe'er my state may be,
All things through Christ who
strengthens me!
So, in whatever state I am,
I live contentedly;
In all things now, and anywhere,
Through Christ who strengthens me,
This secret hath my soul sufficed:
I find sufficient strength through Christ!
—*Selected*

But, there were disappointments. The three older boys had no interest in the things of the Lord. They loved, however, to come home to Jessie, which they did on a regular basis. She dearly loved them and always welcomed them, cooked for them, and generously shared her hospitality with them.

Sadly, her son Mervyn died while still a young man. His widow, Rene, and their two young children moved to Toronto but always kept in touch with Grannie Corrigan. To illustrate their love and affection they had for Jessie, every year, Rene would send a lovely bouquet of roses to Jessie, even after she re-married in Toronto.

Mervyn and Rene had two children, Graham and Lois; both are living today. Their son Graham and his family live in Vancouver, B.C., and their daughter Lois and her son live in Toronto. I am including a poem that Lois wrote on the bus coming home from church. Divorced from her husband and with a son who was ill, Lois wrote:

Soul

When trouble hits our soul,
What do we see?
How do we face the battle—
Is it on bended knee?
When trouble hits our soul,
What do we hear?
As our world crashes round us—
Like thunder to our ear.
When trouble hits our soul,
What do we feel?
As our heart is breaking—
Are we ready to kneel?
When trouble hits our soul,
There is no other way
But to surrender to God—
Let Him have sway.
When trouble hits our soul
Like a bolt out of the blue—
God is waiting
For me and for you.
With love to sustain
Wisdom to reach our goal,
Compassion to comfort—
When trouble hits our soul.
—Lois Corrigan

Another meaningful poem:

Happiness keeps you sweet,
Trials keep you strong
Sorrows keep you human
Failures keep you humble,
Success keeps you glowing,
BUT ONLY GOD KEEPS YOU GOING
—Author unknown

Jessie needed God and leaned heavily upon him during the next years of her life. On November 28, 1933, Alex, her dearly beloved husband, was accidentally killed as he put his pipe into his pocket, forgetting he had dynamite caps in that pocket. What a shock! What *loss* to Jessie and their whole family! Jean, my wife, was only eight years old; her brother Graham, eleven years of age. Jessie, though barely fifty at this time, had become quite frail and the trauma of Alex's sudden death left her in a state of shock, and the road back to wellness was long and difficult.

Trust His Heart

All things work for our good,
Tho sometimes we can't see how they could;
Struggles that break our hearts in two
Sometimes blind us to the truth.
Our Father knows what's best for us,
His ways are not our own;
So when your pathway grows dim,
And you just can't see Him,
Remember, you're never alone!
God is too wise to be mistaken;
God is too good to be unkind.
So when you don't understand,
When you don't see His plan,
When you can't trace His hand,
Trust His heart!
He sees the master plan.
He holds the future in His hands.
So don't live as those who have no hope;
All our hope is found in Him.
We see the present clearly,
But He sees the first and the last.
And like a tapestry, He's weaving you and me,
To someday be just like Him!

He alone is faithful and true,
He alone knows what is best for you.
—Eddie Carswell and Babbie Mason

Mrs. Charles Cowman in her well-known book, *Streams in the Desert*, quotes Psalm 27:13 in part: *"I had fainted, unless I had believed to see the goodness of the LORD."* The author goes on to say:

> What do you do when you are about to faint physically? In your faintness you fall upon the shoulder of some strong loved one. You lean hard. You rest. You lie still and trust...God's message to you is not, 'Be strong and of a good courage,' for He knows our strength and courage have flown away, but it is that sweet word, 'be still and know that I am God.'

Mrs. Cowman goes on to write about Hudson Taylor, that great missionary to China, who was so feeble in the closing months of his life. He wrote to a dear friend these words: "I am so weak, I cannot write; I cannot read my Bible; I cannot even pray. I can only lie still in God's arms like a little child and trust."

Mrs. Cowman concludes with these precious words: "God keeps His choicest cordials for our deepest faintings." Psalm 27:14 admonishes each one of us: *"Wait on the Lord: be of good courage, and He shall strengthen thine heart: wait, I say, on the Lord"* (KJV).

It was during these years that Jessie decided she would begin reading her Bible in Genesis and follow it right through to the last book, Revelation. As a matter of fact, Jessie read the Bible through at least four times during the latter part of her life.

When You Read the Bible Through

I supposed I knew my Bible,
Reading piecemeal, hit or miss,
Now a bit of John or Matthew,
Now a snatch of Genesis,
Certain chapters of Isaiah,
Certain Psalms (the twenty-third),

Twelfth of Romans, First of Proverbs—
Yes, I thought I knew the Word!
But I found that thorough reading
Was a different thing to do,
And the way was unfamiliar
When I read the Bible through.
You who like to play at Bible,
Dip and dabble, here and there,
Just before you kneel, aweary,
And yawn through a hurried prayer;
You who treat the Crown of Writings
As you treat no other book—
Just a paragraph disjointed,
Just a crude, impatient look—
Try a worthier procedure,
Try a broad and steady view;
You will kneel in very rapture
When you read the Bible through!
—Amos R. Wells

A quote from Rev. A. B. Simpson's book, *Days of Heaven Upon Earth,* says: "So often God bids us tarry ere we go, and fully recover ourselves for the next stage of the journey and work." And this is exactly what Jessie did, for there were times ahead that would truly test her faith and trust in God. But she survived!

You see, Jessie was a true student of the Word of God and she well knew the Scripture in the King James Version. *"It is good for me that I have been afflicted that I might learn Thy statutes"* (Psalm 119:71). Jessie not only read the Bible, she learned the blessedness of meditating upon God's Word.

Jessie regained her strength and a measure of health as the years slipped by. Her daughter, Elsie, carried on the trucking business her father had established and was able to sustain the little family financially and provide for all their needs.

Elsie, with her mother's permission and gratitude, had a contractor build a lovely, year-round sunroom at the front of the house, enabling Jessie to enjoy the sunshine, even on the coldest of days. She was disappointed that Elsie became seriously involved with a young man who was not a Christian and who later became alcoholic. But Jessie loved this man, shared her gracious hospitality almost every Sunday for years and did so until his untimely death while still a comparatively young man.

Sometime during these years her son Art left his wife and child and moved to Montreal. From that time on Jessie rarely saw or heard from him. Fortunately, her son Clem, with his wife Delta and their two children, Bob and Elsie, came often from their home in Schumaker to spend quality time with Jessie and the family. This meant a lot to Jean and Graham since they were close in age to their niece and nephew.

Again I quote from *Streams in the Desert*:

"O Lord, I know that the way of man is not in himself: it is not in man that walketh to direct his steps." (Jeremiah 10:23)

"Lead me in a plain path."
(Psalm 27:11)

> Many people want to direct God, instead of resigning themselves to be directed by Him; to show Him; to show Him a way, instead of passively following where He leads.
> —*Madame Guyon*

I said: "Let me walk in the field."
God said: "Nay, walk in the town."
I said: "There are no flowers there."
He said: "No flowers, but a crown."
I said: "But the sky is black,
There is nothing but noise and din."
But He wept as He sent me back,
"There is more," He said, "there is sin."
I said, "But the air is thick,
And fogs are veiling the sun."
He answered: "Yet souls are sick,
And souls in the dark undone."

I said, "I shall miss the light,
And friends will miss me, they say."
He answered me, "Choose tonight,
If I am to miss you, or they."
I pleaded for time to be given;
He said: "Is it hard to decide?
It will not seem hard in Heaven
To have followed the steps of your Guide."
I cast one look at the fields,
Then set my face to the town;
He said: "My child, do you yield?
Will you leave the flowers for the crown?"
Then into His hand went mine,
And into my heart came He;
And I walk in a light Divine,
The path I had feared to see.
—*George MacDonald*

It was wintertime, and Jessie, in her seventies by this time, was entering the church. The vestibule was wet with melted snow. She fell and broke her back. She was put in a body cast and remained in bed for many, many weeks. It was doubtful that she would make a recovery from this dreadful accident and was advised that her ability to walk was very unlikely.

I made a special trip at this time to visit her. We read God's Word and prayed fervently and we both believed and trusted that God would raise her up to walk again and live a relatively normal life. And God did!

I Needed the Quiet

I needed the quiet so He drew me aside,
Into the shadows where we could confide,
Away from the bustle where all the day long
I hurried and worried when active and strong.
I needed the quiet tho at first I rebelled
But gently, so gently, my cross He upheld
And whispered so sweetly of spiritual things
Tho weakened in body, my spirit took wings

To heights never dreamed of when active and gay,
He loved me so greatly He drew me away.
I needed the quiet. No prison my bed,
But a beautiful valley of blessings instead—
A place to grow richer in Jesus to hide.
I needed the quiet so He drew me aside.
—*Alice Hansche Mortenson*

David Roper in the devotional *Our Daily Bread*, wrote the following, which I quote in part:

> Far from being an obstacle to our spiritual growth, pain can be the instrument of it—if we're trained by it. It can push us closer to God and deeper into His Word. It is a means by which He graciously shapes us to be like His Son, gradually giving us the compassion, contentment, tranquility, and courage we long and pray for. Without pain, we wouldn't be all that God wants us to be. His strength shines brightest through human weakness.

The author of the devotional adds the following for our admonition:

> Has God set you apart today to receive instruction through suffering and pain? Endure this training patiently. He can turn the trial into a blessing. He can use it to draw you close to His heart and into His Word, teach you the lessons He intends for you to learn, and use it to bestow His grace on you.
>
> God is making more of you—something much better—than you ever thought possible.

Let me relate an incident to you that was so typical of Jessie in her long life. My wife, Jean, became very deaf after the birth of our daughter Judith. This necessitated an operation called Fenestration. This was complicated microsurgery involving a hole drilled into the skull to the inner ear. It was not only an extremely painful operation but also involved a long and slow recovery due to the upset of the equilibrium.

Our two children were in the care of Jessie and Elsie at this time. As I remember, it was well over two months before the children returned. Then, after the birth of our second son, Kevin, Jean lost the hearing in the other ear. We, of course, were dreading the ordeal of the fenestration surgery again!

However, by this time a new procedure was developed called the Stapes Surgery. It was far less invasive than the previous operation and, if successful, meant that Jean's pain would be greatly reduced and her recuperation would be short-lived. We were so excited about this possibility and its outcome.

The surgery was performed at St. Michael's Hospital in Toronto. But, because of severe scar tissue in that ear, the doctor explained that the operation was unsuccessful and Jean would need to return in about a year's time for the major surgery if her hearing was to be restored. Later that night I phoned Jean's mother and sister with the disappointing news.

Later, and this is why I have related this incident in such detail, Elsie told us that when their mother learned the news the next morning from Elsie, she took her Bible and quickly retreated to her room. She spent the whole day meditating upon the Word and communing with the Lord until she could finally leave the burden at the foot of the Cross.

Jessie knew the following gospel song and sang it many times during her lifetime. (I have sung this song many times in my youth and would often chuckle when I sang the last verse, but I'm not laughing anymore, just thankful that the Saviour will go with me to the end!)

Leave It There

If the world from you withhold of its silver and its gold,
And you have to get along with meager fare,
Just remember, in His Word, how He feeds the little bird;
Take your burden to the Lord and leave it there.
Leave it there, leave it there,
Take your burden to the Lord and leave it there.
If you trust and never doubt, He will surely bring you out.
Take your burden to the Lord and leave it there.

If your body suffers pain and your health you can't regain,
And your soul is almost sinking in despair,
Jesus knows the pain you feel, He can save and He can heal;
Take your burden to the Lord and leave it there.
When your youthful days are gone and old age is stealing on,
And your body bends beneath the weight of care;
He will never leave you then, He'll go with you to the end.
Take your burden to the Lord and leave it there.
—*Charles Tindley*

During the latter years, as I mentioned earlier in the chapter, Jessie would come to visit and we always enjoyed her presence. I only remember one time when she became frustrated with any of our children. Russell was around two years of age, still in his highchair, and Jessie thought it was time for him to use a bread plate. Well, as soon as she would put it on his tray he would promptly drop it on the floor. She finally gave up on that one!

Whenever Jean and I would have a disagreement, Jessie would never interfere but I must admit that when she gave her opinion, it was always in my favour. No wonder I loved her so!

When Jean and Graham were young, whenever either one did something wrong, Jessie would quietly quote an appropriate verse of Scripture which would apply to their misdemeanor. Jean has told me that she had such love and respect for her mother growing up that all her mother had to say was "tut-tut" and that ended the wrong she must have been doing.

With all of the heartache, pain, untimely family deaths, and sorrow she had in her life, did Jessie ever ask God "Why?" I don't really know, to be honest, but I do know that many of God's children have asked that question. Some of us put on the mask and say, "Well someday we'll understand!" For several years, Ruth Graham Bell wrote in the publication of the Billy Graham Association called *Decision*. She wrote one article which she entitled, *Asking God Why?*

Sometimes the question *Why?* is *wrenched* from a person—even from earnest believers.

While I was growing up in China, one of our fellow missionaries committed suicide. Overworked and under unbearable pressure, this dear Christian broke.

Left untended for a brief moment, a child of missionaries fell into a tub of scalding water. Not long after that the daughter of those same missionaries died after eating poisonous beans.

Sometime later a missionary friend was shot and then beheaded by bandits.

When I was in high school in Korea, a fellow student was killed by a train. His death affected the entire student body.

From time to time throughout our lives, our cry of anguish goes up to God: "Lord God, take away our pain."

But still, pain—unexpected, unendurable, unexplained—continues to strike us.

Nor has our Billy Graham Team "family" been exempted from pain—one son was shot accidentally by his cousin... one daughter suffered severe brain damage from taking illegal drugs...an ideal son died on an operating table...an unexplainable suicide...broken marriages...*Is it wrong for us to ask, "why?"*

When Moses asked "Why?" God's answer was "Now shalt thou see what I will do."

Even our Lord Jesus once asked "Why?"—on the cross at Calvary.

Someone has said that faith never asks why. But surely, involuntarily, one must often cry out, "Why?"

We need to pray for courage to ask the right questions so that we will be prepared for the answers.

This might be a good time for all of us who are true believers in Jesus Christ to ask ourselves the question, "Do I really know the blessing of prayer in my own personal life?" Read the following by Leonard Ravenhill, from *Why Revival Tarries*. Then let us honestly search our hearts concerning this necessity in our lives if we are to grow more like Jesus, who so many times went alone to pray, often all night.

NO CHRISTIAN IS GREATER THAN HIS PRAYER LIFE

The church has many organizers, but few agonizers; many who pay, but few who pray; many resters, but few wrestlers; many who are enterprising, but few who are interceding. People who are not praying are playing.

Two prerequisites of dynamic Christian living are vision and passion, and both of these are generated in the prayer closet. The ministry of preaching is open to a few. The ministry of prayer is open to every child of God.

Don't mistake action for unction, commotion for creation, and rattles for revivals.

When we pray, God listens to our heartbeat.

Hannah's lips moved, but her voice was not heard (1 Samuel 1:12, 13). When we pray in the Spirit, there are groanings which cannot be uttered (Romans 8:29).

Tithes may build a church, but tears will give it life. That is the difference between the modern church and the early church. Our emphasis is on paying, theirs was on praying. When we have paid, the place is taken. When they had prayed, the place was shaken (Acts 4:31). In the matter of effective praying, never have so many left so much to so few. Brethren, let us pray.

In John's Gospel Chapter 10, verse 3, we read from the King James Version, *"...and he calleth his own sheep by name, and leadeth them out."*

Proverbs 4:12 says, *"When thou goest, thy steps shall not be straightened, and when thou runnest, thou shalt not stumble"* (KJV). The computer had a hard time with the King James Version in this verse. But, it was Jessie's version and she knew it well!

Years ago, a good friend of mine, a pastor without a church, became a member of the church I was pastoring. From time to time, as a means of encouraging him, I invited him to preach. On one particular Sunday morning Worship Service, all I remember about the message was his over-stating of the word "verities." In my ignorance I asked a confidante of mine, "What in the world was he talking about?"

Well, now I can tell you, for in Isaiah 40:8 we read: *"The grass withers and the flowers fall, but the word of our God stands forever."* There are some everlastingly dependable truths found in the Bible—eternal verities, which we can rest on with utter confidence.

Mary A. Lathbury wrote the hymn, *Break Thou the Bread of Life.* Jessie knew and sang it many times. I quote only one verse:

Break Thou the bread of life, dear Lord, to me,
As Thou didst break the loaves beside the sea;
Beyond the sacred page I seek Thee, Lord;
My spirit pants for Thee, O living Word!

A woman by the name of Jan Turner was in a serious car accident and the horrific results of the accident left her a quadruple amputee. Both hands and feet were removed because of complications during the period she was in a coma. Depending on the truth of God's Word in Philippians 4:13, *"I can do all things through Christ which strengtheneth me,"* she prayed, "Lord, with your perfect strength, a full and productive life will become my reality."

Another verse from which this woman drew strength was Psalm 103:2 and 4, *"Bless the Lord, O my soul, and forget not all His benefits… who redeemeth thy life from destruction; who crowneth thee with loving kindness and tender mercies"* (KJV). Jan Turner gave good advice when she said: "Gaze at the promises; glance at the problems. Remember—God is faithful. He'll always see us through."

Jessie's life's motto must surely have been: Never too old or spiritual to keep growing. This could very well have been Jessie's testimony:

In My Father's Hand

I'm in my Father's hand,
He safely holds me there,
He shelters me with His great love
And keeps me in His care.
I'm in my Father's hand,
The place of perfect rest,
No harm or foe may enter in

And nothing can molest.
I'm in my Father's hand,
I never need to fret.
He's promised to supply my needs,
He never will forget.
I'm in my Father's hand,
It's where I'd rather be
Than any place in all the world—
He knows what's best for me.
I'm in my Father's hand,
He ever holds me there,
He shelters me with His great love
And keeps me in His care.
—*Alice Brill*

The year Jessie turned eighty was to be a milestone in her life. My wife, Jean, had made arrangements for the two of them to go to Britain. Jessie was ecstatic for they would be renting a car and from London they would tour the British Isles including her beloved Scotland.

She came to our home in Hamilton a few weeks before the scheduled departure. All the plans were made, hotel bookings in London, etc., when Jessie fell and broke her wrist. This was only two or three weeks before they were to leave! Should the trip be cancelled? Not on your life! As far as Jessie was concerned, they were going! The cast was removed and Jessie massaged and exercised her swollen wrist, determined to proceed with the trip.

Let me relate for you an incident that happened in London that caused Jessie to giggle many times throughout the trip. Jean had booked one room for the two of them. Upon arriving at the hotel—for sure it was not a five-star—they had reserved separate rooms. This was not at all satisfactory, so Jean, tired after the long trip, (propeller planes in those days), left her mother resting and went out to find more suitable accommodation for the next night.

This she was able to do and returning home was ready for a good night's sleep. She asked Jessie to awaken her at eight o'clock the next morning in time for breakfast and then sightseeing. Now, you need to remember that Jessie had been sleeping all day while Jean was searching for another hotel.

At eight o'clock, Jessie knocked on Jean's room and, though Jean was still exhausted, they went down to the dining room for breakfast. Jean glanced at the menu and noticed it was the dinner menu. Thinking it was a mistake on the waiter's part, she asked for a breakfast menu. The waiter replied in his cockney accent, "Lady, I don't know where you've come from, but it is evening here in England and it's dinner time!"

Both Jessie and Jean burst out laughing. You see, since Jessie had slept away most of the day and she awoke at eight o'clock seeing daylight, she assumed it was morning. Jean was glad to be able to go back to bed and get a good night's sleep!

Although they toured much of Britain, including Scotland, Ireland, Wales, and of course England, the highlight of the trip was Glasgow, Scotland. Jean and her mother returned to the Homes where Jessie had been placed when she was orphaned.

They attended the church service on the Sunday they were there, sat in the pew where she sat as a little girl and visited the cottage where she lived. After the service the pastor and his wife invited them to their home on the grounds of the campus. They informed Jessie that she was the oldest former resident who had ever visited the Homes. The Quarrier Homes are now used as a facility for unwed mothers and their babies.

A few years later, Jessie fell in her home and broke her hip. She came through the surgery with flying colours, but, sadly, the shock of the fall, the operation, and no doubt the anesthetic left her senile. She remained in the hospital for the duration of her life.

She almost always recognized us when we visited but she could no longer carry on a conversation. However, when we would read God's Word with her, she could repeat from memory the very words we were reading and praised God with us as we prayed.

Let me relate a really funny incident showing what a sense of humour she had. I mentioned Rene earlier in this chapter, who dearly loved Jessie and kept in close touch with her even after her husband died (Jessie's oldest son, Merv).

Rene had remarried. Jean brought Rene up to Rouyn from Toronto to visit "Grandma" as Rene called her. Jessie finally realized who Rene was and that she was now married to G. A. as he liked to be called. Jessie whispered in Rene's ear, "And which one did you love the best?" to which Rene replied with tears streaming down her face, "Why Grandma, your son!"

A New Psalm

Blessed is the Senior, whose Bible is worn
Its spine nearly broken, its bindings torn
There are words penciled in at many a line,
Where they found help and blessing time after time.
Like a favourite tool in a tradesman's hand
It falls open quickly to salvation's plan,
Underlined and marked are the verses of hope
"Praise the Lord" written in, when the Spirit spoke.
Crumpled pages there, from a youngster's hold
Made when Mom or Dad read to them stories of old,
Of Moses and Joshua, David and 'Dan'
And prayed that their son would become such a man!
There's some strange puckered spot, evidence of tears
When they prayed over the Word and the answer took years;
The pages are edged not in gold but brown
And there is a list of unsaved friends in town.
There's a coffee stain from a hurried devotion,
Before the whole house awoke to commotion,
Yes, blessed the Senior whose Bible is tattered
Their faith will endure, though often battered.
And through generations their voice will be heard
"It's not just a book, child, it's really God's Word."

—J. Stokes

In the latter months of her hospitalization, Jessie went completely blind. She lay in her bed, no longer recognizing anyone but Elsie. She never stopped quoting Scripture, another favourite being Psalm 23 (KJV). She would quote the entire Psalm.

The LORD is my shepherd; I shall not want.

He maketh me to lie down in green pastures: he leadeth me beside the still waters.

He restoreth my soul: he leadeth me in the paths of righteousness for his name's sake.

Yea, though I walk through the valley of the shadow of death, I will fear no evil: for thou art with me; thy rod and thy staff they comfort me.

Thou preparest a table before me in the presence of mine enemies: thou anointest my head with oil; my cup runneth over.

Surely goodness and mercy shall follow me all the days of my life: and I will dwell in the house of the LORD forever.

Then she would sing,

Only believe,
Only believe,
All things are possible,
If you'll only believe.
This is the victory
This is the victory
This is the victory
If you'll only believe.
—Author Unknown

The following story reminds me of the way Jessie led her life, not ever complaining and feeling sorry for herself in those final days of complete senility and blindness. The only thing coming out of her mouth was her beloved Scripture verses by memory and the hymns and choruses she so dearly loved.

When just a baby, Fanny Crosby was mistakenly prescribed an ointment by an imposter physician for her reddened eyes from a cold. The treatment caused permanent blindness and the imposter fled in a panic.

Though blind, Fanny Crosby wrote over eight thousand hymns during her lifetime. She testified, "I am the happiest creature in all the land." In spite of this blindness she wrote the following poem when she was just eight years old:

O what a happy soul am I
Although I cannot see,
I am resolved that in this world
Contented I will be;
How many blessings I enjoy
That other people don't,
To weep and sigh because I'm blind,
I cannot and I won't.

One day at the Bible conference in Northfield, Massachusetts, Miss Crosby was asked by D. L. Moody to give a personal testimony. At first she hesitated, then quietly rose and said, "There is one hymn I have written which has never been published. I call it my soul's poem. Sometimes when I am troubled, I repeat it to myself, for it brings comfort to my heart." She then recited while many wept:

Someday the silver cord will break,
And I no more as now shall sing;
But oh, the joy when I shall wake
Within the palace of the King!
And I shall see Him face to face,
and tell the story—saved by grace!

1 Corinthians 2:9 says, *"But as it is written, eye hath not seen, nor ear heard, neither have entered into the heart of man, the things which God hath prepared for them that love him" (KJV);* and Isaiah 33:17 reads, *"Thine eyes shall see the king in his beauty: they shall behold the land that is very far off" (KJV).*

My Savior First of All

Oh, the soul-thrilling rapture when I view His blessed face,
And the luster of His kindly beaming eye;
How my full heart will praise Him for the mercy, love and grace,
That prepare for me a mansion in the sky.

I shall know Him, I shall know Him,
And redeemed by His side I shall stand,
I shall know Him, I shall know Him,
By the print of the nails in His hand.
Through the gates to the city in a robe of spotless white,
He will lead me where no tears will ever fall;
In the glad song of ages I shall mingle with delight;
But I long to meet my Savior first of all.
—*Fanny J. Crosby*

Bear with me as I tell you about another faith-filled woman and relate to some things that remind me of Jessie. Corrie ten Boom is known all over the world as the author of *The Hiding Place.* Her remarkable ministry has become known through this book and the movie that tells her story.

I am not what you would call a "Name Dropper," but I would like to mention here how we had the privilege of having Corrie ten Boom in our church in Hamilton, Ontario, when she first came to North America. It was long before she became widely known throughout the world. She became loved and respected by many of the V.I.Ps of not only the Christian world but also scores of talk show hosts, entertainers, etc. Many were touched, not only by her testimony but her clear and unique exposition of the Word of God.

The ten Boom family, devoted Christians, decided to hide Jews in their home in the Netherlands until they could escape to safety from the Nazi occupiers of their country during World War II. Corrie, her sister Betsie, and their father were imprisoned in Holland and then when the Allies were getting close to liberating Holland, the prisoners were crowded into railway cars and transported to Ravensbruck in Germany. Throughout this dreadful incarceration, Corrie and Betsie continued to read God's Word, witness to and lead many to a saving knowledge of Jesus Christ as personal Saviour. Sadly, because of the cold, lack of food, and the cruelty of the guards, both Betsie and their father died.

Billy Graham, who knew Corrie ten Boom well and had her give her testimony at many of his crusades, wrote the following as an introduction to a book written by Joan Winmill Brown:

> This is one of the most amazing lives of the century! It constantly shows how God's grace and love can sustain us in the worst of time. Corrie ten Boom and her family stood up for persons in a minority group—the Jews. It cost most of them their lives. It is amazing how these Dutch Christians speak to all of us in our world, our society, our lives today.
>
> Corrie ten Boom's story has a strong message for Christians. The greatest need in the church today is to realize that judgment is coming, troubles are coming, and we must have disciplined, hardy Christian lives. This is the example of the experience of Corrie ten Boom and her family—of Christian lives disciplined by the Word of God and the power of His Spirit giving strength and courage to fight evil and to triumph over it!

After the war, she returned to the family home in Haarlem and to the warm welcome of nieces and nephews and many friends who had miraculously survived those years of enemy occupation. Before the war, Corrie had been adequately trained by her father to do clock repairs. Though she could have remained there and continued the family business of clock repairs, Corrie heard the call of God.

She realized she must leave home and family and follow the Lord's leading wherever it might take her. She needed to share the message of salvation and forgiveness, including enemies. Of course, the rest is glorious history of a woman God used to travel throughout the world, sharing the good news of salvation and encouragement, all found in Jesus Christ alone.

The Lord provided a modest but lovely home with a beautiful garden for Corrie in California, which she named Shalom, where she spent the remaining years of her life, continuing to be a blessing and encouragement to everyone who visited her.

The following quotations are taken from the book *Corrie—The Lives She Touched* by Joan Winmill Brown. Corrie's father would often say to her as she was growing up: "When Jesus takes your hand, He keeps it tight. When He keeps it tight, He leads you through life. And when He leads you through life, He brings you safely Home."

Corrie would sometimes quote:

When I enter that beautiful city,
And the saved all around me appear,
I hope that someone will tell me
"It was you who invited me here."

I have related all of this to tell you how the following quote reminds me of Jessie's spiritual character. It comes from one of the many books Corrie wrote entitled *Each New Day*:

> Some people think that I have great faith, but that is not true. I do not have great faith—I have faith in a great God! Jesus said that if we have faith no bigger than a mustard seed, it is sufficient to move mountains. We understand that to mean not quantity but quality is important. The joy is that the Holy Spirit is willing to bring faith into our hearts. His faith in us has power, just as a mustard seed is small but has power to bring forth fruit.
>
> 'The kingdom of heaven is like a grain of mustard seed…' (Matthew 13:31 RSV).
>
> Holy Spirit, may the faith You bring us blossom and be fruitful.

Jessie remained in the hospital until her death several years later. It was obvious to all who went to visit her that she was dearly loved by the entire staff. They loved to hear her sing, which she did most of her waking hours. She was extremely well cared for by the nurses and her daughter Elsie. Her son, Graham, who at this time lived in California, made the long trip many times to visit his mother and support Elsie as much as he could.

Actually, as it turned out, he was only back home in his California home a short time when his mother slipped home to heaven, but, loving her so much, he returned to be at her funeral service. Jessie died at the age of ninety-six on February 1, 1979. We weren't with her to bid her a fond farewell, but this we knew, the Saviour, the one whom she loved and served for so many years, welcomed her into her eternal home.

It was my privilege to conduct the funeral service for Jessie. The chapel was packed with family, friends, and several of the nurses who cared for Jessie over those many years she was under their care. Ironically, none of these women spoke English but I guess it is true that love has no barriers.

The service really wasn't a funeral service as such, but rather a celebration of the long and fruitful life of one of God's quiet but faithful servants. Jessie was a shy and to some extent timid woman, so this hymn would have meant a great deal to her knowing full well she would be able to praise this way in her heavenly home. She knew the truth of the words of that great hymn written by Charles Wesley.

O for a thousand tongues to sing
My great Redeemer's praise,
The glories of my God and King,
The triumphs of His grace!
Jesus! the name that charms our fears,
That bids our sorrows cease;
'Tis music in the sinner's ears,
'Tis life, and health, and peace.
He breaks the power of canceled sin,
He sets the prisoner free;
His blood can make the foulest clean,
His blood availed for me.
Hear Him, ye deaf; His praise, ye dumb,
Your loosened tongues employ;
Ye blind, behold your Savior come,
And leap, ye lame, for joy.
My gracious Master and my God,
Assist me to proclaim,
To spread through all the earth abroad
The honors of Thy name.

As we committed her frail body to the grave, we did so knowing full well that some day we would see her again. 1 Corinthians 15:53–58 says:

For this corruptible must put on incorruption, and this mortal must put on immortality. So when this corruptible shall have put on incorruption, and this mortal shall have put on immortality, then shall be brought to pass the saying that is written, Death is swallowed up in victory. O death, where is thy sting? O grave, where is thy victory? The sting of death is sin; and the strength of sin is the law.

But thanks be to God, which giveth us the victory through our Lord Jesus Christ.

Therefore, my beloved brethren, be ye stedfast, unmoveable, always abounding in the work of the Lord, forasmuch as ye know that your labour is not in vain in the Lord. (KJV)

Billy Graham, in his book, *Death and the Life After,* tells the story of a little girl walking with her father in the country.

> No neon signs, no automobile headlights, or street lamps marred the stillness of the crisp evening. As she looked into the deep blue velvet sky, studded with an array of diamonds which put the most dazzling Tiffany to shame, she said, "Daddy, if the wrong side of heaven is so beautiful, what do you think the right side will be like?"

A quote from the same book talks more about getting to heaven.

When Will We Go To Heaven?

The believer's passage to heaven is a direct route. As soon as we are dead, we will be with the Lord. Jesus told the repentant thief on the cross, "I tell you the truth, today you will be with me in paradise" (Luke 23:43).

Paul declared, "I desire to depart and be with Christ" (Philippians 1:23). He also affirmed, "Therefore we are always confident and know that as long as we are at home in the body we are away from the Lord. We live by faith, not by sight. We are confident, I say, and would prefer to be away from the body and at home with the Lord" (2 Corinthians 5:6-8).

The moment we take our last breath on earth we take our first in heaven. We are absent from the body and immediately present with the Lord. Then in God's time we receive our glorified bodies at the Second Coming of Christ.

1 Corinthians 15:43, referring to the body we place in the grave, says, *"It is sown in dishonor; it is raised in glory: it is sown in weakness; it is raised in power."*

I have quoted these verses from the Word of God and the helpful comment Evangelist Billy Graham has written to encourage and bless you. I want to help you to understand death for the believer, as the Apostle Paul said in Philippians 1:21, *"For to me to live is Christ, and to die is gain."* Paul also gave us great encouragement and a blessed hope when he wrote to the Christians at Thessalonica and said:

> *But I would not have you to be ignorant, brethren, concerning them which are asleep, that ye sorrow not, even as others which have no hope.*
>
> *For if we believe that Jesus died and rose again, even so them also which sleep in Jesus will God bring with him.*
>
> *For this we say unto you by the word of the Lord, that we which are alive and remain unto the coming of the Lord shall not prevent them which are asleep.*
>
> *For the Lord himself shall descend from heaven with a shout, with the voice of the archangel, and with the trump of God: and the dead in Christ shall rise first:*
>
> *Then we which are alive and remain shall be caught up together with them in the clouds, to meet the Lord in the air: and so shall we ever be with the Lord. Wherefore comfort one another with these words.* (1 Thessalonians 4:13–18, KJV)

In the devotional *Our Daily Bread* we read: "Good-byes are the laws of earth; re-unions are the laws of heaven." Praise God!

There are so many beautiful, meaningful gospel songs about heaven in our hymnals. One that is a favourite of so many of us and I am sure was one that Jessie learned and loved throughout her long life is the following:

When We All Get To Heaven

Sing the wondrous love of Jesus,
Sing His mercy and His grace.
In the mansions bright and blessed
He'll prepare for us a place.
When we all get to Heaven,
What a day of rejoicing that will be!
When we all see Jesus,
We'll sing and shout the victory!
While we walk the pilgrim pathway,
Clouds will overspread the sky;
But when traveling days are over,
Not a shadow, not a sigh.
Let us then be true and faithful,
Trusting, serving every day;
Just one glimpse of Him in glory
Will the toils of life repay.
Onward to the prize before us!
Soon His beauty we'll behold;
Soon the pearly gates will open;
We shall tread the streets of gold.
—Eliza E. Hewitt

I would like to quote a Psalm. I have taken the Scripture from Peterson's translation, *The Message.*

Just as each day brims with your beauty,
my mouth brims with praise.
But don't turn me out to pasture when I'm old
or put me on the shelf when I can't pull my weight.
My enemies are talking behind my back,
watching for their chance to knife me.
The gossip is: "God has abandoned him.
Pounce on him now; no one will help him."
God, don't just watch from the sidelines.
Come on! Run to my side!

My accusers—make them lose face.
Those out to get me—make them look
Like idiots, while I stretch out, reaching for you
and daily add praise to praise.
I'll write the book on your righteousness,
talk up your salvation the livelong day,
never run out of good things to write or say.
I come in the power of the Lord God,
I post signs marking his right-of-way.
You got me when I was an unformed youth,
God, and taught me everything I know.
Now I'm telling the world your wonders;
I'll keep at it until I'm old and gray.
(Psalm 71:9–18)

As I am now an octogenarian, I have never complained about growing old. I told my wife once that I would never talk about my health unless it was good. Well, I haven't always kept my word on that point but on aging, I always remember someone saying "Don't complain about growing old; some people never had the privilege." How true that is!

Billy Graham, in his book, *Death and the Life After*, which I have already referred to, quoted this in part, a message preached many, many years ago by Evangelist D. L. Moody:

Five Minutes After...

It may be a moment, or after months of waiting, but soon I shall stand before my Lord. Then in an instant all things will appear in new perspective.

Suddenly the thing I thought important—tomorrow's tasks, the plans for the dinner at my church, my success or failure in pleasing those around me—these will matter not at all. And the things to which I gave but little thought—the word about Christ to the man next door, the moment (how short it was) of earnest prayer for the Lord's work in far-off lands, the confessing and forsaking of that secret sin—will stand as real and enduring.

Five minutes after I'm in heaven I'll be overwhelmed by the truth I've known but somehow never grasped. I'll realize then that it's what I am in Christ that comes first with God, and that when I am right with Him, I do the things which please Him.

I'll sense that it was not just how much I gave that mattered, but how I gave—and how much I withheld. In heaven I'll wish with all my heart that I could reclaim a thousandth part of the time I've let slip through my fingers, that I could call back those countless conversations which could have glorified my Lord—but didn't.

Five minutes after I'm in heaven, I believe I'll wish with all my heart that I had risen more faithfully to read the Word of God and wait on Him in prayer—that I might have known Him while still on earth as He wanted me to know Him.

A thousand thoughts will press upon me, and though overwhelmed by the grace which admits me to my heavenly home, I'll wonder at my aimless earthly life. I'll wish…if one may wish in heaven—but it will be too late.

Heaven is real and hell is real, and eternity is but a breath away. Soon we shall be in the presence of the Lord we claim to serve. Why should we live as though salvation were a dream—as though we did not know?

'To him that knoweth to do good, and doeth it not, to him it is sin.'

There may yet be a little time. A new year dawns before us. God help us to live now in the light of a real tomorrow!

Billy Graham also quotes in this book:

At the beginning of the book I quoted my father-in-law's comment, "Only those who are prepared to die are really prepared to live." I want to know how to live so that I may learn how to die. Final exams may, in fact, be tomorrow.

I'm not afraid to die, for I know the joys of heaven are waiting. My greatest desire is to live today in anticipation of tomorrow and be ready to be welcomed into His home for all eternity. Will you be making the journey with me?

For any of my readers who are not sure of their eternal destiny, I quote the following verses for your sincere and thoughtful consideration:

There is a way which seemeth right unto a man, but the end thereof are the ways of death. (Proverbs 14:12, KJV)

But your iniquities have separated between you and your God, and your sins have hid his face from you, that he will not hear. (Isaiah 59:2, KJV)

For all have sinned, and come short of the glory of God. (Romans 3:23, KJV)

But now the good news:

For Christ also hath once suffered for sins, the just for the unjust, that he might bring us to God. (1 Peter 3:18, KJV)

But God commendeth his love toward us, in that, while we were yet sinners, Christ died for us. (Romans 5:8, KJV)

But as many as received him, to them gave he power to become the sons of God, even to them that believe on his name. (John 1:12, KJV)

That if thou shalt confess with thy mouth the Lord Jesus, and shalt believe in thine heart that God hath raised him from the dead, thou shalt be saved. (Romans 10:9, KJV)

For whosoever shall call upon the name of the Lord shall be saved. (Romans 10:13, KJV)

For by grace are ye saved through faith; and that not of yourselves: it is the gift of God: Not of works, lest any man should boast. (Ephesians 2:8–9)

The Victor

The Vict'ry I have in Jesus,
That's why I'm glad today,
Though trials deep should face me,
He'll surely lead the way.

I've conquered sin and sadness,
All by His life in me.
And when He's brought me safely home,
A Victor I will be.
The Vict'ry over trouble
O'er conflicts pressing in,
His might has kept me midst the foe
The battle steep to win,
A conqueror like Jesus,
His power has set me free,
And when I've finished the campaign,
I know He waits for me.
The Vict'ry o'er the grave and death,
In Him already won,
Awaits me in the promised rest,
When battle's fully done;
A conqueror forever,
When His blest face I see,
And there proclaim how Christ has made
A Victor out of me.
—Paul Durham

Dear reader, you no doubt know by this time that I am a lover of poems that have both message and meaning in them. Therefore I trust you will forgive me and read on and be blessed by the following two that I feel have a special message.

On the Shore

The day is done: beyond the distant mountains
The sunset light dies slowly in the sky,
Only the pine trees break the deep night silence and whisper softly as the wind goes by.
No human voice breaks on the solemn stillness;
Yet long I linger on the sanded beach
Watching the deep, dark ocean rolling onward
To lands which thought alone, not sight, can reach.

I have no fear of the blue waves before me
That strive to touch and clasp me as I stand;
Do I not know that He whose care is o'er me
Holdeth the waters in His mighty hand?
But to my spirit comes a calm, deep rapture,
The while I watch this wide, unresting sea,
The sense of something pure and full and changeless,
Of something unfulfilled and yet to be.
I think, perhaps, that when my feet turn slowly
Forth from the mortal ways of sin and strife,
When I shall leave behind earth's pain and pleasure
To stand and wait upon the shore of life—
That I shall stand with this same nameless rapture
And wait His bidding from the land above,
Content, until He comes, to gaze in silence
Out o'er the boundless ocean of His love.
—from *For His Name's Sake* (1878) by Millie Colcord, who died at age 18 after several years of illness.

Vance Havner, who was one of the most quotable pulpiteers of his time, said, "I'm homesick for heaven. It's the hope of dying that has kept me alive this long." Heaven is a wonderful place and the benefits for the believer are out of this world!

The Other Side

This isn't death—it's glory!
It is not dark—it's light!
It isn't stumbling, groping,
Or even faith—it's sight!
This isn't grief—it's having
My last tear wiped away;
It's sunrise—it's the morning
Of my eternal day!
This isn't even praying—
It's speaking face to face;
Listening and glimpsing

The wonders of His grace.
This is the end of pleading
For strength to bear my pain;
Not even pain's dark memory
Will ever live again.
How did I bear the earth-life
Before I knew the rapture
Of meeting face to face
The One who sought me, saved me,
And kept me by His grace!
—*Margaret Snell*

It was in Ottawa, Ontario, that I first began attending Sunday school. It was held in the Imperial Theatre on Bank Street. My first Sunday I attended I was given a Bible. I was too young to even read it but my Grannie Dalzell wrote in it: "To lose one's health is much, to lose one's life is more; But to lose one's soul is such a loss, that nothing can restore."

Corrie ten Boom said, "Do not be afraid…read the last pages of the Bible. Jesus is Victor."

We are living in a day of unprecedented violence. Young men and women are being killed, abducted, and abused both sexually and emotionally. No matter what newscast we watch or listen to, what magazine or newspaper we read, it seems no one is guaranteed safety and security anymore. This ought not to surprise us, although, in one sense it grieves us, for we read in 2 Timothy 3:1–4:

> *But mark this: There will be terrible times in the last days. People will be lovers of themselves, lovers of money, boastful, proud, abusive, disobedient to their parents, ungrateful, unholy, without love, unforgiving, slanderous, without self-control, brutal, not lovers of the good, treacherous, rash, conceited, lovers of pleasure rather than lovers of God.*

Those of us who are believers in the Lord Jesus Christ have the comfort of the Saviour's words in John 14:1–3:

> *Do not let your hearts be troubled. Trust in God; trust also in me. In my Father's house are many rooms; if it were not so, I would have told you. I am going there to prepare a place for you. And if I go and prepare a place for you, I will come back and take you to be with me that you also may be where I am.*

To one who might be reading this chapter of Jessie's story and not certain of their eternal destiny, remember, there is only one bridge between you and God and that is the Lord Jesus Christ who said in John 14:6, *"I am the way and the truth and the life. No one comes to the Father except through me."*

If Jessie were still with us, she would make sure that you knew about her Saviour. Her body and mind had failed her, but her daily walk with the Lord could not be silenced or crushed within this earthly frailty. Jessie had spent a lifetime reading her Bible, praying and trusting the God she read about and talked to. There came a moment when the life went out of her weakened, worn body and she entered into the presence of God, her final resting place.

> In changing times, the greatest comfort we have is the fact that our God is a mighty fortress—a strong tower and an unconquerable stronghold. The Psalmist writes, "I call upon the Lord, who is worthy to be praised, and I am saved from my enemies."
>
> —*Selected*

ALL THE *Way* FROM BULGARIA

"You then, my son, be strong in the grace that is in Christ Jesus. And the things you have heard me say in the presence of many witnesses entrust to reliable men who will also be qualified to teach others. Endure hardship with us like a good soldier of Christ Jesus."

(2 Timothy 2:1–3)

"While the past remains part of our lives, it doesn't have to determine our future."

—Selected

Back some two or three years ago, I attended a Pastoral Care Ministry School at Wheaton College in Wheaton, Illinois. Leanne Payne was teaching this course.

One particular evening, I was late for supper and sitting at a table by myself. As I was finishing up, a young man came over and asked if he could join me. I invited him to sit down and was surprised to see that he was packing his meal into his backpack. He explained to me that in his country, Bulgaria, they didn't eat until later in the evening.

He was planning to go to the gym and have a swim before attending the evening class.

I doubt if he did either activity that evening for thus began a friendship that has continued to this day. I will call him Andrei. I suppose, in a sense, one could say I have mentored him ever since our brief time together. We exchanged email addresses and by the time I arrived back in Toronto he had already written to me. We have been in constant touch ever since.

The following is a quotation I jotted down and eventually sent to Andrei. The author is unknown.

Whether by strange coincidence or Divine guidance,
In the course of our life
We cross paths with many people.
Some move towards us,
Others move away.
Some we choose to remember,
Others to forget.
But with a special few
We seem to have no choice
For each has made an impact on the other,
And their memory will live on forever.
These people we call friends—
You, to me, are such a friend.

Andrei was already at seminary in Bulgaria and he spoke excellent English. I asked him how it was he was picked to come over to the United States and take the course at Wheaton College. His answer will reveal to you just how godly a young man he is. Andrei earnestly believes that it was just one of the merciful presents from God to him. He later wrote to me further, and I quote: "…this was an unmerited gift from the Saviour." These are the words of a humble man whom God is using to His honour and glory.

Bulgaria, after World War II, was in the eastern block of Europe and therefore came under the influence and control of the Soviet Union. Although Andrei was born after the liberation from communism, he learned that under communism, it was very difficult for Christians. All the churches were closed and it was necessary for believers to gather together for worship, Bible study, and prayer in homes. This, of course, was opposed by the officials and resulted in many Christians being persecuted and many being killed for their faith in the Lord.

Andrei's parents were atheists but taught him and his younger sister strong moral values. It was one year after Andrei's conversion that his sister accepted Christ as her Saviour. Subsequently his mother and father became believers.

God Sent Us a Savior

If our greatest need had been information,
God would have sent us an educator.
If our greatest need had been technology,
God would have sent us a scientist.
If our greatest need had been money,
God would have sent us an economist.
If our greatest need had been pleasure,
God would have sent us an entertainer.
But our greatest need was forgiveness,
So God sent us a Savior.
—*Author Unknown*

But now I want to relate to you how and when Andrei himself came to a saving knowledge of Jesus Christ; how he came to that point in his life when he surrendered completely to the Lord and dedicated himself to Jesus.

As I read the first chapter in the latest book written by evangelist Billy Graham, *The Journey*, I almost felt as if this noted evangelist and author was writing about Andrei before he became a Christian and true disciple of the Lord Jesus Christ.

> Perhaps your journey has been marked by disappointment, sorrow, and heartache. You yearn for something different, something better in life—but lasting happiness and peace have eluded you. Or perhaps you decided years ago to spend your

life pursuing excitement, pleasure, fame, or success. For a time those may have satisfied you—but eventually (if you're honest) you discovered they led only to boredom, disillusionment, emptiness, or even self-destruction.

Or you may have found yourself overwhelmed by crushing problems beyond your control: sickness, financial pressures, broken relationships, fear, guilt, loneliness, despair. Life for you has become a hopeless burden with no end in sight. Or perhaps you are one of those whose journey has been relatively free from problems yet aimless and empty, without any real purpose or direction. You may even believe in God and consider yourself a sincere Christian, and still you're discouraged and confused, overwhelmed by circumstances you don't understand and don't know how to escape. Tragically, every year thousands decide they can't bear life any longer and decide to end it. You may even have been tempted to follow them.

Andrei was twenty-three years old when he came to Christ. Up until that time he considered himself an atheist. God had allowed him to fulfill all his dreams, but did not forsake or forget him. You see, as God told the prophet in Jeremiah 1:5, he also had Andrei in mind: *"Before I formed you in the womb I knew you."*

David, Israel's greatest king, also knew this truth, for he wrote in Psalm 139:16, *"You saw me before I was born and scheduled each day of my life before I began to breathe. Every day was recorded in your book!"* (TLB) Andrei tried all the world had to offer thinking it would make him happy and bring some meaning to his life.

He sought after and obtained many material things he had longed for growing up. But nothing really satisfied, and actually so disappointed him that real happiness eluded him. His heart was empty and he had no peace within. He even came to the place where he contemplated suicide! He confessed that, in anger, he would even beat up on his father.

Bud Elford is one of the missionaries that I have written about in this book. For many years, and up until he recently went to be with the Lord, he wrote what he refers to as *Minute Message.* It is published on the back page of the *Northern Canada Evangelical Mission* monthly magazine. I quote one of these short messages, seemingly appropriate for this part of Andrei's story.

> On one occasion I was giving a ride to a man who said he was a Satanist. When I asked him why he worshipped the devil, he remarked, "Oh, that's because he is going to win in the end."
>
> I said, "Son, someone has sold you a bill of goods. Do you know what happened at Calvary? Your god is not only going to lose in the end, but he has lost already." I quoted Colossians 2:15, emphasizing that Christ 'triumphed' over the enemy, actually making him a laughing stock. Christ did not just barely win, but He triumphed! It was a slam dunk!
>
> I said, "There is no battle to come. It is over, finished, done. Someone has been leading you down the garden path. Why don't you ask Satan what happened at Calvary?"
>
> My next statement was, "Why not confess your sins and join the Real Winner?"
>
> "But you don't know the things I've done," he replied. "No problem, God does," I said. "He won't listen to me," he argued. "But I know Him and I'll introduce you," I said. "Here, I will tell you what to say."
>
> We were riding north on Highway 21. His voice had been raspy and gruff, but as he confessed his sins and opened his heart to the Lordship of Jesus Christ, his voice changed a whole octave upwards. When he opened his eyes, he said, "Oh, look how green the fields are, and see the birds!"
>
> He then simply announced to Satan what he had done and told him he could no longer have his body, but that he now belonged to Jesus Christ forever.
>
> Such is the glorious triumph of the Cross.

God, in His great love and mercy, saw Andrei in the pit of degradation and despair and His Holy Spirit urged him to start to read the Word of God. He began reading the New Testament and at the same time performing good works which, in his thinking, would please God. That only added to his anxiety.

Charles H. Spurgeon once said: "I looked at Him; He looked on me; and we were one forever." A contemporary of this great preacher took these words and wrote the following lyrics which were eventually put to music:

I Looked to Jesus

I looked to Jesus in my sin,
My woe and want confessing;
Undone and lost, I came to Him,—
I sought and found a blessing.
I looked to Him;
'Tis true—His "Whosoever;"
He looked on me:
And we were one forever.
I looked to Jesus on the cross;
For me I saw him dying;
God's Word believed that all my sins
Were there upon Him lying.
I looked to Jesus there on high,
From death upraised to glory;
I trusted in His power to save,
Believed the old, old story.
He looked on me—oh, look of love!
My heart by it was broken;
And with that look of love He gave
The Holy Spirit's token.
Now one with Christ, I find my peace
In Him to be abiding;
And in His love for all my need,
In childlike faith confiding.

Several months later, God sent a deacon from the local evangelical church, who clearly explained to Andrei that salvation is only by grace, not of any good works as quoted in Ephesians 2:8–9. *"For it is by grace you have been saved, through faith—and this not from yourselves, it is the gift of God—not by works, so that no one can boast."*

He then fell on his knees, asked God to forgive him of all his sins, and accepted Jesus Christ as his personal Saviour.

> *That if you confess with your mouth, "Jesus is Lord," and believe in your heart that God raised him from the dead, you will be saved. For it is with your heart that you believe and are justified, and it is with your mouth that you confess and are saved. As the Scripture says "Anyone who trusts in him will never be put to shame." For there is no difference between Jew and Gentile—the same Lord is Lord of all and richly blesses all who call on him, for, "Everyone who calls on the name of the Lord will be saved."*
>
> (Romans 10:9–13)

Broken Things

My Savior specializes
In mending broken things;
He takes the heart that's shattered
And gives it songs to sing.
He pieces it together
With His sweet gracious touch;
He mends the heart that's broken
Because He loves so much.
He mends the broken Spirit,
Then lifts that spirit up
And pours the oil of gladness
Into the upturned cup.
The broken lives He reshapes;
Those lives so wrecked by sin,
When in their crushed condition
They turn in faith to Him.
The broken dreams that crumble
To ashes at our feet
That seemed so fair and lovely,

That made life taste more sweet,
Those broken dreams He rebuilds
And fashions them anew;
Then gives us faith to trust Him
To see new dreams come true.
What of the broken plans then
The broken health that comes?
Is He not ever mindful
When life's swift pendulum
Dashes to scattered pieces
The plans that we have made?
Above it all, He whispers;
"I shall come to your aid."
He restores broken spirits,
Binds broken hearts and dreams,
Repairs the shattered pages
Of lives that He redeems,
He stands ready to help us
No matter what life brings
Because He specializes
In mending broken things.
—*Georgia B. Adams*

So since Christ suffered in the flesh for us, for you, arm yourselves with the same thought and purpose [patiently to suffer rather than fail to please God]. For whoever has suffered in the flesh [having the mind of Christ] is done with [intentional] sin [has stopped pleasing himself and the world, and pleases God], so that he can no longer spend the rest of his natural life living by [his] human appetites and desires, but [he lives] for what God wills. For the time that is past already suffices for doing what the Gentiles like to do—living [as you have done] in shameless, insolent wantonness, in lustful desires, drunkenness, reveling, drinking bouts and abominable, lawless idolatries. They are astonished and think it very queer that you do not now run hand in hand with them in the same excesses of dissipation, and they abuse [you]. But they will have to give an account to Him Who is ready to judge and pass sentence on the living and the dead.

(1 Peter 4:1–5, Amplified)

These verses bring to mind the words the Saviour spoke to the Sadducees and Pharisees who were constantly nagging Him and trying to trap Him. In Matthew's Gospel Chapter 22, verses 36-38, Jesus made it abundantly clear to whom our love and allegiance belonged. *"Teacher, which is the greatest commandment in the Law?" Jesus replied: 'Love the Lord your God with all your heart and with all your soul and with all your mind.' This is the first and greatest commandment."*

Our Daily Bread devotional quotes the following:

> To grow in your love for God, keep God in your thoughts. We are living in a day when it is very difficult to keep our minds and our thoughts focused on God and thus it should be our prayer: "Lord, I desire to love you with all my mind. Help me to discover new ways to show my love for You in my thought life, in my worship and in all my relationships."

Bill and Gloria Gaither wrote a gospel song that has blessed millions of people. It is entitled *He Touched Me.* Just about every Christian artist and group has recorded this song. Even many other professionals like Elvis Presley and Kate Smith (do any of my readers remember her?). She always sang the American anthem at every National Hockey League game. Surely this song describes Andrei and the difference it made in His life when God "touched him."

He Touched Me

Shackled by a heavy burden,
'Neath a load of guilt and shame.
Then the Hand of Jesus touched me,
And now I am no longer the same.
He touched me,
Oh, He touched me,
And oh the joy that floods my soul.

Something happened and now I know,
He touched me and made me whole.
Since I met the Blessed Saviour,
Since He cleansed and made me whole,
I will never cease to praise Him!
I'll shout it while eternity rolls.

Andrei wrote me one day not too long after he arrived back in Bulgaria to tell me he wanted to become engaged to his girlfriend, Pavlina, and just how would he go about it. Well, I told him what usually happens here in the west—engagement ring, etc. I then explained to him that our cultures were probably considerably different and it would be difficult for me to give him counsel on this matter.

Andrei had met Pavlina at a youth retreat and after a significant time of prayer and fasting they received the assurance from the Lord that they were for one another. Pavlina, at the time, was working with children who had physical and mental problems, teaching them to read and write.

The next thing I knew, the wedding was planned and the main emphasis in this union was to bring honour and glory to the Lord. With this in mind Andrei made sure the gospel was clearly spoken and they had prayed that the unsaved guests, friends, and relatives would be prompted by the Holy Spirit to accept Jesus Christ as personal Saviour. While I have attempted to mentor and encourage this young man, I have also learned much from him. His life reminds me of the gospel song James J. Small wrote, back sometime during his lifetime, 1817–1888.

I've Found a Friend

I've found a Friend, O such a friend! He loved me ere I knew Him;
He drew me with the cords of love, and thus He bound me to Him;
And round my heart still closely twine those ties which naught can sever,
For I am His, and He is mine, forever and forever.
I've found a Friend, O such a friend! He bled, He died to save me;
And not alone the gift of life, but His own Self He gave me!
Naught that I have mine own I call, I'll hold it for the Giver,
My heart, my strength, my life, my all are His, and His forever.

I've found a Friend, O such a friend! All pow'r to Him is given,
To guard me on my onward course, and bring me safe to heaven.
The eternal glories gleam afar, to nerve my faint endeavor;
So now to watch, to work, to war, and then to rest forever.
I've found a Friend, O such a friend! So kind and true and tender,
So wise a Counselor and Guide, so mighty a Defender!
From Him who loves me now so well what power my soul can sever?
Shall life or death, shall earth or hell? No! I am His forever.

Andrei has not really told me a great deal about Pavlina, other than the fact that she was a godly young woman. She was facing a painful operation, and was abiding in the ever-present arms of the Lord she loved dearly and longed to serve.

> *Woman*
>
> The best example of self-denying liberality in the Bible is recorded of a woman. The best example of loving service in the Bible is recorded of a woman. The best example of conquering prayer in the Bible is recorded of a woman. It was no great gift, no great service, no great prayer. The gift was a widow's mite. The service was the anointing of Jesus with a box of ointment. The prayer was a mother's prayer for a daughter possessed with a devil. But the gift and service and prayer were in self-denial and love and faith. And so in the sight of God they were of great service.
>
> *—Herrick Johnson*

The church in which Andrei and Pavlina were members was established almost 130 years ago by American missionaries. They had been without a full-time pastor for almost ten years. A deacon, a very shy humble countryman, had been leading the services.

The church invited Andrei to become the pastor after his graduation from the seminary in June 2006. Andrei and Pavlina were keenly looking forward to going home to Haskova to begin full-time ministry. He asked me to pray for this challenge before them as it was going to involve much hard work and strength from the Lord for an awakening of this pillar of faith.

Andrei, while studying at the Evangelical Institute in Sofia, told me that God had given him a wonderful wife who was fully committed to the Lord. He expressed the hope that with her help he would be better able to serve the Lord. He also testified, and we should take note of this, that "being a Christian is a bilateral issue—privilege and responsibility. Privilege because I have been chosen of God for salvation; therefore as chosen I have the responsibility to lead a life that shows that I am really a chosen one to reflect the incredible character of Jesus. This means that I am to strive to become like my Lord and Saviour in all aspects of my life in order that He may be glorified in all areas of my life."

Joy in Serving Jesus

There is joy in serving Jesus
As I journey on my way
Joy that fills my heart with praises
Every hour and every day.
There is joy, joy
Joy in serving Jesus
Joy that throbs within my heart
Every moment, every hour
As I draw upon His power
There is joy, joy
Joy that never shall depart.
There is joy in serving Jesus
Joy that triumphs over pain
Fills my heart with heaven's music
Till I join the glad refrain.
There is joy in serving Jesus
As I walk alone with God
'Tis the joy of Christ my Saviour
Who the path of suffering trod.
There is joy in serving Jesus
Joy amid the darkest night
For I've learned the wondrous secret
And I'm walking in the light.

Jude 20–23 says,

> *But you, dear friends, build yourselves up in your most holy faith and pray in the Holy Spirit. Keep yourselves in God's love as you wait for the mercy of our Lord Jesus Christ to bring you to eternal life.*
>
> *Be merciful to those who doubt; snatch others from the fire and save them; to others show mercy, mixed with fear…*

In 1869 or thereabout, Fanny Crosby was asked to speak to a group of blue-collar workers in Cincinnati, Ohio.

> Near the end of her address, she had an overwhelming sense that "some mother's boy in the crowd must be rescued that night or not at all." She mentioned this to the crowd who had gathered, pleading, "If there is a dear boy here tonight who perchance has wandered away from his mother's home and teaching, would he please come to me at the end of the service?"
>
> Afterward a young man of about eighteen years of age approached her. "Did you mean me?" he asked. I promised to meet her in heaven, but the way I have been living, I don't think that will be possible now!" Fanny had the joy of leading him to Christ.
>
> Returning to her room that night, all she could think about was the theme, "rescue the perishing," and when she retired that night she had written the complete hymn. The next day, Howard Doane wrote the music, and it was published the following year in his *Songs of Devotion.*
>
> Many years later, Fanny was speaking at the YMCA in Lynn, Massachusetts, and she recounted the story behind "Rescue the Perishing". After the service, a man approached her, his voice quivering, "Miss Crosby," he said, "I was that boy who told you more than thirty-five years ago that I had wandered from my mother's God. That evening you spoke, I sought and found peace, and I have tried to live a consistent Christian life ever

since. If we never meet again on earth, we will meet up yonder." He turned and left, unable to say another word. But Fanny later described it as one of the most gratifying experiences of her life.

—Then Sings my Soul *by Robert J. Morgan*

Rescue the Perishing

Rescue the perishing, care for the dying,
Snatch them in pity from sin and the grave;
Weep o'er the erring one, lift up the fallen,
Tell them of Jesus, the mighty to save.
Rescue the perishing, care for the dying,
Jesus is merciful, Jesus will save.
Though they are slighting Him, still He is waiting,
Waiting the penitent child to receive;
Plead with them earnestly, plead with them gently;
He will forgive if they only believe.
Down in the human heart, crushed by the tempter,
Feelings lie buried that grace can restore;
Touched by a loving heart, wakened by kindness,
Chords that were broken will vibrate once more.
Rescue the perishing, duty demands it;
Strength for thy labor the Lord will provide;
Back to the narrow way patiently win them;
Tell the poor wand'rer a Savior has died.

Andrei, at the beginning of his theological training, began to preach as often as possible in his home church as there was such a need for men, women, and children to hear the gospel message. During his second year at the seminary he was invited to another church in a different city. He began working with young people and started home Bible study groups with older folks as well as students.

At the end of this second year he started a new initiative with the young adults. He called it "Young Samaritan." The purpose of this kind of ministry was twofold—on one hand he was trying to make a flowing, easy transition from the teen group to the young adults who would then fulfill the second part of his plan—to provide time for informal meetings between teens and young adults.

The purpose of these meetings was to visit in the homes of the sick and the elderly. They would clean their houses, buy food, but most of all spend time with them. They would encourage them with prayers and songs of worship and strive to comfort their hearts by reading from the Word of God. Andrei's desire was to put into practice what he preached!

Quoting from a book entitled *The Joy of Following Jesus*, written by J. Oswald Sanders:

> **Conditions of Discipleship**
>
> *Anyone who does not carry his cross and follow me cannot be my disciple.* (Luke 14:27)
>
> As usual, Jesus was surrounded by the thronging crowds, who were listening to His every word. "Large crowds were traveling with Jesus" (Luke 14:25), fascinated by the novelty, winsomeness, and challenge of this new teaching, for it was still in the days of His popularity.
>
> The situation presented Him with a unique opportunity to capitalize on their feverish interest. The whole nation was looking for a charismatic leader who would help them throw off the galling Roman yoke—and here was someone superbly qualified for the task. All He needed to do was to perform a few spectacular miracles and then lead them in a great insurrection.
>
> Did He flatter them, offer some inducement, perform some miracle to win their allegiance? It seemed as though He were intent on alienating their interest and actually discouraging them from following Him. He began to thin their ranks by stating in the starkest of terms the exacting conditions of discipleship.

When graduation came and Andrei and Pavlina were preparing to leave for the church to which they had been called, the church informed them they really couldn't afford to pay them any salary. Andrei emailed and asked me what he should do. He could get a job as could Pavlina, but this would take time away from the ministry and his ability to preach and teach the saving gospel of the Lord Jesus Christ.

I wrote back to Andrei and told him of my own personal experience. I was called to a small church, just having gone through a difficult time, and the salary was to be twenty-five dollars a week. Albeit the church did provide a large apartment over the church. They also paid for the telephone, heating and hydro. But my wife Jean and I, with our young son Russell, accepted the call and went.

We were never sorry and God blessed so wonderfully that it would take pages to tell you of the goodness and faithfulness of God during the years we spent there. We were very young and inexperienced. Obviously we had learned the truth that Samuel told King Saul when he disobeyed God's command given to him by Samuel. 1 Samuel 15:22 says, "*But Samuel replied: 'Does the Lord delight in burnt offerings and sacrifices as much as in obeying the voice of the Lord? To obey is better than sacrifice, and to heed is better than the fat of rams.'*"

God wants complete obedience–
Excuses will not do;
His Word and Spirit point the way
As we His will pursue.
—*Author unknown*

My advice to Andrei was to go and forget about finding a job. I reminded him of God's promise in Philippians 4:19: *"And my God will meet all your needs according to his glorious riches in Christ Jesus."* I also challenged this dear young man with the words the Apostle Paul wrote to his son in the faith found in 2 Timothy 4:1b–2, *"I give you this charge: Preach the Word; be prepared in season and out of season; correct, rebuke and encourage—with great patience and careful instruction."*

Martin Luther King Jr. once said: "Take the first step in faith. You don't have to see the whole staircase. Just take the first step." I also urged Andrei, as I would urge all young men and women who take the gospel message, to clearly emphasize the saving and *keeping* power of the blood of the Lord Jesus Christ shed for all mankind on the cross of Calvary.

A well-known contemporary gospel songwriter by the name of André Crouch wrote a song called *The Blood will Never Lose Its Power.* Those of us who are believers know this truth very well.

The blood that Jesus shed for me
Way back on Calvary
Oh the blood that gives me strength
from day to day
It will never lose its power
Cause it reaches to the highest mountain
And it flows to the lowest valley
It's the blood that gives me strength
from day to day
It will never lose its power
It soothes my doubts
And calms my fears
And it dries all my tears
Oh the blood that gives me strength
from day to day
It will never lose its power

In Exodus 12:13, God gave very explicit instructions to the children of Israel through His servant Moses. During the plagues brought on the Egyptians, they were to sprinkle the blood of a perfect animal on the doorposts of their homes. If they were obedient to God and did this, when the death angel passed over Egypt, the children of Israel would be spared. The promise was *"...and when I see the blood I will pass over you..."* Jesus Himself said in Mark 14:24, *"This is my blood of the covenant, which is poured out for many..."* There are scores of verses in the Word referring to the blood and I quote only one more found in Hebrews 9:12: *"He did not enter by means of the blood of goats and calves: But He entered the most Holy Place once for all by His own blood, having obtained eternal redemption."*

I would also encourage Andrei and every young person starting out in the ministry to indeed teach and preach the Word in sincerity and clarity. Paul also exhorted Timothy in the second epistle he wrote to him in Chapter 4, verse 5, *"do the work of an evangelist."*

The best known and most widely used evangelist of the twentieth century is Dr. Billy Graham. God has used him to reach millions of people around the world. Through his preaching of the gospel millions have come to a saving knowledge of the Lord Jesus Christ. What many people do not realize is that Billy Graham was also a personal evangelist. By this, I mean that he would witness to individuals whenever the opportunity arose and many times would lead the individual to accept Christ as personal Saviour.

On one occasion, several years ago, when the Billy Graham Foundation team and staff were on a ferry leaving Minneapolis to go to an island for their annual picnic, Dr. Graham noticed two women standing at the back of the ship, smoking and chatting away. He went up to the women, introduced himself (they had no idea who he was) and, after briefly talking with them for a few minutes about the weather, etc., began to explain the gospel to them. He then led both women to the Lord.

Harvest

I want to see you work, dear Lord
with a quick decisive stride.
I want conversion of the world—
then catch away the church, your bride!
Yet, there are fields where many souls
have not awakened to your Word...
How can I want to fly away
when they have not heard?
So send me, Lord, by SIGHT OR PRAYER
to many souls caught in despair,
To learn that as the many come
They enter in, just one by one.
—*Darlene Laubrech*

I am in no way minimizing the work of a pastor, but I am trying to show Andrei and every servant of the Lord, both at home and abroad, that the work of an evangelist is of the utmost importance. I just learned the following interesting story recently and want to pass it on to you.

A Sunday school teacher in the city of Chicago led one of his pupils, a shoe salesman, to the Lord. That man was Dwight L. Moody, the best-known and most widely used evangelist of the 19th century. At one of his meetings in New York City, a famous, professional baseball player by the name of Billy Sunday accepted Christ as his personal Saviour and became an outstanding evangelist in the latter part of the 19th and 20th centuries. In one of his meetings, a man by the name of Mordecaiah Ham accepted the Lord and became a lesser-known evangelist, but an able preacher of the Word. Mr. Ham held meetings in a small town in South Carolina. At the last meeting, and on the last verse of the invitation, a young farm boy went forward and accepted Christ as his Saviour. That young farm boy was Billy Graham.

When I was in our young people's group back in Ottawa, we often used to sing fervently and sincerely:

Lead me to some soul today;
Oh, teach me Lord, just what to say;
Friends of mine are lost in sin
And cannot find their way.
Few there are who seem to care,
And few there are who pray
Melt my heart and fill my life,
Give me one soul today.
—*Wendell P. Loveless*

Sadly, many of us sang that chorus as a prayer but few of us put feet to our prayer and witnessed as we should have done for the Lord.

Stir My Heart in Passion for the World

Stir me, O stir me, Lord, I care not how
But stir my heart in passion for the world;
Stir me to give, to go, but most to pray;
Stir till the blood-red banner be unfurled
O'er lands that still in heathen darkness lie,

O'er deserts where no cross is lifted high.
Stir me, O stir me, Lord, till all my heart
Is stirred in strong compassion for these souls,
Till Thy compelling "must" drives me to prayer;
Till Thy constraining love reaches to the poles,
Far north and south in burning, deep desire;
Till east and west are caught in love's strong fire.
Stir me, O Lord, Thy heart was stirred
By love's intensest fire till Thou didst give
Thine only Son, Thy best-loved One
E'en to the dreadful cross that I might live;
Stir me to give myself back to Thee
That Thou canst give Thyself again through me.
—Selected

David Brainerd had such an intense compassion for souls, and was so earnest for their salvation, that he said, "I cared not where or how I lived, or what hardships I went through, so that I could but gain souls for Christ. While I was asleep I dreamed of these things, and when I awoke the first thing I thought of was this great work. All my desire was for the conversion of the heathen, and all my hope was in God."
—Selected

For many years I added to my personal library books that instructed and encouraged growth, numerically, financially and spiritually. I gained considerable help from most of these books, but I came to find out early in the ministry that as important as preaching, teaching, evangelizing, and visiting were, the most important for the pastor and the people was prayer.

God's Word has made it so very clear that prayer is of the utmost importance in the life of the servant of God and the entire church body. 2 Chronicles 7:14 is a classic: *"If my people, who are called by my name, will humble themselves and pray and seek my face and turn from their wicked ways, then will I hear from heaven and will forgive their sin and will heal their land."*

The Apostle James emphasized prayer in James 5:13–18:

> *Is any one of you in trouble? He should pray. Is anyone happy? Let him sing songs of praise. Is any one of you sick? He should call the elders of the church to pray over him and anoint him with oil in the name of the Lord. And the prayer offered in faith will make the sick person well; the Lord will raise him up. If he has sinned, he will be forgiven. Therefore confess your sins to each other and pray for each other so that you may be healed. The prayer of a righteous man is powerful and effective.*
>
> *Elijah was a man just like us. He prayed earnestly that it would not rain, and it did not rain on the land for three and a half years. Again he prayed, and the heavens gave rain, and the earth produced its crops.*

William Barclay said it so well when he wrote: "Prayer is not a way of making use of God; Prayer is a way of offering ourselves to God in order that He should be able to make use of us."

Corporate prayer, which is a group meeting together (we used to call it "Prayer Meeting"), was practiced by the early church as recorded in the Book of the Acts of the Apostles. In Acts 1:14, when it was time to replace Judas, the one who had betrayed Jesus and hung himself, we read: *"They all joined together constantly in prayer, along with the women and Mary the mother of Jesus, and with his brothers."* In Acts 2:1 we read, *"When the day of Pentecost came, they were all together in one place."*

Later in this chapter I intend to emphasize the importance of the Spirit of God in the life of every Christian, but just now I want to emphasize the need for prayer in the church. Peter, filled with the Spirit and endued with this marvellous power, was totally fearless and preached the gospel. We read, continuing in Acts 2:42: *"They devoted themselves to the apostles' teaching and to the fellowship, to the breaking of bread, and to prayer."* In Acts 4:31, *"After they prayed, the place where they were meeting was shaken. And they were all filled with the Holy Spirit and spoke the word of God boldly."* Please note that after they were filled with the Holy Spirit they spoke the Word of God boldly. The Amplified Bible puts it this way, *"…and they continued to speak the Word of God with freedom and boldness and courage."* How very important, yes necessary, that Andrei and all young pastors and Christian leaders realize the importance of prayer.

Tis the Blessed Hour of Prayer

Tis the blessed hour of prayer, when our hearts lowly bend
And we gather to Jesus, our Savior and Friend
If we come to Him in faith, His protection to share
What a balm for the weary, O how sweet to be there!
Blessed hour of prayer, blessed hour of prayer
What a balm for the weary, O how sweet to be there!
'Tis the blessed hour of prayer, when the Savior draws near
With a tender compassion His children to hear
When He tells us we may cast at His feet every care
What a balm for the weary, O how sweet to be there!
'Tis the blessed hour of prayer, when the tempted and tried
To the Savior Who loves them their sorrow confide
With a sympathizing heart He removes every care
What a balm for the weary, O how sweet to be there!
At the blessed hour of prayer, trusting Him, we believe
That the blessing we're needing we'll surely receive
In the fullness of the trust we shall lose every care
What a balm for the weary, O how sweet to be there!
—*W. H. Doane*

In his book, *The Journey*, Billy Graham devotes an entire chapter to the importance of prayer. After quoting 1 John 5:14, *"This is the confidence we have in approaching God: that if we ask anything according to his will, he hears us,"* he begins the chapter with these significant words, "Prayer is not an option but a necessity."

Dr. Graham indicates that he had a great affection for his wife's father, Dr. L. Nelson Bell, who for many years served the Lord in China as a medical missionary. I quote his words as to his relationship with his father-in-law: "After Ruth and I were married, he became one of my closest friends and advisers, someone whose wise counsel I always respected." He concluded his paragraph on this godly man by saying:

> Prayer for Dr. Bell wasn't a hurried sentence or two at the end of the day or a hasty afterthought when facing a crisis. Prayer for him was a constant, moment-by-moment practice that penetrated his whole life. Prayer for him was also a joyful experience, an opportunity to come daily into God's presence.

In this same chapter, Dr. Graham states that "Every man or woman whose life has ever counted for God has been a person of prayer." He then said:

> Most of all, Jesus demonstrated the importance of prayer by His own example. His whole ministry was saturated with prayer. On one occasion, "very early in the morning, while it was still dark, Jesus got up, left the house and went off to a solitary place, where he prayed" (Mark 1:35). On another occasion, "Jesus was praying in a certain place. When he finished, one of his disciples said to him, 'Lord, teach us to pray'" (Luke 11:1). He responded by giving them what came to be His most-quoted words, the Lord's Prayer. As His death approached, He withdrew to the Garden of Gethsemane, a secluded place outside the walls of Jerusalem, to pray, "And being in anguish, he prayed more earnestly, and his sweat was like drops of blood falling to the ground" (Luke 22:44). His last words from the cross were a prayer: "Father, into your hands I commit my spirit" (Luke 23:46). If prayer was this important to the Son of God during His journey on earth, shouldn't it be important to us?

I have been told that Korean believers gather every morning before they go to work to pray. Is it any wonder, then, that God has blessed them and prospered them and kept them safe through all these fearful years in the Orient; that God has prospered them spiritually as they have placed such importance and emphasis on corporate prayer?

I want to pass on to you the outline Dr. Graham gives us in this chapter on prayer:

Learning to Pray

First, have the right attitude. A friend of mine likes to define prayer as "a declaration of dependence"—and he has a point.

Prideful, self-sufficient people will never pray, because they don't believe they need God's help. The Bible reminds us that "God opposes the proud but gives grace to the humble" (1 Peter 5:5).

Second, seek God's will in your prayers. God wants us to bring our every concern to Him in prayer and to be persistent in our praying.

Third, bring everything to God in prayer. The Bible says, "In everything...present your requests to God" (Philippians 4:6).

Fourth, learn to pray at all times, and in all situations. Nothing can replace a daily time spent alone with God in prayer. The Bible says, "Pray continually" (1 Thessalonians 5:17). When Daniel's life was in danger because he refused to stop worshipping God, "he went home to his upstairs room... Three times a day he got down on his knees and prayed,...*just as he had done before"* (Daniel 6:10, emphasis added).

Fifth, trust God for the outcome. Sometimes God answers "Yes" when we ask Him for something. But sometimes His answer is "Not yet" or even "No." And sometimes His answer is simply "Trust Me, even if you don't understand."

Ruth's father, Dr. Bell, always kept a list of people for whom he was praying. After his death Ruth found one of his prayer lists. ("Mostly illegible," she commented. "You know how doctors write!" (On it was a specific concern about one of our children. Not until five years after his death was that prayer answered—a vivid reminder of God's faithfulness in answering prayer according to His timetable, not ours.

Finally, learn to listen. Prayer is speaking to God—but sometimes He uses our times of prayerful silence to speak to us in return. The Bible says, "Be still before the Lord and wait patiently for him" (Psalm 37:7).

Begin today making prayer central in your life. Pray because of Jesus' example. Pray because God has commanded it. Pray because Christ died to give us access to the Father. Pray because God is worthy of your praise and thanksgiving. Pray because you need His forgiveness and cleansing and His guidance and protection. Pray because others need your prayers.

Pray most of all because God *wants* your fellowship and you *need* His fellowship on this journey He has set before you.

Some readers may feel I have spent an inordinate time on this subject of prayer, but, if I am to hear of blessing upon blessing as Andrei serves the Lord in Bulgaria, he must encourage his people, though few in number, to pray. Matthew 14:23 expresses this need: *"After he had dismissed them, he went up on a mountainside by himself to pray. When evening came, he was there alone."*

Andrei must also remember that it is absolutely necessary that he keep his personal prayer time with the Lord a vital priority. He is our Father and as loving and obedient children we must maintain intimacy with Him. After all, He could have let us all die and go to hell. Because He loved us so much He gave His beloved Son, the sinless Lamb of God to take our punishment which we deserved, and made it possible for us to become children of the Most High God.

> *But because of his great love for us, God, who is rich in mercy, made us alive with Christ even when we were dead in transgressions—it is by grace you have been saved. And God raised us up with Christ and seated us with him in the heavenly realms in Christ Jesus, in order that in the coming ages he might show the incomparable riches of his grace, expressed in his kindness to us in Christ Jesus. For it is by grace you have been saved, through faith—and this not from yourselves, it is the gift of God—not by works, so that no one can boast. For we are God's workmanship, created in Christ Jesus to do good works, which God prepared in advance for us to do.*
>
> (Ephesians 2:4–10)

Recently, I heard someone say that this word "workmanship" actually means "masterpiece." Why then, are we so reluctant to maintain and take advantage of this intimacy with the God of the Universe? 2 Peter 3:18 (Amplified Bible): "*But grow in grace (undeserved favor, spiritual strength) and recognition and knowledge and understanding of our Lord and Savior Jesus Christ (the Messiah). To Him [be] glory (honor, majesty, and splendor) both now and to the day of eternity. Amen (so be it)!*"

Morning Prayer

I get up in the morning
To face another day,
And wonder what's in store for me
Along life's traveled way.
Before I start to do my work
With all its toil and care,
I stop and lift my eyes to God
And offer up a prayer.
I thank Him for the life I have,
The strength to do my work.
I ask Him to assist me
With the things I shouldn't shirk.
I also pray for others,
The sick, the lame, the blind,
For those who work with people
A better life to find.
This little talk I have with God
Just starts my day off right.
The things I do seem easier
From morning until night.
So first thing in the morning
Do this without delay;
Ask God for strength and guidance,
You'll have a better day.

—Ed Partington

We don't know the struggle King David was going through when he wrote Psalm 42, but it is apparent from the first two verses it was extremely difficult.

As the deer pants for streams of water,
so my soul pants for you, O God.
My soul thirsts for God, for the living God.
When can I go and meet with God?
My tears have been my food
day and night,
while men say to me all day long,
"Where is your God?"

The following quote is taken from a book written by Dutch Sheets, *Intercessory Prayer.*

Two frogs fell into a can of cream,
Or so it has been told.
The sides of the can were shiny and steep,
The cream was deep and cold.

"Oh, what's the use," said number one,
"It's plain no help's around.
Good-bye, my friend, good-bye, sad world"
and weeping still he drowned.

But number two, of sterner stuff,
Dog paddled in surprise
The while he licked his creamy lips
And blinked his creamy eyes.

"I'll swim at least a while," he thought,
or so it has been said.
It really wouldn't help the world
If one more frog were dead.

An hour or more he kicked and swam,
not once he stopped to mutter.
Then hopped out from the island he had
Made of fresh churned butter.
—*Author Unknown*

Lessons from Three Men and a Frog

I first heard this witty poem 20 years ago in a message by John Garlock, one of my professors at Christ for the Nations Institute, on the subject of tenacity.

Brother Garlock mentioned the story found in 2 Samuel 23:8–12 about three of David's mighty men: Shammah, Adino and Eleazar. Shammah had tenacity in the face of a humble assignment, defending a small plot of lentils from a bunch of Philistines. Adino personified tenacity in the face of overwhelming odds as he killed 800 Philistines single-handedly. Eleazar pictured tenacity in the face of incredible overwhelming fatigue as, after fighting for several hours, his hand had to be pried from his sword.

Thanks Professor Garlock, for teaching me through three men and a frog the importance of perseverance and endurance. "Hang in there" didn't make it into the Ten Commandments, but it did into the nine fruits of the Spirit.

In this day of instant everything—from 'fast foods' to 'get rich quick schemes' to 'how to have the biggest church in town overnight' conferences to 'four easy steps to answered prayer' seminars—we are rapidly losing the character trait of hanging in there. We cook faster, travel faster, produce faster and spend faster…and we expect God to keep pace with us, especially in prayer.

Many married couples today, at some point in their marriage, reach a stage where there is a lack of intimacy. This could be in their communication, decision-making or perhaps in their sexual life. This is always an unfortunate situation and quite often, without godly counselling, leads to separation and divorce. This is indeed sad.

But what about our intimacy with God, our Father? Many men and women never experience a closeness with their father. Many of us never knew our fathers and thus we have had to learn that God, as our Father, has saved us and longs to be intimate with us. The hymn-writer put it so beautifully for us when he urged us to "Tell it to Jesus."

Are you weary, are you heavy hearted?
Tell it to Jesus, tell it to Jesus.
Are you grieving over joys departed?
Tell it to Jesus alone.
Tell it to Jesus, tell it to Jesus,
He is a Friend that's well known.
You've no other such a friend or brother,
Tell it to Jesus alone.
Do the tears flow down your cheeks unbidden?
Tell it to Jesus, tell it to Jesus.
Have you sins that to men's eyes are hidden?
Tell it to Jesus alone.
Do you fear the gathering clouds of sorrow?
Tell it to Jesus, tell it to Jesus.
Are you anxious what shall be tomorrow?
Tell it to Jesus alone.
Are you troubled at the thought of dying?
Tell it to Jesus, tell it to Jesus.
For Christ's coming kingdom are you sighing?
Tell it to Jesus alone.
—Edmund S. Lorenz

There is an interesting passage of Scripture found in Hosea 2:19–20: *"And I will betroth you to Me forever; yes, I will betroth you to Me in righteousness and justice, in steadfast love, and mercy. I will even betroth you to Me in stability and faithfulness, and you shall know (recognize, be acquainted with, appreciate, give heed to, and cherish) the Lord"* (Amplified Bible). This verse indicates to us God's unconditional love and longing for closeness and intimacy.

Another old gospel song, not found in many of our hymnals, is *Teach Me to Pray.*

Teach me to pray, Lord, teach me to pray;
This is my heart-cry, day unto day.
I long to know Thy will and Thy way;
Teach me to pray, Lord, teach me to pray.
Living in Thee, Lord, and Thou in me,
Constant abiding, this is my plea;
Grant me Thy power, boundless and free,
Power with men and power with Thee.
Power in prayer, Lord, power in prayer!
Here mid earth's sin and sorrow and care,
Men lost and dying, souls in despair,
O give me power, power in prayer!
My weakened will, Lord, thou canst renew;
My sinful nature Thou canst subdue.
Fill me just now with power anew,
Power to pray and power to do!
Teach me to pray, Lord, teach me to pray;
Thou art my pattern day unto day.
Thou art my surety, now and for aye;
Teach me to pray, Lord, teach me to pray.
—Albert Simpson Reitz

Leanne Payne, in her book, *Restoring the Christian Soul,* has included a chapter entitled *Listening Prayer: The Way of Grace and the Walk in the Spirit*. She states in the opening paragraph, "The extraordinary wonderful thing about listening prayer is that it is not only the vital step we take toward self-acceptance, but it is also the same step that begins the walk in the Spirit for all of us, no matter what our psychological needs may be."

Quoting again from *Intercessory Prayer*, by Dutch Sheets:

> Father, please forgive us and deliver us. Set us free from being hearers of the Word only, and not doers. Give us homes and churches that are founded on the rock of obedience to Your Word. Rise up in Your people with the stubborn tenacity that Jesus had, that the Early Church walked in. Cause us to cast off

everything that would oppose Your Spirit and move us into a realm that pays a price and lays hold of the kingdom of God.

Fill us with Your Spirit. Baptize us in fire. Let there be an impartation of the Spirit of grace and supplication. Let there be an anointing that comes from Your throne to hungry people who are tired of status quo, of mediocrity, of death and destruction. We are tired of it, God. We are tired of being defeated by a defeated enemy. We are tired of being held back from our destiny, both individually and as a nation. We are tired of lack and disease. We are tired of sin. We are hungry for something—the God of the Bible!

Perhaps, and sadly, the poem below has often been true in our lives!

The Difference

I got up early one morning,
and rushed right into the day;
I had so much to accomplish
That I didn't take time to pray.
Problems just tumbling about me
and heavier came each task
"Why doesn't God help me?" I wondered,
He answered, "You didn't ask."
I wanted to see joy and beauty
but the day toiled on, gray and bleak.
I wondered why God didn't show me,
He said, "But you didn't see."
I tried to come into God's presence,
I used all my keys at the lock;
God gently and lovingly chided,
"My child, you didn't knock."
I woke up early this morning
and paused before entering the day;
I had so much to accomplish
that I HAD to take time to pray.

—Selected

Before I move on from this important subject of intimacy with our Heavenly Father, let me point out to you a truth God impressed upon my heart just today during my "quiet time" alone with God. I was reading from *The Message* (the Bible in contemporary language) from Hebrews 11:7, in that great chapter on the subject of faith. *"By faith, Noah built a ship in the middle of dry land. He was warned about something he couldn't see, and acted on what he was told. The result? His family was saved. His act of faith drew a sharp line between the evil of the unbelieving world and the rightness of the believing world. As a result,* ***Noah became intimate with God****"* (Emphasis mine).

Noah's intimacy with God was based on his faith. Hebrews 11 makes this very clear. But also, this intimacy with God was based on Noah's obedience to his God. In Genesis 6:22 we read, *"Noah did everything just as God commanded him."* Faith, obedience, intimacy with God, they are all linked together as we draw nigh to God. And the promise is given in James 4:8, "*and He will draw nigh to you*" (KJV). In 2 Peter 2:5 Noah is called *"a preacher of righteousness,"* although none of his sermons are recorded in Scripture. It is plain to see that he was a man who "walked the talk." Obviously, it was his godliness, faith, and obedience to God that spoke out to the wicked around him.

Jesus Himself exhorted us in Matthew 6:6, *"But when you pray go into your (most) private room, and, closing the door, pray to your Father Who is in secret; and your Father, Who sees in secret, will reward you in the open."* Mrs. Charles Cowman said it so beautifully in these words: "Prayer is not overcoming God's reluctance, but laying hold of His highest willingness."

There are countless numbers of books written by esteemed godly men and women on the subject of prayer, but we must learn to just do it! God will be pleased and we will be blest. One of the favourite phrases Leanne Payne uses often in her ministry and books is: "Practice the presence of Jesus." I jotted down some notes from a teaching session she gave concerning Listening Prayer.

1. Open and meditate upon Bible text.
2. Ask God to speak to you through His Word.
3. Then, quietly and patiently listen for God to speak.

Oswald Smith, founder of the Peoples Church in Toronto and missionary statesman wrote a hymn many years ago, long since forgotten and no longer found in newer hymnals. One statement I have always remembered: "...will not someone stop and listen?"

Chapel of My Heart

There's a place where God is very near,
Where His gentle touch I feel;
A place where I can speak to Him,
His presence very real.
—*Selected*

At the beginning of this chapter you will have noted that I quoted 2 Timothy 2:1–3. Further, in 2 Timothy 4:2, Paul exhorts his son in the faith, *"Herald and preach the Word! Keep your sense of urgency [stand by, be at hand and ready], whether the opportunity seems to be favorable or unfavorable [Whether it is convenient or inconvenient, whether it is welcome or unwelcome, you as preacher of the Word are to show people in what way their lives are wrong.]. And convince them, rebuking and correcting, warning and urging and encouraging them, being unflagging and inexhaustible in patience and teaching"* (Amplified). *Our Daily Bread* devotional has put it well when it said: "In a changing world you can trust God's unchanging Word."

There's never a lack of God's power
In prayer and reading God's Word;
For Jesus in Heaven is listening
Your prayer will always be heard.
—*Author Unknown*

The Psalmist over and over again emphasized the importance of the Word of God in his life. Of the many recorded, Psalm 119:105–106 says, *"Your word is a lamp to my feet and a light for my path. I have taken an oath and confirmed it, that I will follow your righteous laws."* I urged Andrei to make the preaching and teaching of God's Word a priority in his ministry.

Holy Bible, Book divine,
Precious treasure, thou art mine;
Mine to tell me whence I came;
Mine to teach me what I am.
Mine to chide me when I rove;
Mine to show a Savior's love;
Mine thou art to guide and guard;
Mine to punish or reward.
Mine to comfort in distress;
Suffering in this wilderness;
Mine to show, by living faith,
Man can triumph over death.
Mine to tell of joys to come,
And the rebel sinner's doom;
O thou holy Book divine,
Precious treasure, thou art mine.
— *John Burton, Sr.*

Evangelical scholar Lewis Drummond has written a recently published book, *The Evangelist, The Worldwide Impact of Billy Graham*. The Foreword of the book was written by a well-known British preacher, John R. W. Stott, who said, "No single person in the twentieth century has been more influential for Christ than Billy Graham." John Stott commenced his foreword of the book with the following paragraph:

> It was, I believe, an Episcopal [Anglican] clergyman who lodged a complaint against Billy Graham during the 1949 "Christ for Greater Los Angeles Crusade." His criticism was that Billy Graham had set back the cause of religion a hundred years. Billy Graham's rejoinder was typical. "I did indeed *want* to set religion back," he said, "not just 100 years but 1900 years, to the Book of Acts, when first century followers of Christ were accused of turning the Roman Empire upside down."

Matthew 7:24–25 says, *"So everyone who hears these words of Mine and acts upon them [obeying them] will be like a sensible (prudent, practical, wise) man who built his house upon the rock. And the rain fell and the floods came and the winds blew and beat against that house; yet it did not fall, because it had been founded on the rock."*

Again I quote from Evangelist Billy Graham: "Study the Bible constantly…" and then he goes on to explain and compare the Old Testament with the New Testament. "The New Testament is *contained* in the Old Testament. The Old Testament is *explained* in the New Testament."

Further to all I have said above in exhorting Andrei to be the humble and successful pastor/evangelist God wants him to be is to acknowledge the explosive power and absolute necessity of being filled with the Spirit of God. The Apostle Paul also made it abundantly clear in Romans 5:5 that we are indwelt with the Holy Spirit upon salvation. Most Bible readers are well acquainted with the text in the Old Testament that Zechariah heard from an angel of the Lord, *"'Not by might nor by power, but by my Spirit,' says the Lord Almighty"* (Zechariah 4:6).

So many of us are in danger, while not intentionally, of serving the Lord in our own limited strength, forgetting that we have been clearly instructed in Ephesians 5:18, *"…be filled with the Spirit."* I have sung the following gospel song so many times and I want to share it with you now:

Come, Holy Spirit

Come as a wisdom to children,
Come as new sight to the blind,
Come, Lord as strength to my weakness,
Take me soul, body and mind.
Come, Holy Spirit, I need you,
Come sweet Spirit, I pray,
Come in Your strength and Your power,
Come in Your own gentle way.
Come as a rest to the weary,
Come as a balm for the sore,

Come as a dew to my dryness:
Fill me with joy evermore.
Come like a spring in the desert,
Come to the withered of soul,
O let Your sweet healing power
Touch me and make me whole.
—Bill and Gloria Gaither

I wish I could conclude this chapter on my young friend, Andrei, on a more positive note, but being honest and real, I must tell you where he is at in his ministry and life today. As I mentioned near the beginning of this chapter, Andrei was called to be the pastor of his home church.

The church had an apartment attached to the church building for their pastor. They spent considerable time fixing, repairing, painting, and furnishing the apartment for this young couple. With a full-time pastor, the church started to grow, with souls being saved and backsliders restored.

However, after less than a year, Andrei was faced with a dilemma. His wife was lonely for her home and parents and wanted to take their small son and return to her family home. Andrei was devastated. He expected this would end in divorce and could very well hurt or even make it impossible to serve the Lord full time. Pavlina's parents even offered to give them a piece of land and build them a house if they would return. So Pavlina and the baby left and went back to her parents' home.

I then suggested to Andrei that he join them and commute back and forth to the church, spending a long weekend at the church and the rest of the time with his family. He felt this would be somewhat difficult because of the drive of several hours and the cost of the gasoline. Eventually he decided this would be the best alternative to what was a heartbreaking situation for him.

A few months after this arrangement, Andrei sent me several pictures of the baby, and one of them was Andrei himself holding his son. I didn't recognize him and thought it must be another member of the family. He was very thin and looked very haggard. When he replied to my concern he confessed that he was completely exhausted and was busy putting the finishing touches on the new house into which they planned to move in a matter of days. Going back and forth to the church, helping with the baby and building the house was taking its toll. I assured him of my continued prayers for him and his little family. He thought that the Lord might very well open a door of ministry nearer to where they lived.

Andrei told me he was offered a scholarship to take a Masters Degree in Theology at a Presbyterian seminary in South Carolina in the United States. He would be in the "distance program," which meant he would spend one month at the seminary in the spring and one in the fall and the rest of the program would be through the Internet. He was seeking the Lord's will as to what he should do. Although tuition, books, room and board were all included he would have the expense of the airfare and other incidentals.

When I last heard from Andrei, he was struggling with what he should do. He confessed to me he had doubts about taking up this offer but I suspect it was the expense that most concerned him.

I am reminded of a portion of Scripture found in Psalm 50:14–15: *"Offer to God the sacrifice of thanksgiving, and pay your vows to the Most High, and call on Me in the day of trouble; I will deliver you, and you shall honor and glorify Me"* (Amplified Bible). This is what Andrei has done all through his seminary training and ministry. He has glorified and honoured God in all he has sought to do.

I wrote Andrei and quoted a short poem by Dr. D. Dehaan of the Day of Discovery Ministry:

Thank God in your disappointment,
Celebrate His grace and love;
Know that He will never leave you
And will bless you from above.

Andrei has set before us an example of a young and godly man. I trust that the life of this young man will be a challenge to each one of us. Andrei has struggled in his journey, facing tremendous odds, in a country still suffering from decades of communism. Yet he is still focused on Jesus and the call to the ministry to which God has prepared him.

I trust the words of the writer to the Hebrews will comfort and invigorate Andrei to follow where God leads him. Hebrews 13:5b, "*For he Himself has said, 'I will never leave you nor forsake you.'*"

> "I am learning to step out of God's way and just do nothing but say, 'Yes, Lord.'"
> —*Selected*

"For I know the plans I have for you,' declares the LORD, 'plans to prosper you and not to harm you, plans to give you hope and a future. Then you will call upon me and come and pray to me, and I will listen to you. You will seek me and find me when you seek me with all your heart.'"

(Jeremiah 29:11–13)

I have asked my daughter (and editor) to write her own story of her journey. Judith is a remarkable woman who has learned what Paul experienced when he said in Philippians 4:10–13, *"For I have learned to be content whatever the circumstances…I have learned the secret of being content in any and every situation…I can do everything through him who gives me strength."*

Dad has quoted a number of stories from the book *Goforth of China* by Rosalind Goforth. Mom and Dad have visited me in Winnipeg over the years. On what was to be their last visit in August 2004, Dad brought me his copy of this book. I was thrilled to receive it as a gift from him because I remembered this book from when I was an eight-year-old child!

I asked Dad to write in it before he and Mom left to go home because it had such special meaning for me (which you will understand from his note). This particular copy was printed in 1937. I was expecting some small sentiment from Dad and it wasn't until after they went home that I opened the book to read what Dad had written. I was very touched by his words and writing and from that time on considered it to be Dad's blessing to me as his daughter.

If as a dad you have never said or written a blessing to your children, I would encourage you to look into the impact this can have on your children. In the meantime, here is Dad's blessing to me:

> August 17, 2004
>
> Dear, dear Judith, Many, many years ago when you were a very little girl, we experienced a real crisis in our home in Hamilton. Your Mom was very sick and although both Grannie Corrigan and Grannie Russell came to help it seemed all our attention and care was focused on your Mom.
>
> You and the boys were well looked after with all the physical needs you required but sadly, not the emotional and spiritual help you needed. You were aware of how sick Mom was and down deep in your heart you longed for her to get better and things return to normal.
>
> Well, thanks be to God, Mom did get better and as usual soon was as busy as ever in our home and her work in the church. And then you became sick and landed in the hospital.
>
> When you were just learning to walk and talk I would ask you if you wanted Daddy to rock you in our little rocking chair and you responded, "I go get my banket." (blanket). Those were precious days in Meaford when I had the time to sit and rock you and many times you would drop off to sleep. Those were precious memories.
>
> Now you were older and with all the books I might have chosen for you that would have been more appropriate and more for your age level, I brought this book, and for hours every day you would cuddle on my knees with a blanket wrapped around

you and I would read and you would listen. We were anxious for your well-being and it was a stressful time for our whole family. As we got into the book, we would both be wiping tears from our eyes. But through a period of great concern it was a precious time.

Well, life hasn't turned out as we thought or would have liked. You have suffered excruciating pain and a tremendous challenge to carry on since your injury. But you keep 'coming back' after every set back and carry on. You can certainly sing, "Through it all, through it all, I've learned to trust in Jesus, I've learned to read His Word…" and you have become a spiritual woman who just carries on loving and serving the Lord as well as your family and friends.

We are proud of you and love you dearly. You have been a blessing. And in spite of ups and downs in our lives we are still a family and God has been so good and so faithful.

God bless,

Affectionately, Dad

As you can see from what Dad has written above, crisis in our family is not something new. We have had so many serious illnesses and events in our lives over the years, but each and every time we have known and experienced the hand of God in everything. So at the time of my injury, there was already a long history of God's faithfulness to look back on and be encouraged by—stepping stones of faith.

I also realize and acknowledge that any time I share my story there are many others who have had or are experiencing suffering in their own lives. My story is an avenue for all who hear or read it to become vulnerable within their own spirits to ask God to do what Isaiah wrote about in Chapter 61, verses 2b–3, "*…to comfort all who mourn, to provide for those who grieve in Zion—to bestow on them a* ***crown of beauty*** *instead of ashes, the* ***oil of gladness*** *instead of mourning, and a* ***garment of praise*** *instead of a spirit of despair. They will be called oaks of righteousness, a planting of the LORD for the display of his splendour*" (emphasis mine).

So I tell this story to encourage you and to remind us of how much God loves us and uses *all* of our difficult circumstances for His glory. Life sometimes seems like a long journey, but this part will end when we meet Jesus face to face.

When God lead me to Bible college in a small town just outside of Winnipeg, little did I know how much He would use this experience in my life to show me so much of Himself in the lives of people I would meet. I was confused with what was Scripture and what was "Church" and it was my intention to begin sorting out some of these things.

I met Steve and Jackie Masterson at Providence Bible College. They took me in and made me a part of their family. I did lots of babysitting and spent as much time with them as I could. They taught me through example what God's heart was for me and began a process in me through the Spirit of God. It was a progression of events over time that brought me to where I was by the time I arrived at this next critical event that took place in my life.

God has taught me much through this experience, and continues to do so. Biblical teaching is no longer just something I learned in church, Bible school, or seminary. It has become a way of life.

I love the way these verses in Peterson's translation, *The Message*, popped out for me. It is in Matthew 8 where a leper came to Jesus and asked for healing. After Jesus healed him, he told him not to talk about it all over town. *"Just quietly present your healed body to the priest, along with the appropriate expression of thanks to God. Your cleansed and grateful life, not your words, will bear witness to what I have done."*

Come with me as I share my gratefulness for the grace of God and His strength as He lives His life through me in my wheelchair. If you are in the midst of your own difficult circumstances, let God use these thoughts to begin healing in your own heart.

Just before my injury occurred, I was struggling with years of chronic back pain, now known as fibromyalgia. I was stressed with this pain causing so much misery in my job and actually dictating whether I stayed in nursing or not. As a registered nurse, the physical toll was forcing me to make some difficult decisions. Some friends had been talking to me about having healing prayers with anointing of oil but I was very hesitant about this as I was not sure what I would do with God if healing did not happen. I was also trying to shield myself from further disappointment if one more thing did not work. I did not think life could get any harder! I definitely felt at a crossroads.

It was 1988. I was at a Bible camp on a church retreat over the weekend; it was Father's Day and we were just finishing up with games and soon heading home. The bell tower, made up of 2 x 10s and a cedar roof, lifted off the base and collapsed. The pole it was on hit me and fractured and crushed my vertebrae, damaging the spinal cord. Famed theologians would turn over in their graves at the simplicity of my theology, but I believe the tower fell as a result of us living in a fallen world and at the moment of impact God's Sovereignty took over. God ultimately decided the extent of my injuries and what He was asking me to live with.

When I became conscious, I knew the people who were talking to me in spite of some other memory loss and I could still move my hands and arms. I knew enough to know I was paralyzed but told them I would be alright as I could still knit and hold babies! I've mostly given up on the knitting but still do the baby thing! The injury left me paralyzed from the mid-chest down, and I have no sensation to touch, pain or temperature.

God made me very aware of his presence in the Emergency room. They had put a tube down my nose into my stomach. This was extremely uncomfortable and I was panicking trying to catch my breath. I knew they would just have to put it back in but panic was greater than logic. My eyes were closed as I reached up to pull it out. I suddenly felt someone pulling my hands away from my face and forcing them down to my side. I opened my eyes to see who was there and the cubicle was empty! That was the beginning of the ride of my life!

The first night in hospital was physically critical. My friend Jackie spent the night with me. We had a very special time together in those first hours following the injury. During that time, as I began thinking over what had just happened, I realized my whole life had been turned upside down never to be the same again. Yet I lay there, feeling so peaceful and calm. There was no reality denial—I was very well aware of the gravity of the situation. No, this was different. I knew this peace came from God—peace that passes all understanding (Philippians 4:7). I finally knew what this verse really meant! Here I was in circumstances that seemed unbelievable, and yet peace pervaded and gave me comfort while the world looked on and mourned for the loss.

I believe it was during this first night and over the next few days that God miraculously took me through inner healing. It was realizing I was the most helpless I had ever been yet so aware of God and friends and family still loving me in spite of this helplessness.

There was nothing in all of my years as a registered nurse that prepared me for what I was about to go through. I had looked after paraplegics and quadriplegics in my early days of nursing and vowed then I would rather die than live through such a tragedy. But oh, the grace of God! Lamentations 3:21–23 says: *"Yet this I recall to mind, and* ***therefore I have hope****. Because of the Lord's great love we are not consumed, for His compassions never fail. They are new every morning;* ***great*** *is your faithfulness"* (emphasis mine).

I remember within the first few days of my injury asking for my book by Corrie ten Boom, *The Hiding Place*. Dad has referred to her in previous chapters. Having met her as a child, her story had always been meaningful to me. I remembered something in it that I wanted to look up.

Here it is: As a child, Corrie had been frightened by visiting a home where a baby had died in the night. When her father came up the stairs to tuck her in she burst into tears, afraid that her father would leave her by dying.

> "Corrie," he began gently, "when you and I go to Amsterdam—when do I give you your ticket?" "Why, just before we get on the train."
>
> "Exactly. And our wise Father in heaven knows when we're going to need things, too. Don't run out ahead of Him, Corrie. When the time comes that some of us will have to die, you will look into your heart and find the strength you need—just in time."

This is what God was doing in me. I didn't need to know any sooner than the moment it happened that I could live through it. God's grace gives us what we need when we need it, and in the proportion it is required. People often said to me in those early days they wouldn't "handle" it as well. Oh yes they would! God's grace is there for you, too, in your painful moments, if you choose to allow God to make it available to you.

I was in hospital for three-and-a-half months. It was a long, arduous task and the situation surrounding the staff on the ward was less than ideal. But God gave me a roommate Dad had met at the first hospital and we were a constant source of encouragement to each other.

There were difficult days during the six weeks on bed rest. My body coped with the stress and trauma through nausea and vomiting. This plagued me throughout my entire hospital stay with only an occasional break. I also had two bouts of anxiety attacks, when my body shook from the inside out, and it wouldn't stop for days. Dr. Taylor, a former professor of mine at Bible college and member of my church, came to visit during one of those spells, and read Isaiah 43:2: "*When you pass through the waters, I will be with you; and when you pass through the rivers, they will not sweep over you. When you walk through the fire, you will not be burned…*"

These were such words of comfort to me. I couldn't expect God to necessarily take away these hard things, but I could count on His promise of staying and going through it with me. I clung to this promise. It became my hope.

As I began thinking about coming off bed rest and getting up in the chair, I became aware of the grim facts. I had to start all over again. I didn't know how to sit up, turn over, get dressed, look after my personal needs, and the list went on. My prayer on waking each morning, once I started getting up, was for God's grace to face the day, for His strength to do the task at hand, and most of all, for great courage to keep fighting, work hard and not give up. I was always good at starting things but not a great finisher.

My mom was able to stay with me for three months and kept me encouraged. I realized well after the fact how difficult it must have been for her during those months. She was away from Dad and my sister all that time and missed them. I was also aware that she sat there every day in physiotherapy, watching me learn how to do these basic activities all over again. These were all the things she had lovingly watched me do as a growing baby but in these extreme circumstances was watching me start all over again!

The rehabilitation process continued long after I left the hospital. It took a very long time to regain upper body strength and over the years that has fluctuated. But I am also doing things I thought would never be possible. I am wheelchair-independent, and in my own home. This has not come about without dealing with the harsh reality and pain that this is how I am spending the rest of my life. But in all of this, God knows what He is doing.

People would often warn me that I would probably have to deal with depression at some point. This was often a caution voiced as I was doing so well emotionally and spiritually. It seemed there was concern that I would come off of this "high" and eventually crash.

I had dealt with depression before because of my chronic pain and I knew the darkness it could bring. I did not want to have to go there again but knew it could happen as part of the process of this injury.

I was at my kitchen sink one night. It was in the dead of winter when it seemed there were barely any hours of sunlight. In the early months of my discharge I had very long, deep sleeps in the afternoon and by the time I woke up it was dark out. As I was doing the dishes I saw a picture of a black cloud coming toward me. I knew it was the black cloud of depression and I could feel the darkness and heaviness settling in.

I started to cry and then pray. I acknowledged this was a normal part of the process and if God was asking me to bear this burden then I would enter into it. But as I was praying, God brought some other things to mind. I realized that as supportive and loving as my friends and family had been there was a part of my heart and soul that they could not enter into with me. It was a level of pain and anguish that only God could reach and He had been there with me every step of the way.

Because of these thoughts I realized I did not have to go through depression. It had not yet happened because God was already doing a work in my heart that was very deep and very real. As these thoughts came to mind, I saw the black cloud start to move away and then disappear. My heavy heart became lighter and I have not had to deal with any major depression.

None of this is to say I do not have any bad days. God has never promised that days always come trouble-free. But He gives grace for each and every day, and at the end of a day, whether it be good or bad, there is the realization that God has brought me through and allowed me to finish the tasks that He set before me for that day.

Many years have now passed since those early months and years in the wheelchair. There are so many blessings that God keeps pouring into my life. There are constant reminders of how much God's timing and grace is set before me.

I have always had what I call a "wheelchair" baby! God has put families into my life who have had the courage to leave me with a newborn and go out on "date night"! These different babies have grown with the chair, and my lap is a favourite place for children to this day.

I have been in and out of the hospital many times over the years. God has seen me through each of these life-threatening illnesses, giving my spirit a sense of trust and well-being for whatever the outcome.

One of those hospitalizations was in the summer of 2000. I was hospitalized for what ended up being a life and death battle with my body. I was in the hospital for seven weeks. It happened on holidays in Ottawa where I had spent my teen and early adult years (I now live in Winnipeg). What a gift that time became for me.

It was such a special time to have visits with friends I had known for years. We had lots of "catch-up" time that only added to the warmth of past memories. It was also a time of returning to God's grace for the moment and the day; to trust Him once again with the physical consequences of what my body was putting me through.

Once healing had taken place, I experienced a sense of urgency in my spirit. It is difficult to describe, but it reminded me very clearly that all we have is *now* and each day must be spent directing that urgency to the things that are eternal.

In January of 2002 I was hit with another physical complication, testing again how much I would trust God for each day. I started having stiffness and pain in my upper body joints where I had feeling. It seemed to progress with each day and within a few weeks I could no longer do my transfers in and out of bed.

My dad had come out for a visit and was soon going to be returning to Toronto. When we realized I could not be left alone for more than a couple of hours at a time, Mom and Dad decided he would stay with me until things improved.

In the morning, when it was time to get up, there was excruciating pain in my joints. It felt like ripping apart a chicken bone at the joint where the gristle is. One morning, as I was part way up, I stared at the wall trying to get up the courage to put my weight onto my arms to push the rest of the way up. It was at this point of my transfer that it hurt the most. I then began praying. I asked the Lord to give me back my one-day-at-a-time and even one moment at a time.

God is so faithful in our suffering. If God was asking me to live with this level of pain, then my prayer became one of asking Him to teach me how to do this. I was eventually diagnosed with severe rheumatoid arthritis. It seemed a much more difficult diagnosis to live with than my paralysis. Other than acute illnesses and eventual complications, my paraplegia is fairly stable. Rheumatoid arthritis is progressive and very debilitating, especially not having my lower body to help out.

I felt a great sense of loss as my activities had been greatly limited and reduced. I could no longer look after myself. I went through so much with the process of finding the right combination of medications without the side effects being too dangerous.

As my limitations continued, God gave me pictures of other people with severe arthritis—people I had met long before my own diagnosis. These were pictures of people very severely crippled and yet having a wonderful attitude in spite of their pain, finding ways to impact their world from the confinement of their beds.

What a loving God we have. He would later bring them to mind and use them in my own life to reassure me there would always be purpose in everything he allowed. Once again, God used pain and suffering to teach me deeper truths and greater dependence on Him.

It was three-and-a-half months later that my dad was able to leave and return back home. It must have been Dad's turn to spend time with me while Mom was left at home! It was not at all what we had planned, but God's timing is always perfect and there was further healing and blessing brought about in Dad's life because of my illness.

The following is part of a devotional by John Fischer, who writes the daily devotional for *Purpose Driven Life*. I quote this as it expresses my heart so much more eloquently and clearly.

God's Economy

God's economy is all about turning our hardship into help for someone else. There is a purpose in pain. It's never pleasant at the time, but it bears fruit for others. The process is quite simple really. I go through something that necessitates my receiving resources from God to get through it. And while God is strengthening me, the strength that He gives me is something I can share with someone else, especially someone going through a similar difficulty.

Paul puts it this way in 2 Corinthians 1:3–5. "Praise be to the God and Father of our Lord Jesus Christ, the Father of compassion and the Lord of all comfort, who comforts us in all our troubles, so that we can comfort those in any trouble with the comfort we ourselves have received from God. For just as the sufferings of Christ flow over into our lives, so also through Christ our comfort overflows."

There you have it. Overflowing comfort. When we're going through a hard time, God gives us more than enough to cope, so we'll have something leftover to share with someone else, thus giving us a purpose even in our hardship. This is so important because one of the tendencies when things go bad is to think that our life is suddenly pointless and wasted. We find it hard to wrestle anything good out of the bad things that happen to us. But the good is always there, and if we can't see it, it's because we aren't tuned into God's economy. We are just looking at the situation from one point of view, and it happens to be the most depressing one.

Did you notice, also, that our sufferings and comfort both come from the same source? We share in the sufferings of Christ so that we can share in the comfort that comes from Christ as well. That's God's economy.

So are you going through it right now? Are you asking God, "Why?" and not getting any answers? Well, at its most basic level, the unique set of circumstances that set you up for this are such that they will qualify you to help someone else in a similar situation. So if that someone should say to you, "You can't possibly know what I'm going through," you will be able to say, "Oh yeah? Let me tell you my story and show you how God met me." It keeps circling around like that. That's part of God's economy.

Eventually the right medication was established, and along with a healthy, specific diet my arthritis has stabilized. God has given me a level of physical function and strength that I have not had for many years. After seven years (now nine) with this disease, I have minimal to no joint damage. I can still make a tight fist with no pain and realize how much God has protected my body from the ravages of this disease.

In the summer of 2005, God once again brought difficult circumstances to bear on our family. My sister and her husband were expecting their third child, already having a four-year-old son and a two-year-old daughter. I needed to pick a date to leave Winnipeg and drive to Toronto, as I wanted to be there to help when this baby arrived.

It had been four years since I was last able to travel and so I was thrilled with the prospect of being able to make this trip and thankful God had given me this measure of health. I prayed a very simple prayer when I chose the date to leave Winnipeg. Little did I know the huge impact this prayer would have. My prayer was asking God to work out the details of the baby's birth (being a high-risk pregnancy) and the timing of my departure.

By the time I left for Toronto, my brother-in-law had been diagnosed with malignant melanoma (the most serious skin cancer). He had a few surgeries, all of which happened very quickly as God had given them a doctor friend who was able to see them through all the details of this illness.

When I arrived, my dad was in the hospital for the third time over a short period and was even more seriously ill than before. My brother-in-law had been home a few days from his final surgery and the baby was to be induced in a couple of days.

When my nephew was born, there were no risks or complications and he was able to come home the next day instead of being in Intensive Care. The first two babies had been in Intensive Care so we were thankful in the midst of already very difficult circumstances God had blessed us with no complications. He was very well aware of our limits.

To summarize this very long summer, Dad's health continued to deteriorate, Mom suffered a small stroke a week after the baby was born, and my sister's husband still had to go through a month of intravenous treatment at the hospital! We were definitely in overload!

I am still amazed as I look back over that summer how God took care of each little detail. His timing was so perfect in so many ways. One of the incredible ways he cared for us through this time was giving me the strength to be able to help at such a huge level. It was beyond anything I had been able to do for many years.

As demanding as the crises were, I would not have traded any of the time I had with the little ones and other family members. We built some wonderful memories that cannot be taken from us.

In early September 2008, my wheelchair-accessible van was stolen out of my garage during the night! There are no words to describe the astonishment of those moments and the realization that it was *gone!* Little did I know the path this would take. It became high profile through the media and along with amazing family and friends I was surrounded and loved and very sure of God's hand in this process. I knew I was covered by many prayers raised to the Father on my behalf. At first it looked like I might get a new van through fundraising, but within three weeks of the theft it was found abandoned in the streets of Edmonton! Certainly none of this made sense and there are absolutely no definitive answers as to whom or why, other than they obviously wanted to get to Edmonton!

During the time I was waiting for the van to be repaired, I also had an appointment with Rehab Seating Clinic. My purpose for this visit was to get a new custom seat and back for my wheelchair to correct the way I was sitting in the chair. The muscles needed to hold my spine straight are paralyzed and over the last year or so there had been a lot of deterioration and I had become very crooked. This was causing increased fatigue, pain, and weakness.

This rehab visit with my Community Occupational Therapist (OT) and the Rehab OT resulted in not just needing new seating but also needing to change to a different wheelchair! Not something I was expecting and it certainly left me feeling overwhelmed. I am in a program where I have a free wheelchair.

My OTs were asking if I could go outside the program, which, translated, means I would have to pay for it. They wanted me to try a "Cadillac" wheelchair so I could see the difference—the "Cadillac" version costing five-thousand dollars! The therapists suggested that we look into some fundraising options.

I left, still feeling very overwhelmed. As I was waiting for my taxi, I saw a man who looked to be quadriplegic wheeling past me. I also realized that he had whizzed past me with only one or two strokes of his arms in his manual wheelchair! Over the next few minutes I began processing what I had just seen. This must be one of those titanium light-weight wheelchairs (the "Cadillac" version), and the ease with which he was able to wheel, with more limited arm strength than I have, totally amazed me. I knew in those moments this was the way to go. But there was the issue of five-thousand dollars!

Just after I came in the door, the phone started ringing. It was my friend Steve Bell, checking in on me to see where the van repairs were at. Before I knew it I was telling him the events of the morning. This wheelchair was the difference between functioning and barely functioning.

Steve was very understanding with what this chair would mean and because we were not doing a fundraiser for the van he turned it into a wheelchair fundraiser. I was hesitant to even expect anyone to do this, but Steve was more than willing.

Steve Bell is a Christian singer/songwriter/storyteller extraordinaire. It is said of him, "Beyond the numbers and the crowded trophy shelf lies the fact that his songs, music, and concerts resonate deeply within the hearts and souls of his fans, providing both solace and inspiration. It is this connection, rather than platinum plaques to hang on the wall, that is Bell's true goal and his most real achievement."

This description of him is what translates from the stage into real life. Steve is not one persona in a performance and another sitting in your living room. It is this genuine spirit of kindness and giving that is "Steve."

In all of this I was overwhelmed with his love and care for me. He and his wife Nanci had been walking through this journey of the van along with so many others. No "coincidence" that Steve was on the phone when I got home from Rehab! He is always on the road and a very busy man, never mind having time to be calling and checking on me!

Mid-November I was set up with a new trial system—new seat, new back, new wheelchair! OT had me go for a wheel in the department. There were some practice ramps in another area and I was able to get up them by myself with very little effort! I could not believe the difference. This trial was to be approximately two weeks.

There was certainly some adjusting with balance and pain from moving my body into a new position. I was amazed at how easily I could get through the snow and ice when winter set in. I was able to keep up with all of my errands again.

Then the community OT called and said the retailer was letting me keep the chair over the holidays until my mid-January appointment back at rehab. What a gift and a real blessing.

The time came in mid-January to give back the trial chair and seating. I would then wait for the fundraiser in April and order my new chair. The Sunday before this appointment, someone at church came to me and said there was a group of businessmen who were willing to give me the money for the chair upfront so I could order it right away and then pay them back when we had the fundraiser! I was blown away! It was yet another clear way God was reminding me of how he cares for me time and again!

This friend told me to just stay in the chair on Tuesday and tell him he couldn't have it back because I was not getting out of it! He also suggested the retailer might let me keep it since I was going to order it right away. But I knew from my OT that he already needed the trial chair for someone else.

The night before my appointment was very stressful and teary. I prayed that God would give me the grace to face the huge change and embrace whatever that meant. I realized this was the first winter since getting rheumatoid arthritis that I was not having a winter flare-up. My joints had started aching quite badly on a regular basis just before I got the trial chair and the ease of functioning in this chair seemed to have actually helped my joints! I was only having occasional mild pain and swelling.

And so the morning began! The community OT told me that she had told the retailer before Christmas about this Christian musician who was going to do a fundraiser for me. That's when he told her, "Oh no! She's got God on her side. I better let her keep it!" Wow! (A few tears on hearing that!)

OT had a different chair back I could use so I was grateful for that. One of my biggest concerns had been about going back to the old one. The OT and I started going through all the options related to ordering the new chair while the retailer was setting up my old chair. They were all thrilled when they found out I could order it right away.

The retailer was having a hard time getting the brackets to work on my old chair and it took well over an hour to get that part of it done. Besides the problems with the mechanics of doing the new back on my chair—my own seat cushion with the gel had frozen in the van overnight and it still wasn't thawing! I should not have left it in the van but never thought about it at the time! The OT said she could not let me keep the current seat I was using for the trial as it was already overdue and had to go back to the department.

Then it became clear that my cushion was not going to thaw in time so she got a different seat that was a bit oversized and we then began stuffing it with all the extras it needed to try to keep me straight. Then the time finally came for me to get into my own chair.

Absolutely *nothing* could have prepared me for what happened when I got into that chair! Because my body had been in a completely different position for two months—I had *no* idea where most of my body was. I didn't know how to move to put it anywhere and I could not let go without falling over. It felt like I was sitting almost completely sideways!

We just all stared at each other in disbelief, then the OT said we had to do a number of things to my chair to try to get it so I could sit in it! The retailer then said, "You're ordering it today?" "Yes." "Oh just keep it till your new chair comes—it's too much work to make all the changes to your chair." Then the OT said, "You can't sit on your cushion, it's too cold. I am going to let you keep the same cushion on the condition that if I have an emergency come up I get it back right away."

By this time I was in shock and very quickly got out of my chair and back into the "trial" chair! We had been at this for a total of *four* hours! We had all definitely had enough at that point! But out of this frustration and weariness came this huge blessing and gift!

All things work together for good. It was all this hard stuff with the back not going together easily and my cushion not thawing and the fact that if I hadn't been told there were funds to order the chair right away…God's timing is so perfect! This is all so amazing to me. What an incredible gift! This was a two-week trial that turned into two months and will now go on for another six weeks! God loves doing what we see as impossible!

As I got home and started trying to process all of this it seemed it all started with the van being stolen…God took something so hard and brought good out of it…the idea of a fundraiser being a possibility for the van…which brought about being able to fundraise for the wheelchair… right through to that Sunday at church with the funds being available right away.

Most of the time we only see the messy side of life. We don't always know what God is doing with the big picture. I love that every once in awhile we get to peak around the corner from the back side of the tapestry and see some of the beautiful weaving that is all part of his incredible plan for our lives.

It's not that I am surprised God would do all of this—I think it is more that I am overwhelmed with the fact that he cares so much about the everydayness of our lives and chooses to bless us in ways we don't expect. He delights in loving us lavishly and using all of our circumstances (good and bad) to bring about his best for us.

A quote by an unknown author which summarizes this and so many other events in my life says:

> I know discouragement comes easy, but I also know things happen when God is ready for them to happen and not a second sooner. God knows why he wants things to happen in the order they have to. We just need to be ready when they come.

I can look back over the years and see how God's hand was on my life and the ways in which he was looking after me and helping me find my way to his heart and his joy and contentment. I am somewhat of a wounded warrior.

I know there were people praying for healing. Their prayers were for physical healing because they could not bear the tragedy of what was happening. But I saw no need to be healed of my paralysis. The inner healing that had taken place was so real and I knew if I were healed of my paralysis we would give God the glory and over time life would become normal and busy and once in awhile we would remind ourselves of divine healing…but as long as I remained in this chair it would be a constant reminder of my need for God and his faithfulness in my life.

I am more blessed in this chair than I ever was on my feet. I know who I was then and I know who I have become through this chair. More importantly, I know who God is. God continues to pour blessing into my life. I truly believe that I am one of those people who needs to be reminded on a regular basis I cannot live my life without being connected to my Father. It is a constant reminder of God's faithfulness and overwhelming love and delight for me. There is nothing I can ever do that will stop his extravagant love for me.

The Lord is my light and my salvation—
whom shall I fear?
The Lord is the stronghold of my life—
of whom shall I be afraid?
I am still confident of this:
I will see the goodness of the LORD
in the land of the living.
—Psalm 27:1,13

Joni Eareckson Tada has written many books. Friends gifted me more recently with one I had not yet read entitled *The God I Love.* I cannot help but give you the following quote—not because I can even come close to experiencing her years of suffering, but because she expresses my heart so much more clearly than my own words. Those of you who walk the road of suffering on a regular basis will most likely be able to connect to her words as well.

> "Lord, your no answer to physical healing meant yes to a deeper healing—a better one. Your answer has bound me to other believers and taught me so much about myself. It's purged sin from my life, it's strengthened my commitment to you, forced me to depend on your grace. Your wiser, deeper answer has stretched my hope, refined my faith, and helped me to know *you* better. And you are good. You are so good."
>
> I let the tears fall.
>
> "I know I wouldn't know you…I wouldn't love and trust you…were it not for—"
>
> I looked down at my paralyzed legs.
>
> "—for this wheelchair."
>
> …There are more important things in life than walking.

I want to close this chapter with a song that I want sung at my memorial service when God calls me home, unless I meet Him in the air! No matter what any of us are going through, it is only for a time. Someday all will be revealed and, in light of God's glory and being in His presence, I doubt our earthly struggles and pain will even bear any weight!

If You Could See Me Now

Our prayers have all been answered. I finally arrived.
The healing that had been delayed has now been realized.
No one's in a hurry. There's no schedule to keep.
We're all enjoying Jesus, just sitting at His feet.
If you could see me now, I'm walking streets of gold.
If you could see me now, I'm standing strong and whole.
If you could see me now, you'd know I've seen His face.
If you could see me now, you'd know the pain is erased.
You wouldn't want me to ever leave this place,
If you could only see me now.
My light and temporary trials have worked out for my good,
To know it brought Him glory when I misunderstood.
Though we've had our sorrows, they can never compare.
What Jesus has in store for us, no language can share.
You wouldn't want me to ever leave this perfect place
If you could only see me now.
—*Kim Noblitt*

Postscript

So much has happened since I wrote this chapter. I made a decision to not keep adding to it. Then this morning, I felt the Spirit prompting me to share what is happening right now as this book is being submitted to the publisher. It has been a time of soul searching and at the onset of this crisis often asking the question "Why?" I haven't asked this very much along the journey of my paralysis and rheumatoid arthritis, but it is these diseases that are responsible for the journey I am on right now.

Briefly, I made a trip with a friend to Bolivia to visit a family involved in missions there. Near the onset of our holiday I fell out of my wheelchair, very gracefully I might add, from missing a small step. I was back in my chair in no time with help and on we went.

Within a couple of days my leg had become very hard and swollen. I went through two clinic visits and a hospital stay. I ended up being treated for what would later be revealed as two misdiagnoses.

There was a settling of trust and peace for my circumstances, but at times a very loud *"why, God?!"* would cross my heart and mind. We were at the other end of the world and all of this was only adding *huge* stress to my friends with absolutely *nothing* making any sense.

I knew during my last week in Bolivia that my lower right leg had broken. Originally it was probably a stable fracture but with no immobilization both bones broke away at the fracture sites just below the knee.

After years of paralysis, the bones become very weak and will break unknowingly as I have no feeling there. The fractures only became clear after they broke off from each other. Some breaks are never identified. An x-ray also showed an old fracture in my ankle that I had no knowledge of until now.

I eventually made the long trip home and to the hospital here in Winnipeg. I was x-rayed and had a cast put on. It was hoped that high-risk surgery could be avoided by lining up the bones with the cast holding them in place. They were slightly misaligned, but with not walking there would be no problem going this route.

I needed my wheelchair adapted to keep my leg elevated. I was also non-weight-bearing and was devastated when I found out. It meant *not* putting my foot down on the foot rest to do my transfer independently. I am thankful for homecare, and God has provided some wonderful caregivers. The only time I can get into my wheelchair is when someone is here to hold my leg while I transfer.

This adds up to long hours on the bed. I find the time goes by very quickly most days. I have coffee in bed listening to Steve Bell's newest CD, *Kindness!* Yes, *every morning!* One of the reasons for listening to this particular album is the first three songs. When Steve brought the CD to the hospital and had it downloaded onto my walkman (yes, I do know what an iPod is!) it seemed those songs had been written just for me lying in that hospital bed!

Its words and music with the beautiful arrangements help settle me deep down and get my day off to a quiet, prayerful start. Here is one of the songs that gives me so much encouragement:

Changes

Changes coming upon us
It keeps moving, moving around us
Got to keep dancing knowing
He loves us
Got to keep joy in our hearts,
He knows all of our needs and
He will meet them following His plan
Even the changes turning in His hand
Soon will be part of it all
So we enter a new time
There are places where it's a hard climb
But there are faces carrying sunshine
Warming our path as we go.
Sometimes we may be lonely
It's a hard job making us holy
But in the long run there will be glory
Glory to rival the sun.
—Jim Croegaert

These words help to sum it up. God is always meeting our needs, and nothing we receive comes to us except through his hand. It comes back to our suffering and its purpose—to make us more like Christ and to prepare us for the glory that is yet to come—"Glory to rival the sun."

As I pen these words, I have just come through surgery after three-and-a-half months in the cast. There has been little to no bone growth. This is where the paralysis and arthritis come in. With paraplegia, there is decreased circulation, which in turn slows down healing. Added to that, the medication needed to control my arthritis suppresses the immune system. This opens me up to possible serious infections and slows down the healing process! Getting the picture?

There are no easy answers to any of this. I am still non-weight bearing and we wait another two to three months to see if the bones will heal. Therefore I purpose in my heart the wise wisdom Jesus gave in Matthew 6:31–34:

So don't worry about these things, saying, "What will we eat? What will we drink? What will we wear?" These things dominate the thoughts of unbelievers, but your heavenly Father already knows all your needs. Seek the Kingdom of God above all else, and live righteously, and he will give you everything you need.

So don't worry about tomorrow, for tomorrow will bring its own worries. Today's trouble is enough for today.

Friends who are brave drive my full-sized van—most drives taking me to the hospital for appointments. My garden has been cleaned up, my grass is cut regularly, my flowers are being planted, and my meals are being cooked! Is there want of anything more?

Most days I have God's deep joy and contentment. I trust in his greater plan that is beyond anything I can imagine. I receive blessing upon blessing through people who are "Jesus with skin on" (Steve Masterson's descriptive quote!).

Every night Mom and Dad call and on the night they found out there was no further healing, my mom prayed a powerful prayer with strength in her voice, under laden with tears. They continue to pray on the phone regularly with me. My parents are elderly and so these are precious moments we never would have had if not for this leg!

This book is finally being published because I have been able to put the final pieces to it while lying on my bed. Dad is most thankful for that one! There are so many more special things mixed with the hard things. But God sees fit to keep changing us and preparing us to long for him and to look homeward to our final resting place.

I have a beautiful plaque hanging on my wall. It is a purposeful reminder of what life is all about here and the limited vision we have with what God is doing.

The Tapestry of My Life

My life is but a weaving
Between my Lord and me.
I cannot choose the colors
He works so steadily.

Oft times He weaves in sorrow
And I, in foolish pride,
Forget He sees the upper
And I, the underside.
Not till the loom is silent
And the shuttles cease to fly,
Will God unroll the tapestry
And explain the reason why.
The dark threads are as needed
In the Weaver's skillful hand,
As the threads of gold and silver
In the pattern He has planned.
—*Author Unknown*

There is such intense suffering going on around the world every day. There seems no end to it. I cannot even begin to offer any answers or solutions. My fractures pale in comparison and it is so easy to get wrapped up in our own little world. I usually manage to do that many times during the day.

But Psalm 33:12–14 gives us assurance that we are not alone or ignored: *"What joy for the nation whose God is the Lord, whose people he has chosen as his inheritance. The Lord looks down from heaven and sees the whole human race. From his throne he observes all who live on the earth."*

I felt helpless and boxed in just a few nights ago and was on the phone in tears. Following our conversation, my friend Nanci emailed me her morning devotional. It was just what I needed!

> In a world of unrelenting changes, I am the One who never changes. I am the Alpha and the Omega, the First and the Last, the Beginning and the End. Find in Me the stability for which you have yearned. I created a beautifully ordered world: one that reflected My perfection. Now, however, the world is under the bondage of sin and evil. Every person on the planet faces gaping jaws of uncertainty. The only antidote to this poisonous threat is drawing closer to Me. In My Presence you can face uncertainty with perfect Peace.

I am the Alpha and the Omega, the First and the Last, the Beginning and the End" (Revelation 22:13, NLT).

—*Selected*

My leg is a mess. There are many complications going on right now. Do I believe God could miraculously heal me right now? *Absolutely!* Do I believe God has purpose to this suffering? *Definitely*!

Tomorrow my leg will probably still be a mess. So I choose life; I choose joy; I choose contentment; I choose to believe God's commitment to His many promises and to me; I choose to believe that He loves me with an everlasting love and at all times.

I cannot imagine my life any other way but in this chair. I continue to learn lessons that can only be experienced in the confinement of a wheelchair. But it is this same confinement that has given me the most freedom I have ever known. Why? Because it is part of the story that God continues to write—a story not finished—one that is eternal! It is all to the glory of God. God receives glory each moment I choose Him!

May this encourage you to know Christ, His sacrifice and the punishment He bore to give us eternal life; to know God, a loving, just, and faithful Father. All glory to Jesus, the Lamb of God who takes away the sin of the world. There is no greater love but a man laying down his life for another. Thank you, Jesus.

"Therefore go and make disciples of all nations, baptizing them in the name of the Father and of the Son and of the Holy Spirit, and teaching them to obey everything I have commanded you. And surely I am with you always, to the very end of the age."
(Matthew 28:19–20)

Greg Constable submitted a wonderful account of the work that God is doing in India at King's College. It is reminiscent of what Christ asked his followers to do in the New Testament—*make disciples* and they in turn will go out and teach and train others!

King's College—www.kingscollegeindia.org

King's College is a holistic ministry devoted to the mentoring of future leaders in India, strategically positioned to invest in the lives of a nation on the cusp of dominant global influence. As King's College continues to invest in the lives of its students, its growing alumni body continues to flourish and influence the emerging generation of a nation coming of age. To this end, King's College recruits disadvantaged young men, ages sixteen to seventeen, for two years of residential training.

During the program the young men are spiritually mentored and academically educated.

Through their training, King's College students are equipped to overcome their backgrounds of poverty and social discrimination. Consequently, King's College graduates look forward to lives of hope, opportunity, and leadership within their churches and communities.

Spiritual Mentoring

The students of King's College are selected based upon their desire to be trained as disciples of Christ. Their spiritual growth is nurtured through personal devotions, Bible teaching, and personal mentoring. Each weekend King's College students are partnered with village pastors and become proficient in sharing their faith, teaching Sunday school, leading worship, and discipleship instruction.

Educational Opportunity

Once admitted, the students are intensively instructed in their academic subjects and the English language. Due to the college's high standard of education and practice of English immersion, the majority of King's College graduates are able to go to university and do so with success.

Social Justice

Students are selected for admission to King's College based on, among other factors, economic need. Consequently, all students come from poor and disadvantaged families. The student body regularly includes orphans, children of single-parents, and those from abusive homes. Although the largest percentage of the college students come from the Dalit community, there is representation from a cross-section of social castes.

Results

King's College was founded in 2000. Since then it has graduated about sixty young men. Alumni of the college have completed post-graduate studies, entered full-time ministry and acquired full-time employment. There is no doubt that students and graduates of King's College are excelling scholastically. Spiritually, continued growth can be gauged as we see many of our graduates demonstrating ministry initiative in their churches and individual lives.

During the summer of 2009, the twenty students of King's College conducted Vacation Bible Schools for 1,043 students in eight villages. This, in itself, is one of the exciting annual fruits of this ministry. But over the last few years some King's College alumni have chosen to initiate the organization of VBS programs throughout the state as well. This past summer twelve of our alumni banded with some of their friends, and on their own initiative, conducted VBS programs for 1,380 children in eighteen distinct programs. We praise God that our disciples are now sowing seeds and starting to teach new little disciples throughout their own country.

Henry Ford

It was the privilege of King's College to host Henry Ford during the summers of 2002 and 2003. Henry made himself available to travel to India to assist the students in the learning of English. King's College students, coming from poor rural backgrounds, do not speak English when they come to the college. However, because the ability to function in English is an important skill for its students to acquire, the college operates as an English-medium institution.

To help prepare the students for the impending subjects to be taught in English, Henry volunteered himself for two consecutive summers. Henry quickly endeared himself to the students and was soon affectionately known as '*Henry Uncle.*' Despite his advanced age (seventy-five and seventy-six at the time) and physical challenges, Henry was a trooper and braved the heat of both the climate and the local spicy foods.

Henry has proven to not only be a great friend of King's College, but also an inspiration to the staff and students as they marveled at his desire to engage world missions in a practical way at a time when most people are in retirement mode. The staff and students of King's College will forever be grateful for the friendship and encouragement of '*Henry Uncle.*'

employment. There is no doubt that students and graduates of Kings College are excelling, holistically, spiritually; continued growth can be expected as we see many of our graduates in outreaching ministry in other churches and in individual lives.

During the summer of 2009, the twenty students of Kings College conducted Vacation Bible School for three hundred in eight villages. This, in itself, is one of the exciting components of the ministry. But over the last few years some Kings College students have chosen to pursue the organization of VBS programs throughout the area as well. This past summer twelve of our students banded with some of their friends, and on their own initiative, conducted VBS programs for 1,500 children in eighteen different programs. We praise God that our students are now sowing seeds and starting to reach new little disciples for Jesus in their own country.

Henry Ford

It was the privilege of Kings College to host Henry Ford during the summers of 2012 and 2013. Henry made himself available to travel to India to assist the students in the learning of English. Kings College students, coming from poor rural backgrounds, do not speak English when they come to the college. However, because the ability to function in English is an important skill for the students to acquire, the college operates as an English-medium institution.

To help prepare the students for the impending subjects to be taught in English, Henry volunteered himself for two consecutive summers. He quickly endeared himself to the students and was soon affectionately known as *"Henry Uncle."* Despite his advanced age (seventy-five and seventy-six at the time) and physical challenges, Henry was a trooper and braved the heat of both the climate and the local spicy foods.

Henry has proven to not only be a great friend of Kings College but also an inspiration to the staff and students as they observed his desire to engage world missions in practical ways at a time when most people are in retirement mode. The staff and students of Kings College will forever be grateful for the friendship and encouragement of *Henry Ford*.

Editor's NOTE

As Dad's physical body began deteriorating from his post-polio syndrome, his heart and desire for ministry certainly did not. Not being actively involved as a pastor in a church anymore, he longed for ways to reach out and mentor other young men.

Dad met Greg Constable at Peoples Church in Toronto, Ontario. Greg was asking for someone to go with him to help out at King's College with teaching English. Dad was the only one who responded!

Dad's first trip in 2002 was for three weeks. Because there was so much to do and many ways to serve, Dad made a decision to go for six weeks the following summer. He trusted the Lord to provide financially as well as physically and God did just that. By this time Dad was walking with two crutches as well as a walker.

Dad spent one week each summer with a representative from an Indian missionary society. Every night Dad and Edward would go to a different home for prayer and Dad would give a message. The evening always ended with a late dinner.

During the day Edward arranged for Dad to speak in private schools. He was even able to go to a university where he gave a gospel message. After each of these sessions he would have tea with the principal. This is when he met Evangeline Sita, a wonderful Christian woman.

She arranged for him to go to the leper colony and made arrangements to speak at her church. It was a magnificent building with two balconies and no posts to hold them up. It was a Methodist church and the pastor's son led the music. Dad asked to play his keyboard and still hears from this man now and again.

The following are a few excerpts from emails that Dad sent during his second visit to India (edited, of course!).

> June 26, 2003
>
> Dear Family, Friends and Loved Ones,
>
> I can hardly believe that I have been in India for three weeks and that this is my first email. Greg and I were separated for a week and he only had his laptop.
>
> As planned, Greg met me in London and had a wheelchair for me to get on the flight to Dubai, a small Arab Emirate, and then on to Delhi, India. From Delhi (India's capital) we went north overnight to a town called Dehra Dun. I should tell you that the overnight to Dehra Dun was not exactly luxurious. We had bunks but no pillows, sheets or blankets, and no air-conditioning.
>
> Anyway, through the night it had cooled down as we travelled north and I was then wishing I had my jacket. Greg and Principal David dropped me off in this lovely little town. We went from the train by taxi where I stayed at a large, beautiful compound, a Christian school for blind girls. Most were on holidays, but the facilities they have for these girls are incredible. They have the best of equipment, computers, etc. Many who graduate are able to function in offices as well as "seeing" people. The director and his wife were kindness itself—wonderful praying people who show much love and care, not only for the girls and women, but also for the entire staff.
>
> June 13, Greg came by taxi to pick me up to go to Delhi. We took the train to Delhi with a much nicer sleeper, air-

conditioning, sheets, pillows, and blankets. This was overnight. We got stuck in Delhi because of a mix-up in reservations. I was to preach on Sunday a.m. but we didn't arrive in Hyderabad until fairly late Monday evening, June 16.

Mr. Edward, a man of God and a missionary coordinator for an Indian missionary society, picked me up at the railway station. We picked up his wife Grace, a truly gracious Christian woman, and then went to a couple's home where they were expecting us.

After giving a short message and having prayer, the hostess served a full-course Indian dinner! I think we arrived home at about 12:30 a.m. exhausted, but that was just the beginning!

The next morning, poor old Henry is up bright and early and visited two Christian schools with almost all the children either Hindu or Muslim. Parents must agree to a Christian message, Lord's Prayer, and Bible reading once a week, Edward comes with his accordion and sings gospel choruses and gives a gospel message. So every day the same routine, two schools each morning and prayer meeting and Bible message in various homes throughout this huge city, ending with a large Indian dinner.

The traffic, as I said last year, was absolutely indescribable. To arrive anywhere safely is a miracle. The last morning I was there, which was Friday, June 21, I spoke to over 100 masters degree students, both men and women 18-24 years of age. There are one or two Christians in this class and they lead in gospel choruses, scripture and prayer. They must attend this chapel service or they are asked to leave the school immediately. Oh, by the way, the "lift" was being repaired so they carried me up three flights of stairs.

That week I spoke and shook hands with at least 3,000 boys and girls, teenagers and adults. All the children I hugged, and either kissed them on the cheek or had them kiss me on the cheek, and whispered in their ear that God loved them; they were special and precious to Him. Then Friday morning we hurried to Secunderabad where Greg had been having a teacher's workshop and I spoke to this group. Then it was back to Edward and Grace's house in Hyderabad to pack, have tea, rest, and at last, to start off and arrive at King's College to settle in.

The boys were still up when I arrived and I received a very warm welcome. Two of the boys were new to me, having joined the college after I had left last year. But it wasn't long until we were good friends.

This building Greg has leased is very spacious and comfortable. My room is on the ground floor and is very comfortable, with lots of fresh air and a ceiling fan. Upstairs is equally spacious, with two bedrooms for boys, one room for the warden, kitchen, dining room, washroom, prayer room, sitting room, and a large terrace refreshingly cool in the evening. I have breakfast and lunch in my room and then I am literally carried upstairs for dinner, which is served around nine o'clock. Oh yes, we do have tea in the morning and around 5:00 p.m. in the evening. Very English!

The alumni who are here for this week are a group of good spiritual young men. Greg has scheduled an excellent week for them. One of the graduates from last year, perhaps one of the brightest and most promising, sadly, was at home for a visit and went swimming in the Bay of Bengal and drowned. It was a shock to us all because he was loved and respected and held in high esteem by his fellow students as well as the staff. Earth's loss but heaven's gain. How important it is for all of us to be prepared for that time when we have completed life's journey. I had a small part through the day and spoke to them during their devotions last night.

Last Sunday I preached in the church where Principal David's uncle is pastor. It is in a factory district where there are many work shifts but there were around 100 present (ministerial speaking), nearly all sitting on the floor. These people are mostly uneducated, speaking only Telugu and it had to be translated.

The church is finished except for the front, which is completely open. Many asked for prayer. Greg was at the front and I at the back. Greg and I prayed for various needs.

Well again, sorry for this long delay. Thanks again to all of you who have given and made it possible for me to be here. And grateful thanks for all of you who are praying daily. This I need as I serve and live in this needy country. I especially want to serve in the strength of the Holy Spirit and only to the glory of our precious Saviour.

Much love to all.

July 5, 2003

Dear Family, Friends and Prayer Supporters,

Here I am again. It has been a busy time since last you heard from me here in India. You will recall that in the last email I preached in a small church in a factory town with lots of shift work; but even so, there was at least one present. We had tea with the pastor and then I was asked to pray for the pastor's wife. I have no idea what her need was. As a matter of fact, many of the people asked Greg and me to pray for them as we greeted them at the door. How I wish I was some 40 years younger and could minister to these needy people showing love and care through the Lord Jesus Christ.

When we arrived back at the college the alumni had arrived for the week. All came back except one, who was unable to get time off. We had a very moving memorial service for Samson, the boy who drowned just a week ago. It was obvious that he was well loved and highly respected. He was a top student, and spoke English quite well. He was a dedicated believer and shared the gospel with all his relatives and friends.

It brought me immense joy to hear testimonies of these young disciples and realize how they are developing in their Christian lives. I had only met these guys at a picnic last year for a couple of hours so it was a privilege to get to know them. The week consisted of seminars, including character studies, evangelism, personal growth, small group studies, quizzes, and leadership. This was during the morning and afternoon.

Of course, morning and afternoon we had our English tea that is made by boiling the water, milk, and lots of sugar. It was served in small dainty cups. The boys played cricket and volleyball for about an hour. Then there was a devotional service with singing and testimonies and each night a special speaker. I was involved in several of these programs. The last night, which was Friday, we had dinner as usual at 9 p.m. For the final meal, we had a banquet, and dessert was ice cream (thanks to Florence, a special family friend of ours). The boys left on Saturday. They were tired but happy and so were we!

On Saturday, June 28, we left the city to go to a village. Steven, the warden at the college, lives here. He was anxious for me to see his village, meet his family and preach in his church.

It was a distance of 150 km but it took us four hours. The roads were sometimes four lanes and sometimes two lanes. Some roads were paved and some were plain earth but all had numerous potholes; some so bad that Greg, who was driving, was so badly shaken that his hands flew off the steering wheel. I thought that the roads were hectic with cars, scooters, motorcycles, bicycles, thousands of people, oxen pulling heavy loads, and shepherds driving their herds of goats home. There were seven herds all together. Did I mention trucks, buses and cows? A miracle we arrived in four hours.

We arrived in the village around dusk. These dear people had just gone out and bought new plastic summer chairs like we have at home so we would be comfortable, as well as new china teacups and a pretty new tray. You would have to know how poor these people are to fully appreciate this gesture.

As it grew dark, very dark, candles were lit, as the hydropower wasn't due to come on until 9 p.m. Sometime during our introduction to all their relatives, too numerous to count, the mother killed a chicken (I heard the death squawk) and eventually we were served dinner. It was very good, prepared and served so graciously.

They had brought the cow and bull in from grazing, and as the power was on by this time, I wanted to see them. The barn was a wing of the house and at the other end of this small barn was Steven's room. His room was neat and tidy but still in the barn! They wanted to show us the rest of their home but as I was going to have to duck to get through the doorway I declined and they seemed to understand.

By this time it was very late and relatives were going to host us for the night. This was considered a fairly large village but the roads were simply unbelievable. These kind people had cleared out their living room and dining room except for the table and laid out four beds. This family was obviously fairly well off as he had a job as a conductor in a small city a few kilometers from home. By the way, this family had some kind of dispute in the church where I would be preaching and had left and gone to the other church in the village, which happened to be Catholic.

When all the lights were off and all settled in bed it was very late but so nice and quiet compared to the city. There was a little thin kitten running around but thankfully he didn't come near me. I don't know when the others woke up but when I awoke neighbors had already arrived to socialize.

These folks had a shower/bath room a few feet from the house and I was assisted over to the bathhouse where a chair and hot water were ready for me. Greg said that when he was in the bathhouse standing up he could see over the wall.

I was left alone for some thirty minutes to go over my message and pray. I heard a strange noise and looked behind me to see and hear a chicken laying an egg! Greg said it had been there all night. When everyone arrived and sat down, women on one side and men the other, the church was full. To be continued…

Much love, and thanks for your prayers,

Dad, Henry, and Grandpa. XXX OO

This is the third email, a continuation of the July 5 letter.

Hello everyone!

I hope I am not boring you with my day-to-day activities but I am *enjoying* this experience so much and as I speak, share, and fellowship and work with the boys, I myself am being so blessed.

We arrived back from the village church fairly late but had a very warm welcome from the students. They are the kids I worked with last year so it was a joy to see them again. The whole week was called English Week. We were busy with classes, which included pronunciation, comprehension (understanding what they read) drama, grammar, music, and several other worthwhile subjects.

I try very hard to get them to speak English more often but their first language is Telugu and naturally it is the easiest to communicate in. Also, because the principal and the warden have Telugu as their first language, they most often use that. My concern is the fact that all higher education schools without exception teach in English, so it is vital for them to have a working knowledge of English.

A really great week to say the least, but a busy one. We had chapel every night at 7:30 with a different speaker each night. Greg and I took our turn, but two didn't show up (apparently typical). I am still with these boys this week working on English as often as I can and then taking devotions each night; then at 9 p.m. supper.

The cook is Martamma, a dear Christian woman who doesn't speak a word of English but has a lovely smile. She always attends devotions so I have to have my devotional translated. Poor guys—it takes twice as long! I bought her a lovely sari to wear on Sundays to church and she was so thrilled. It cost 100 rupees, which is less than $4.00. She has her own little house attached to the college and, of course, gets all her meals but not a very large salary. But this job is heaven to her because being a widow, life for her would be very hard. The boys love and respect her and she loves them. Most all the meals are vegetarian, except on special occasions we have chicken and every Sunday, beef.

Yesterday, twenty-one pastors came for a special day. The college paid for their bus fare, gave them breakfast and lunch (that's when we served chicken curry) and then Greg and I spoke and another speaker brought an excellent message. This was a real treat for these pastors as they have so little and yet love serving the Lord.

They are making real sacrifices, as are their wives and children. As a matter of fact, we went out to the village last Sunday where the pastor, who coordinates the boys lives. It was some experience. First of all it poured rain and with no gravel in the village it was quite muddy to say the least.

The service was to start at 10 a.m. We arrived around that time but the service didn't start until sometime after 11 o'clock! In fact, the pastor didn't start getting properly dressed until long after we arrived. The service is being held in his home for now.

This is the church we helped raise money for at the bowlorama back in the early spring. This is Friday, July 11, and Greg is out at the village checking out the lot they will buy. Exciting to have had a part in it!

Back to the church service that finally got started and lasted for two hours. Translation took quite a bit of time but they sang a lot. After the service the pastor brought up every family member, some including extended family plus Grandma. I prayed for some as a family and some had special needs. The pastor didn't interpret my prayer so the dear folks had no idea what I was praying, but thank God He knew.

Everywhere I went I assured everyone that God loves them and they are precious to Him. Sometimes in our affluent lifestyles, meager as they might be, we forget that God loves the world and gave His Son to be their Saviour.

Tomorrow is turning out to be a busy weekend—a prayer meeting followed by dinner in the early evening (I hope). If the rain stops I'm going to visit a leper colony. The lady who is arranging it will bring food and I hope to find some clothes for them around here. If not, I may have to give the shirt off my back! On Sunday morning at 7:30—a.m. that is, *[Dad is **not** a morning person, especially with his post-polio syndrome!]* I'm speaking at the English service of the largest Methodist church in Hyderabad. Following that I am speaking at a new church in the suburbs and then home to Edward and Grace's for a rest.

At 6:30 p.m. I will be speaking at the 15,000-member Baptist church. But in case you think India does not need the gospel, remember, the population is now over one billion.

On Monday, I pack in between other activities and Tuesday, all the boys will come to the airport to see us off. I really love it here in India and it is going to be hard to leave all the wonderful friends I have made. But on the other hand, I am looking forward to being home. Please take no offence but after Jean, Aunty to the boys, I can hardly wait to see my little darlings Daniel and Charlotte. *[His grandchildren, Luke not being born yet.]*

Lots of love to everyone and thank you for your prayerful support and making it possible for me to have this very special experience in India, one of the most blessed ministries I have ever had.

Again all my love in Christ,
Henry XXX 000

Dad uses a power chair to get around now but I find it amazing that with such limited use and function of his legs he was able to minister to so many in such rugged and harsh circumstances. All God needs is a willing heart! God certainly protected him through this part of his journey and provided many other servants, including Greg who went out of their way to be Dad's "legs."

Isaiah 61:1 in the Amplified Bible says:

The Spirit of the Lord God is upon me, because the Lord has anointed and qualified me to preach the Gospel of good tidings to the meek, the poor, and afflicted; He has sent me to bind up and heal the brokenhearted, to proclaim liberty to the [physical and spiritual] captives and the opening of the prison and of the eyes to those who are bound.

Matthew 24:14 confirms the need for believers to be in the business of kingdom building: *"And this good news of the kingdom (the Gospel) will be preached throughout the whole world as a testimony to all the nations, and then will come the end."*

I would like to close this chapter with a "Father's Day Tribute" I wrote for sharing in church on Father's Day back in 2003. It is somewhat brutally honest about some of the struggles and pain Dad has endured. He has already shared some things in previous chapters. Let it be an encouragement to each one of you as this tribute reminds us of God's great love and mercy for us—all redeemable by the blood of the Lamb, clothed in righteousness, never beyond the reach of the cross at Calvary.

Dad had asked me to put this tribute in the book at the end of my story but it just didn't seem to fit in there. I set it aside for awhile to ponder and pray about where it belonged. I soon realized it had found its place in this final chapter. It wasn't until I got to the end of the tribute that I saw it was written just before his first trip to India, confirming where it belonged! It also seems fitting to end his book with this, as it shows Dad's heart throughout his life for ministry, dedication, perseverance, and service.

FATHER'S DAY TRIBUTE, 2003

There is so much I have learned from my dad that it is difficult to put it into five minutes, but here is my attempt!

One of the things my dad has passed on to me is his love for music. But my biggest rip in life is that he passed on more of his love for it than he did his talent! I have greater expectations for heaven in that department. To this day, music is a big part of my life, both in healing and everyday life.

When he was eleven years old, Dad was stricken with polio. It paralyzed his legs. He was told he would never walk again. He vowed that he would walk again and serve the Lord, which is what he has done all these years. Over the last twenty years, Dad has dealt with what is called post-polio syndrome. The parts affected by polio wear out and become weaker and can even cause paralysis again. The specialist who saw Dad back then said he couldn't have had polio in the 1930s, because they were seeing people with these changes from the 1950s outbreak and Dad should not have walked into his office! I have seen this perseverance and stubbornness carry Dad through many physical changes and challenges over the years, and even though it is more difficult and limiting Dad is still walking to this day!

It was Father's Day fifteen years ago when I was paralyzed and began my life in this chair. My dad had a heart-wrenching time accepting what had happened to me, but in time he was able to accept more of his own physical limitations along with mine. So we have persevered together and I am thankful for these strengths of his that I learned long before my injury ever took place.

He also taught me to laugh, even if you're flat on your face on the floor! Many times he has fallen over the years when his knees would buckle. As he would recount these incidents to us he would be laughing and we would be laughing right along with him. Many of my stories are now told in the same way.

But it is in the last few years I have probably learned the most from my dad. It is because God has taught me more about who He is through my dad's personal pain. Life is not perfect for any of us, and it is not whether someone else changes but what I do with God because of the pain it has caused in my life. I have learned that we are never so low that God cannot reach down and bring us out. No one is ever beyond redemption. What seemed impossible and limiting to me was God's showcase for His Spirit of truth and healing.

There is a song that reminds me of my dad when I hear it. It sums up what God has done for us as a family and it continues to teach me how deep and how high is the love of God. It doesn't do as much justice without the music but the words are still very powerful:

Mercy Saw Me

The years had left scars,
And the scars had left pain,
How could he recognize me,
For I wasn't the same;
I knew I should pay and I knew the price,
For justice and law had demanded my life.
O but his tender heart heard
my desperate cry,
And he saw all my past through
merciful eyes!

"Beautiful", that's how mercy saw me,
For I was broken and so lost;
Mercy looked at all my faults.
Justice of God saw what I had done,
But mercy saw me through the Son;
Not what I was but what I could be,
That's how mercy saw me!
For sin had stolen all my dignity,
And all my self esteem;
But I was made brand new again,
When mercy looked at me.
Not what I was but what I could be,
That's how mercy saw me!
—*Craig Nelson*

In my Father's Day card to Dad I wrote, "Happy Father's Day, Dad! Your legacy will be the courage you have shown to us over the past year in allowing God to prove his unconditional love to you and proving that nothing is impossible with God. No matter how strong or weak you may feel that will never change. Lots of love to you and prayers as you live this out in India."

Yes, in this kingdom life there is no such thing as retirement. My dad's words in a letter he wrote in April of this year—"I am thrilled and amazed that at my age, and with my limited strength, God is giving me this opportunity of service." He is seventy-six years old next month and armed with much prayer, his crutches, walker, Bible, sermon notes and sun hat, he is in India for six weeks on a missions trip. That's one of the other great things my dad has taught me—how to love people and be involved in ministry. And so the end days of his life are finishing just as they began, serving the King!

CPSIA information can be obtained at www.ICGtesting.com
Printed in the USA
LVOW012146141112

307351LV00003B/8/P